Fly It Like You Stole It

The Early Years

By Kevin Lacey

ISBN 979-8-9864578-0-2 (hardback)

ISBN 979-8-9864578-1-9 (paperback)

ISBN 979-8-9864578-2-6 (e-book)

Book cover by raeghandesigns.com

Dedication

I dedicate this book to my Mom who stood beside me along the way. She did not have much to offer in the way of advice as she knew very little about the aviation industry, but she was always there with an encouraging word and moral support.

I would be remiss if I did not mention Robert Lotero who accepted me as a goofy-ass kid and turned me and my enthusiasm for aviation into a productive member of the aviation community.

I also dedicate this book to my gal Beverly, who often times never knew when or if I would be coming home but stood beside me regardless, and to my close friends Bob and Rosemary, Gary Cobb, Roy Gentry, Ron Roland and Carson Fitzgerald and all those who encouraged me and helped me chase my dreams.

I even acknowledge those who said that I could not do it, along with the others who did everything they could to trip me up in my efforts. Even those who said *'everybody knows that a mechanic can't fly'*, or those who would say *'you must not be a very good mechanic if you are a Learjet pilot.'*

I would like to offer special recognition to those folks out there that volunteer their time and resources to help inspire future generations of aviators. To the thousands of volunteers who help organize and coordinate aviation events and airshows across the country each year such as EAA's AirVenture in Oshkosh, Wisconsin, Sun n Fun Aerospace Expo in Lakeland, Florida and many other events, I salute you!

And finally, to all those who unselfishly dedicate their time, energy, and money to providing EAA Young Eagle flights to young aspiring aviators, the Angel Flight pilots who transport patients in medical need, the Veterans Airlift Command providing free air transportation to our wounded warriors.

To all those seeking a career in aviation, chase your dreams, the sky is not the limit, it is merely a waypoint.

"Repo pilot Kevin Lacey looks and sounds a lot like the Dennis Weaver character from the 1970s TV series "McCloud." Despite the folksy demeanor, Lacey has a reputation as a somewhat Machiavellian aero-sleuth who always gets his airplane."

Stephen Joiner – Smithsonian Air & Space Magazine April/May 2010

Table of Contents

Preface

As a sophomore and junior in high school, I was not exactly what one would call a model student. I always seemed to be in trouble for one reason or another and my grades were not what my parents would have hoped them to be.

Instead of using my time in the third-floor study hall classroom doing homework or studying for an upcoming test, I spent my time gazing out the window at the aircraft in the traffic pattern at Red Bird Airport which was a mere two miles away as the crow flies. If there was nobody in the traffic pattern, I was busy making paper airplanes and tossing them out the window into the courtyard below.

As a family, we were not poor, but we lived a frugal life and were always saving nickels and dimes for that rainy day. It must have been the work ethic my parents instilled in me, if I wanted something, I needed to figure a way to raise enough money to buy it. As a result, I was always working part time jobs. From throwing the morning and afternoon newspapers, mowing lawns, bussing tables, sacking groceries, and even painting industrial equipment, I was always working.

My dad passed away unexpectedly just before the end of my junior year. Even though he and I had a lot of disagreements, it was a devastating life changing event. Mom had to muster the strength and money to look after three teenage kids. With me being the oldest, I took it upon myself to try to set an example for my younger siblings and leave as little financial burden on mom as possible.

I would be graduating high school soon and I needed to figure out what I wanted to be as an adult. Without much in the way of adult supervision, curiosity got the better of me and I soon found myself spending all my spare time and money at the airport in search of a long-term prosperous career.

The Early Years is a series of short stories related to some of the aviation adventures and mis-adventures encountered along the way to becoming a career aviator.

Chapter 1

Inspiration

It was a brisk, bright, blue-sky morning in late September of 1973, when I hopped in the car to take a ride to some exotic dedication ceremony that I heard about on the radio. Living on the south side of Dallas in a suburb called Oak Cliff, it seemed as if I had driven all morning and halfway across Texas to get to the location where this grand event was to take place.

As I got closer to my destination, I got this eerie feeling that I had been here before. I began to recognize the area. It wasn't so much an abundance of landmarks as it was the surrounding terrain that I recognized. Mesquite trees, reasonably flat terrain, some barbed wire fences.

Rounding the corner and driving in from the north down the main road, I realized that I had in fact been here before, and it was just last week, but it was not by car. There were a lot of construction barricades that looked as if they were mostly being used to funnel traffic to a specific location. For a place in the middle of nowhere, there sure were a lot of cars and people here.

Following directions of the folks who were trying to manage the traffic jam, but mostly just going with the flow, I realized that this was going to be some kind of really special event. With the car finally parked, I became part of the crowd, which resembled a herd of cattle making its way to the watering hole. We all just migrated towards this huge semicircular building.

Inside this brandy spankin' new building, there appeared to be a lot of important people milling around. There were mayors, congressmen, the governor of Texas, and all kinds of dignitaries dressed up in suits doing whatever it is that important people do at these events. As a teenage kid with long hair and blue jeans, I really did not fit in, so nobody paid much attention to me.

Little did I know how much this event would impact my future career choices. Not that any of those fancy little gatherings, speeches, and talks held my attention for very long. There was nothing much of interest for me here inside this building so I decided to move along. Off to my right was a door that led outside with a lot of people coming in and out, so I decided to follow the crowd through the door.

Oh boy! This is more like it! This is what I came here for. A fresh, brand-new concrete ramp all littered with airplanes! As I recall, the theme for this event had something to do with welcoming the "Jet Age" to North Texas, but the first airplane I saw was a regal old Convair CV-440 with its massive four-blade propellers, standing tall and proud on her landing gear. She showed signs of many years of loyal service behind her, and considering the company she was keeping on this sunny fall day, she was probably contemplating her upcoming demotion from luxury passenger service to the world of flying cargo for the remainder of her career.

I had to shield my eyes when looking to my left, as the sun's reflection coming off of a glorious shiny new-looking jet airliner was blinding. It was hard to look at from my angle, but I knew that further investigation was necessary.

Making my way over to the Boeing 707, she was all dressed up in American Airlines livery, and looked as if someone had been polishing on her for months. She looked brand new. A stairway led up to an open cabin door with a few people going in and out of the aircraft. Acting as if I knew what I was doing, I marched right up the stairs like I owned the place. To the right of me appeared to be nothing more than a bunch of movie theater seats in this long narrow aluminum tube, but to my left was the marvel of space age technology.

As I stood there in total amazement of the flight deck of that Boeing 707, I thought to myself that there was no way this seventeen-year-old student pilot flying a little Cessna 150 could ever learn what all those switches, buttons, and dials did, much less understand what kind of information was contained in all those little flip charts and manuals that seemed to be everywhere.

All alone in the cockpit, I took a seat at the Flight Engineer's station. There must have been at least a hundred dials and switches.

2

There were these flip-charts that had numbers and graphs that were all way beyond my level of comprehension.

Moving to the Captain's seat, I only recognized a couple of basic instruments such as the airspeed indicator and altimeter on the flight instrument panel. The Flight Manuals and other associated books and documents found in the cockpit were larger in size than all my high school books combined. It was all very intimidating, but motivational at the same time knowing that someone out there knew what all these knobs, dials, and switches did. It would have been nice if that someone was here to explain some of it to me. Inquiring minds wanted to know.

It was really cool to exit the cockpit and walk down the stairs and wander around underneath the aircraft, looking into the jet engine inlets and exhaust and wondering how these things worked. I looked over the landing gear and up inside the wheel wells with all that plumbing. It was amazing trying to figure out what all those components did.

I had only been this close to a jet airplane one time in my life and that was just a few months prior when the family took a trip from Dallas Love Field to DeLand, Florida, to bury my dad, who had recently passed away. I was thankful that on this day, nobody paid much attention to this teenage kid wandering around the ramp all by himself.

Parked next to the American Airlines 707 was a big orange Boeing 747 operated by Braniff International Airways. It was affectionately referred to as 'Fat Albert'. I really wanted to go inside, but the line to go up the stairs was pretty long, so I opted to just walk around underneath and marvel at the engineering that went into creating an aircraft this big and then actually making it fly. As I came around the other side of the airplane, I was stopped dead in my tracks.

Oh wow! There she was! The fastest commercial jet in the world! The Concorde! I had heard and read all about the Concorde, how sleek and fast it was supposed to be, but now here she was, right in front of me, in all her majesty.

I overheard someone say that the very first landing the Concorde made in the U.S. was right here at this little ol' North Texas airport. In spite of the fact that she reminded me of an aardvark, with her nose all bent out of shape, she still looked like she was going the speed of sound just sitting there on the ramp. I later discovered that the nose moved down during take-offs and landings so the pilots could see over it during operations with a high angle of attack.

The line to board the Concorde was even longer than the line to board Fat Albert. To make matters worse, there were a lot of suit and ties that seemed to be given preferential treatment, as they were cutting in line in front of us commoners. I figured that I would simply wander around and under the airplane until the line got shorter. This was an event where I wished I owned a camera.

As I walked back towards the terminal building, constantly looking back at these magnificent flying machines on display, my mind wandered. I thought to myself *if only these airplanes could talk, what amazing stories they could tell.* Just imagine the places they had been and the things they had seen, the pilots and crew members that traveled in these machines. They had truly seen the world. This was what I called excitement!

On this late September day, I realized - perhaps for no other reason than they left the cockpit door open on the 707 and allowed this kid to sit there and daydream the possibilities - why I had been spending every penny I could earn taking flying lessons for the past several months. I found my dream job. I was going to be a pilot for American Airlines!

It all began with a combination of my dad passing away and sitting in the third-floor study hall class at Carter High School. I would pass the time gazing out the window at the airplanes coming and going from Red Bird Airport, which was just two miles away as the crow flies. I always wondered who those people were and where they were going. Curiosity eventually got to me and soon I found myself taking flying lessons.

Kev with flight instructor Dave – summer 1973

As I drove home that afternoon from the Dallas/Fort Worth Regional Airport, my first resolution was to stop using DFW as my practice field for take-offs and landings. Until this day, I really never knew why all that concrete was out there in the middle of nowhere. For a seventeen-year-old kid, all that fresh new concrete made a great place to practice landings, but that had to stop.

My mind then drifted off into subjects like, *What does it take to become an airline pilot? How many flight hours do you need? What ratings are required? College? What about college? Do you need a college degree?* I was not exactly what one would call a model student in high school. *Are there schools that train airline pilots?* So many questions, with no one to turn to for answers.

Since my dad had passed away several months prior and with no real adult supervision, I turned to my high school counselor, Mr. Spruell. I knew that he was a Private Pilot and flew a Mooney out of Red Bird Airport. He might have an idea for a pathway to my newly found career passion.

5

Mr. Spruell was pleased that I was seeking his advice, but my grades really sucked and I was going to have to get off my ass, roll up my shirt sleeves, and start getting better grades. He devised a plan, telling me he would do all he could to help if he saw an improvement in my grades.

I was in a high school program called Coordinated Vocational Academic Education (CVAE). It was a class that taught us how to balance a checkbook, how to file the IRS Forms for income taxes, how to write a resume, and a variety of other useful skills. The teacher even helped us find part-time jobs.

I would leave school at 12:30 and drive across town to my job at American Lift Truck Company. The mechanics performed major maintenance on the engines, hydraulics, and chassis of the fork lifts, and when they were finished, I would strip off all the paint. Then I would assist the painter and make the fork lifts look brand new with a fresh coat of paint.

At school, I actually began studying and doing all my homework. Slowly but surely, my grades began to come up. I was flying as much as the weather, money, and my schedule would allow. Pretty soon, I had met almost all the flying requirements to take my Private Pilot check ride.

After some more consultation with Mr. Spruell, he began parading me around to the recruiting offices for the military. First, we went to the Air Force recruiter's office, then it was off to the Navy, followed by the Marines. It seemed like none of the armed services were interested in an aspiring young aviator wanting to join their ranks. Finally, we went to the Army.

The recruiter asked Mr. Spruell if we had visited any of the other Armed Services recruiters. Mr. Spruell listed everywhere we had been. We were then informed that the government was in the process of closing down their little party in Southeast Asia, and at the present time they were not seeking any new recruits. They had plenty of hardened combat aviators coming home from Vietnam and at this point, they were not sure what to do with all of them.

The recruiter suggested that if I wanted an aviation career, I should research my options in the civilian world.

With Mr. Spruell's help we began looking for an aviation school for me to attend after high school graduation. We began searching the advertisements in the back of *Flying* magazine and the *AOPA Pilot* magazine and found a couple of aviation schools to take a look at during the summer.

Right after graduation, I took a week off and traveled to Tulsa, Oklahoma, and Greely, Colorado, to look at aviation schools. By comparison, the school in Greely appeared all but shut down. It was explained that it was between semesters, but the school in Tulsa was still going full speed ahead.

I chose Spartan School of Aeronautics in Tulsa for a variety of reasons, but probably the biggest deciding factor was that they actually took the time to explain the program and the associated costs involved and the number of flight hours involved for each rating. Besides, I kinda liked the "Dawn Patrol" history and the Black Cat and the number 13 logo on the tail of the airplanes. I had no idea how I was going to pay for all this, but I gave them a check for my first tuition payment with the promise to return in August.

After working as an industrial equipment painter during the day and bagging groceries late into the evening all summer and saving my money, I packed everything I owned in the car, gave Mom a kiss goodbye, and launched out on my own to Tulsa, Oklahoma.

Chapter 2

Let the Adventures Begin

After driving for five hours, I arrived at the Spartan School of Aeronautics Riverside Airport Campus in Tulsa to register for class. After what appeared to be some confusion behind the counter, I was told that I was at the wrong campus. I was supposed to register for class at the Pine Street Campus, which was clear across town by Tulsa International Airport.

Even though my paperwork indicated that enrollment was on this day at the Riverside Airport Campus, they suggested that I had better hurry it up and get moving as it was getting close to rush hour and registration closed at 5 p.m. Spartan had three campuses, so it made sense to me that there could have been some sort of mix-up and they inadvertently sent me to the wrong campus.

Not knowing exactly where I was going, I raced across town and made it to the Pine Street Campus just in time to complete the enrollment process and get my class schedule. They were very helpful as they referred me to a cheap little nearby hotel where I could stay until I found something more permanent.

I thought it was rather interesting in that all my classes for the next six weeks were at the Pine Street Campus and there was no mention of a flight schedule. I figured there must be a lot of book learning necessary to learn what all those switches and dials do on the flight engineers panel to become an airline pilot, so I didn't think much about it.

The remainder of the week was chaotic. Aside from buying my books and attending class, I found a cheap little apartment to rent and moved out of that fleabag hotel that I had been staying in. I then started looking for a job.

Spartan had a job placement office that sent me off to a furniture moving company. After getting hired I was sent off to move some king-size mattresses and several couches up a flight of stairs. Standing at 5'10" and weighing in at 145 pounds soaking wet, I was not cut out for this kind of work. I quit right then and there. The following day they sent me to a tire shop, where I spent the afternoon busting tires off of rims. I quit that job at the end of my shift and went back to the job placement office.

I pleaded for any kind of a job at the airport, just so I could be around airplanes. She continued to assert that she had no aviation-related jobs in her listings, and then she said, "Well, unless you have any painting experience, I do not have anything."

Painting experience!! Hell yes I had painting experience! I'll take it! I explained that I had worked at American Lift Truck during my senior year of high school and all summer painting fork lifts. I even took over the paint shop after the main paint guy called in drunk one too many times.

I was sent to Lot Aero Flying Service at the Sand Springs Municipal Airport in Sand Springs, Oklahoma, which was west of Tulsa and was about a thirty-minute drive from school, so I had to hustle to get out there. Lot Aero was a little aircraft maintenance shop that was run by Robert Lotero along with his dad, Manuel.

After an interesting interview, I was hired for part-time work and instructed to report for work the following day at Harvey Young Airport. That was fine with me as Harvey Young was on the east side of Tulsa and only a few miles from school and my apartment and would save a ton of money on gas.

Lot Aero kind of reminded me of an aviation facility called Modern Aero at Red Bird Airport back home. Rivet guns banging away, air compressor running, people working together on a project, airplanes taxiing in and out - it all looked kind of exciting to me. Due to my class schedule, I was only going to get a few hours of work each day which meant a pretty light paycheck, but at least I would be at the airport.

Life was fairly good for a while, as my time after school was split between working at Harvey Young and Sand Springs airports, but I was rapidly going broke. I had burned through most all the cash I had saved staying in that hotel, getting an apartment, paying the deposit and electricity, paying for school books, and so on. I was beginning to get restless, and was anxious to get the flying part of my training program underway.

After about four weeks of school, I raised my hand in class, and when the instructor called on me, I asked, "So when do we get to start flying?" His eyes locked onto mine as if to say *oh shit*. He looked around the classroom and asked, "Is there anyone else?" which resulted in a show of about four more hands. "We will talk at break time," he said.

Break time brought about the big reveal. You see, the government had this little party in Southeast Asia that was called the Vietnam War, and our troops were returning home and receiving their well-deserved benefits from the GI Bill. The school's financial analysts had determined that the guaranteed money from GI Bill students was much more stable than were the funds from some random kids trying to pay their own way through flight school. They needed to allocate their resources (airplanes, instructors, and flight schedule) accordingly to maximize their profit.

Rather than tell us they did not have room in the flight school at registration and let us review our options, they simply sent us across town to their airframe and powerplant mechanic training campus and had us sign up there. Unfortunately, none of us were informed of this when we enrolled. The class schedule was not very descriptive as provided to us on a piece of paper, with only a three-number class code, a two-word title, the class times, and a room number. After all, we were just a bunch of teen-age kids fresh out of high school doing what the adults told us to do.

They promised that if we stayed in A&P school, they would help us get our commercial, multi-engine, and instrument ratings, but it would not be through their formal FAA Part 141 flight training program. "Look at it like this, when you guys are old enough to own your own airplanes, you will be able to do all the maintenance yourselves and not pay expensive maintenance shop prices."

This was not what I signed up for, but considering that I had already packed up and moved 200 miles away from home, gotten an apartment, and found a job, there was no going back. I tentatively accepted reality and their offer and got busy making some changes.

My first move was to drive down to Riverside Airport and check with Ross Aviation. They were also in the flight training business and had a rather large fleet of training aircraft but, like Spartan, they were booked solid for the foreseeable future with GI Bill students.

My next move was to ask Robert if he would hire me full time if I switched from day classes to night school. With that confirmation, I was off to the admissions office to make the switch from day classes to night classes. Night classes began at 5 p.m. and went until midnight, so if I could get to work by 7 a.m., I could almost get a full day's work in, and with working the weekends, I could get in a full forty-hour work week. That move meant much needed cash for tuition and living expenses.

Little did I know then that I was in for the adventure of a lifetime. After making the switch to night school I began working full-time at the airport. I slowly became a member of the local aviation community. I began meeting our maintenance customers, aircraft rental customers, and aircraft and engine parts supply vendors. It seemed that everyone had a small role to play in the grand scheme of things and I was becoming a part of it.

Lot Aero Flying Service operated out of two locations. We had the little sheet metal shop at Harvey Young Airport on the east side of Tulsa where we drilled apart wings, fuselages, and tail feathers. We would fabricate the appropriate repairs and rebuild the major airframe components. As repairs were completed, we would then transport the repaired components to the airport in Sand Springs on the west side of Tulsa for final assembly and completion.

At Sand Springs we were the airport operator. We had a rental fleet of little Cessna's and Pipers, as well as a maintenance shop where we would perform annual inspections and routine maintenance on customer aircraft and on our own rental fleet. This was also the location where we performed the final assembly and rigging of our rebuild projects. Once we had a completed aircraft, we would then do all the preparation and apply a fresh coat of primer and paint prior to the test flight.

The airport had its cast of characters, and among them was a Mr. Roy Simms. To me, he seemed like he must have been about 150 years old. He would show up at the airport every morning wearing his Stetson cowboy hat, boots that were polished to a bright shine, and a matching pair of slacks and jacket complete with a bolo tie. Roy owned a little 1960 model Cessna 150 with the patroller doors on it and he kept it tied down outside in front of the office/lobby.

Roy would sit in the lobby drinking coffee waiting around for someone to talk to or go fly with. Because he had lost his medical certificate, he could not legally get in the airplane and go fly by himself, but if you walked in the door and had a pilot and medical certificate, you would likely end up flying with him at some point, and I did fly with him on several occasions. He always had great stories to tell.

The two part-time flight instructors were Stan and Jay. Stan had a very easygoing, laid-back demeanor. He had several students and was around the airport quite often even when he was not teaching.

And then there was Jay. Jay was a colorful character who had a rather crusty demeanor as a result of having three helicopters shot out from under him in Vietnam. Jay never missed an opportunity to pick on me. He continuously reminded me that airplanes were designed to kill people, and the trick to survival was to be smarter than the airplane and always stay way ahead of it.

I realized early on that you had to be thick-skinned to run around with this crowd. Being the youngest person at the airport by at least a decade meant that it was open season on me. Being the brunt of all the practical jokes, being the target of anything humiliating or embarrassing was just a part of it. Get used to it or go home. That was just the way it was.

In spite of all that, in the shop, I was becoming part of the crew. Working alongside and learning from Robert and a few others, I had become a sponge for their transfer of knowledge and experience. The proper technique for installing and timing a magneto, or the proper way to rig the flight control surfaces, or simply servicing the brakes, there was always something new to learn, and somehow a lot of that new found knowledge and experience transferred to what was being taught in night school.

We always had three or four rebuild projects at various stages of completion, as well as several annual inspections underway. In the meantime, the rental aircraft also required routine maintenance and inspections. On top of all that, we would routinely load up the truck and trailer and travel to a crash site off in the boonies somewhere to disassemble and haul a wrecked aircraft back to the bone yard for storage and subsequent rebuilding.

Because I was the only full-time employee in the company who actually had a valid pilot's certificate, I was called upon to test fly the freshly rebuilt aircraft. In addition, I was often called upon to pick up and deliver customer aircraft before and after a maintenance event. Never mind if I had never flown that type of aircraft before, if I could figure out how to start the engine, I should be able to fly it. I never knew what kind of adventure each day would bring, but what fun it was.

I was at the airport seven days a week and it seemed as though I just could not get enough. Oftentimes I would be several hours late to night school as I would be engaged in a project at work which had my interest much more than any classroom lecture could. As a result, I often found myself in trouble and was forced into doing special projects in order to make up for all the missed class time.

Fortunately, Robert was very accommodating in allowing me to commandeer junk aircraft parts for special school projects. I made cutaway demonstration examples of a Bendix magneto, a curled up Hartzell constant speed propeller, and a Woodward propeller governor and took them to school and put on a show-and-tell demonstration. Not all instructors were so easy on me, but most appreciated my enthusiasm and realized the value I was gaining from the real-world experience I was getting at my day job.

Being the youngest and least experienced at work, I also got called upon to do all the shit jobs. I cleaned the office and restrooms, swept out the hangar, mowed the yard, fueled all the aircraft, and washed the rental aircraft. In the shop I drilled and bucked rivets, laid out new skins, stripped paint and prepared the surfaces for painting using the harshest chemicals known to man. I assisted with every aspect of rebuilding wrecked aircraft.

I was not always happy with all of my assignments, but at least I was at the airport playing with airplanes and getting paid to do it. That was a lot more than I could say for nearly all my classmates, who were either slinging hamburgers or changing car tires for a living.

Flo, the gal who wrote the paychecks, must have skipped a few math classes when she was in school, because no matter how many hours my time card showed at the end of a two-week pay period, my paycheck was always $98.

Upon pointing out the discrepancies, she was always quick to point out that with my limited experience I should consider myself lucky to even get a paycheck, I should probably be paying her to work there. It didn't help matters any when I discovered that Flo was Robert Lotero's mom.

I often referred to Robert as "Boneyard Bobby," because with all the wrecked aircraft hauling and rebuilding the company did, they had accumulated quite a collection of aircraft parts, including dozens of airframes, wings, engines, and accessories. We referred to this off-airport storage location as the "boneyard".

One man's junk is another man's treasure, and it did not take me very long to recognize the value of the boneyard. I found it to be a great resource when looking for an aluminum fuel line, or flight control pulleys, or some other gizmo needed to complete a rebuild project.

After I'd worked for Boneyard Bobby for just six months, he saw my skills, drive, and determination progress enough to grant me my very own project. I was so proud of that little wrecked 1969 Cessna 150J that bore the tail number N60544. My very first project, start to finish. She was pretty smashed up and the people who were flying the airplane had been seriously injured. It needed a firewall repair, an engine mount, a new windshield, some wing skins and a spar repair on one wing, and an aft fuselage skin. It was my first opportunity to take the lead on a project. Of course, I was closely supervised, but I was let loose with the reins and allowed to identify what needed to be done, in what order the work was to be accomplished, and to execute my rebuild plan.

Upon completing the repairs and assembling the airplane, I was allowed to design and apply my very own paint scheme. A white base coat with red trim, and black accents. She was a pretty little One-Fifty. After the test flight and some final rigging adjustments, the boss decided to put her into the rental fleet until someone came along and offered to buy it. Little ol' Five Four Four quickly became a favorite for many of our customers. I was really proud of that little Cessna One-Fifty.

At eighteen years old, I was working my ass off and living the dream. It was airplanes all day and night, interrupted occasionally by a brief romantic adventure with a local gal that I found somewhere along the way. Financially I was in the poor house but happy to be gaining a lot of knowledge and experience.

Chapter 3

My First Repo

Although I did not know it at the time, one of our customers who really liked Five Four Four was a local banker who financed airplanes. He was a very stylish, fashion-minded young guy from Tulsa. I will never forget the fancy maroon three-piece suit complete with bellbottom pants that he always wore. He had matching red hair cut in the then fashionable shag style and sported a goatee. I know it sounds horrible now, but keep in mind that this was the mid-seventies and Disco Danny was very much in style.

One morning, we were all out in the shop (all four of us) working on the assembly process of a little Cherokee 140 when this banker dude shows up. I remembered thinking to myself that his visit was a little unusual on this particular day, as he normally only appeared on the weekends when he would rent one of our aircraft. It was September 2, 1975.

He cornered the boss man and together the two of them went off to the back office in the shop and closed the door. Now this was very strange, as normally around there the only door that was ever closed was the bathroom door, and then only when it was occupied. Didn't matter to me anyway as I had to get this fuel tank installed and it had a butt load of screws that held it in place and I had a couple of mismatched holes.

A short while later the boss man and the red headed banker dude emerged from the office. The banker man jumped in his car and departed the airport. The boss man, without saying a word, went to the operations office and began making phone calls. I had an instinct to not disturb him, but I kinda needed some advice as to how to make these last couple of screw holes line up.

A short while later, as I was studying my dilemma, the boss man came up from behind me and said, "Hey, Turkey, I need you to do something."

"Well, okay, Boss Man, but let me show you what we have going on here first. I have a problem and need your advice."

After I described my problem with the Cherokee fuel tank, he said not to worry about it right now, he had something else he needed me to do.

I was handed a big wad of "pick keys" and told to go find a Cessna 150 with the tail number of November One One Three Two Nine and fly it back to Sand Springs. He suggested that I might find it at the Tahlequah Airport, or maybe it could be in Pryor, or even at the Wagner Airport out in eastern Oklahoma. It should be all gassed up and ready to go.

Yippee! I was excited that on this pretty September day, I would get to spend the rest of the day putting another few precious flight hours in my logbook, and I didn't even have to pay for the gas.

Now, the request for me to go pick up an airplane and bring it to the shop for an inspection, or to deliver it back to the owner after the maintenance was complete, had become routine and I always enjoyed the opportunity to fly something different. But on this particular occasion, I thought it was kind of strange that Robert was not sure exactly which airport the aircraft was at. He usually had specific instructions for me such as, "The key to the hangar is under the tool box in the pickup truck parked behind the hangar," or other specific clues, but not this time. Just a wad of pick keys and a guess as to which airport to begin hunting for the airplane.

We usually had a flight instructor or two hanging around the lobby area in search of their next student victim and I would usually recruit one of them for a quick trip such as this, but on this day there were no flight instructors to be found.

One of my co-workers had a student pilot certificate so I asked the boss if I could take Rick with me. He replied that I could, and that we should take One Two Sierra because Rick had been flying it and he was most comfortable with that one. He made certain that we understood that I was to fly the new airplane back to Sand Springs.

Now back in those days, this was considered normal, but in today's world of ever-increasing regulations and insurance requirements, Rick would have to have a flight instructor sign off his logbook approving him for the cross-country solo flight home; it was not like he could simply follow me or the high way home. Back then, there never much talk about minimum experience requirements to qualify for the insurance policy or if I had a check-out in the make and model airplane with a flight instructor. If I could get it started, the boss man expected me to fly the airplane, and who was I to argue.

Rick and I knew where we were going as we had been flying all over eastern Oklahoma for the past ten months, and we knew just about every airport, but just for good measure we consulted with the aeronautical chart. We decided to do a low pass at Pryor and if we did not see anything, we would continue on to Tahlequah, and if we did not see our airplane we would go take a look at Wagner.

Pryor was only about forty miles away, which made the flight rather short, and there were a few airplanes there, but no Three Two Nine. Boss Man said it would be tied down outside, but wasn't here. Tahlequah is only twenty-five miles away, so off we went. We buzzed the runway, and on the first pass we were able to identify a couple of the Cessna's on the ramp, so around we went.

We landed on the next pass and taxied to the ramp. We just drove around the ramp looking at each of the Cessna's and verified that none of them were ours. Back out to the runway where we blasted off heading for Wagner. As we broke ground, enroute to Wagner, we began discussing the thought of the airplane being down in Muskogee. The roar of the powerful Continental O-200 engine mounted on the Cessna made it difficult to carry on a detailed conversation as neither of us had headsets, so the consensus was to continue northwest to Wagner.

Entering the traffic pattern at Wagner, I could see that there was only one little Cessna parked outside in the grass. After we landed and taxied up, Rick reminded me that it was a good idea not to have gone to Muskogee. We parked right next to Three Two Nine, shut down One Two Sierra, and climbed out.

Wow, she was pretty. This 'li'l dumplin'' had some ramp appeal and was going to be a real treat for me because it would be the newest aircraft I had ever flown. I got all excited. She was all trimmed out in a new Cessna white and gold paint scheme complete with the new style wheel pants, tubular steel landing gear, and everything. Three Two Nine was a 1973 model Cessna 150 with only about 300 hours on it and it still had the new airplane smell to it.

Rick was happy that we didn't go to Muskogee, because had we gone there and then here, we would probably have needed fuel to get home, and neither of us had any money. After laughing that off, I began fiddling with keys, and in just a few short minutes I had managed to get the door opened. A moment or two later, I found a key that fit the ignition.

As I walked around little Three Two Nine performing my pre-flight inspection, I noticed that there was absolutely nobody at this little airport except us. Kind of typical for small airports, but there was no sign of life anywhere. Just me, Rick, and a couple of Cessna 150s.

Nothing left here for us to do except saddle up and head home. We fired up the little Cessnas and taxied out together with Rick in the lead. After an engine run-up, Rick took the runway and I followed close behind. Even though Rick did not have his pilot's certificate yet, he had soloed multiple times and could handle One Two Sierra just fine.

1973 Cessna 150L N11329

I chased Rick down the runway and as he banked to the west, I joined up on him at his seven o'clock position. The flight back to Sand Springs was a lot of fun as we did a little formation flying, played chase, and did a little dog fighting. What a way for a couple of teenagers to spend an afternoon at work.

Upon arriving back at the Sand Springs Airport, we quickly discovered that nobody was there. Now keep in mind that this was a little country airport and it was not unusual for all the hangar and office doors to be wide open and nobody be there. Since it was fairly late in the day, I figured everybody was down at the boneyard scrounging for parts or off to a late lunch, or maybe decided to go home early.

I took note of the time and figured that if we hustled, we could get Three Two Nine all opened up for an annual inspection and only be just a little bit late for school. Me and my favorite screwdriver got busy and in no time at all I had the cowling off and the oil draining, while Rick was busy pulling the wing and tail inspection panels. I was inside the cabin removing the seats when the Boneyard Bobby and the redheaded banker man arrived.

We were pretty sure the boss would be proud of us for taking the initiative to be productive in his absences, but no, not today.

"WHAT IN THE HELL DO YOU TWO TURKEYS THINK YOU ARE DOING!? What did I tell you? Go find the airplane and fly it here! That was it! I did not tell you to do any maintenance on it or open it up like this!"

"Well, we're opening her up for the annual inspection, Boss. Isn't that why you sent us to get it?" I sheepishly replied.

"My instructions were simple: go find the airplane and bring it home, now look what you have done!"

I had never seen Boneyard Bobby that mad before, but what was really funny was the redheaded banker man was standing out by the wing tip laughing hysterically, while the boss gave us a dressing down.

It was about that point that I suggested that we were already late for school and should probably be leaving.

When I arrived for work the next morning Three Two Nine was all buttoned up and tied down on the flight line. I did not understand that if we were in such an all fired hurry to get the little airplane to Sand Springs, why was it just sitting on the ramp with no work in progress?

Not another word was mentioned about Three Two Nine until one day about a week later at lunch, when the boss man announced that Three Two Nine would be added to our rental fleet. Now I was excited to hear that, as Three Two Nine was nearly new compared to the rest of the fleet, and having been the one who brought her home, I knew she was in very good mechanical condition.

The one drawback for me with this addition to our fleet was that my beloved Five Four Four quickly took the back seat and became the second favorite Cessna 150 in the fleet with our customers. On the other hand, about a month later I overheard the boss man talking to the banker man about the "repossession" of Three Two Nine. They were talking about how it turned out to be a win-win situation for all parties involved. Hearing that new information, I got a sudden rush of adrenaline.

I asked the boss man why he didn't tell me that I was being sent out to repossess Three Two Nine. His reply was, "Would you have done it if I told you it was a repossession? Would it have made a difference in the way you did your job?"

At the time, I did not really have an answer for him. I had never even given it any thought. To me it was just another precious flight hour in my logbook.

Chapter 4

Jay Was Right

As the instructor droned on and on about seemingly useless information, I got the feeling he was doing so for the sole purpose of torturing me and the rest of the class. It was 11:30 p.m. Wednesday night at Spartan School of Aeronautics, and tomorrow was Thanksgiving.

Most of the other instructors had released their classes early and wished them a happy turkey day, but not our instructor. He seemed determined to keep us there until midnight, which was when classes normally got out.

Waiting for me outside was a rapidly approaching blue northern cold front, strong gusty winds, and below freezing temperatures. Thirty miles away at the Sand Springs Airport was a Mooney Chaparral that somehow I convinced my boss, Robert, to let me fly it home to Texas for the long Thanksgiving weekend.

I suppose the Spartan instructor was feeling that he had tortured the class long enough and was feeling generous when he turned us loose at ten minutes to midnight. With that I jumped in my trusty Cutlas Supreme and raced across town to Sand Springs Airport, knowing that if I did not take off soon, I would be forced to drive to Dallas for the four-day weekend.

For now, the weather was VFR with strong winds at twenty gusting to thirty knots out of the north and the temperature dropping into the twenties. The forecast was for deteriorating conditions complete with strong gusty winds from the north, IFR conditions with low ceilings and visibility, and freezing precipitation.

My pre-flight inspection was very difficult and painful. The big part was easy, but due to the rapidly dropping temperatures most of the airplane had a light coat of frost forming that required some attention. I did the best I could at clearing the frost off the wings with a piece of cardboard, but by the time I got around to sumping the fuel tanks, my hands were pretty well frozen. The fuel looked okay at the time,

23

considering the flashlight was rapidly dimming. It seemed like most all of my flashlights were nothing more than dead battery holders.

I was becoming really anxious to get in the cockpit, out of the wind, and get the engine started and getting the cabin heater going. I already knew, from past experience, that it was going to be a turbulent departure.

Sand Springs Airport sits on a hill surrounded by small hills densely covered with trees, with a pair of radio transmission towers about five miles east that stand about 1,500 feet tall. When the wind blows out of the north like it was tonight, it was always a rough ride up to about 2,500 feet.

The engine fired right up on my command and the oil pressure came right up, but it seemed to take forever for the oil temperature gage to come up off the peg. I closed the cowl flaps to help trap the heat in the engine compartment to aid in warming the engine. As the oil temperature began to rise, I began a slow taxi to runway 35, setting the en route VOR frequencies in the navigation radios.

There were no navigation aids along my direct route of flight; they were all offset either to the left or right of my course and were associated with little towns along the way. These towns were easy to spot on a clear night.

By the time I got to the end of the runway, the oil temperature had come up a couple of needle widths off the peg and I was beginning to feel some welcome warmth from the cabin heater, but looking out the window I could see that frost was already beginning to re-form on the wings. Still, I took my time with my pre-departure engine run-up, slowly cycling the propeller several times, checking the magnetos and vacuum system, aligning the directional gyro, and setting the altimeter.

I taxied around in a 360-degree turn, checking the sky to see if anyone else was crazy enough to be out flying at this time of night with this bad weather rapidly approaching. "Sand Springs traffic, Mooney Seven Seven Eight Zero Mike is taking runway three five for departure." I announced on the Unicom frequency.

With that, I taxied onto the runway and lined up on the centerline, held the brakes, and pushed the throttle in to about 2,000 rpm. After one more scan of the instrument panel to verify that all the gauges were in the green, I shoved in full power and let off the brakes.

As I went barreling down the runway, the gusty winds kept trying to encourage the little Mooney to fly well before I knew it should. After the lowest airspeed fluctuation settled in at my desired speed, I lifted the nose off the runway. Once again, Sand Springs Municipal Airport did not disappoint as she tossed the Mooney around like she was in the clothes dryer.

It took three tries for my right hand to finally connect with the landing gear retraction lever in order to retract the landing gear. Out the windshield I could see the opaqueness of the rapidly approaching cloud cover, but I knew once I got established on course, clear skies, smooth air, and a hell of a tailwind was waiting for me.

Climbing out at about 500 feet above the runway, the engine surged once and then completely quit. Dead silence. My heart skipped a few beats and then instinct took over. I immediately reached my hand down between my legs to the fuel selector valve located on the cockpit floor, switched the fuel selector to the left tank, and then hit the fuel boost pump switch. Almost as fast as the engine had quit, it started back up again at full power. Wow! What the hell was that?

I didn't have much time to think about what just happened as I was getting slapped around the sky like a rag doll and needed to focus on keeping the airplane upright and gaining altitude as quickly as possible so I could make it back around for a landing. As I continued climbing, I brought the Mooney around to a southerly heading and could really feel that tailwind kick in.

The engine was running strong and smooth. The engine interruption was not a catastrophic mechanical failure. It had to be either an ignition issue or a fuel problem. Keeping close to the airport, I decided to continue climbing.

Soon I was into smooth air and was able to better concentrate on my situation. The engine was running well so I decided to climb to about three thousand feet over the Sand Springs Airport. My thinking was that if the engine quit again, I could always spiral down and make it back to the home base.

Once reaching about 3,000 feet, I carefully switched the magneto switch from "Both" to "Right", then to "Left". The engine did not run as well on the left or right magneto as it did on both, but both magnetos were functioning properly. I figured the power interruption must have been a fuel issue.

I spotted Riverside Airport to the southeast and decided that with the tail wind I now had, I could easily make it there, so I aimed for Riverside and continued to climb.

Before I got to Riverside Airport, I could see the rotating beacon at Okmulgee Airport, which was about twenty-five more miles to the south of my position, and Bristow Airport, which was a little closer. I kept climbing. Henryetta was just a little further south.

With confidence that I could easily glide to another airport in the event of another engine failure, I continued to climb to 8,500 feet en-route to Red Bird Airport in Dallas. It was not very long before the glow of the DFW Metroplex lights came into view.

The little Mooney scooted along pretty good with a 35-knot tail wind that had the DME bouncing off of 200 knots several times along the way, but I still had an uncomfortable feeling during the entire flight as Jay's words about airplanes being designed to kill us echoed in my head.

The descent into the DFW area and landing at Red Bird was uneventful and quiet, as I must have been the only one out flying around at 2 a.m. The airport seemed abandoned and it was help yourself to a parking spot and tie-down ropes.

Using the payphone on the wall outside the Modern Aero FBO, I called Mom to let her know I had landed safely and in short order, she arrived to pick me up. I was happy to be back in Texas, even if it was only to be for the Thanksgiving weekend.

Curious as to why the engine had failed on take-off, the following morning, I drove out to Red Bird Airport to look the Mooney over. I took a fuel sample from the right fuel tank and did not note anything unusual, but when I took a sample from the left wing, I noticed that the reddish color of the fuel was much more defined and closer to the color of the 80/87 octane fuel that we were using.

I crawled back under the right wing and continued to take fuel samples from the sump drain into the little sample cup. After about ten fuel samples, I decided that this might take a while. I rummaged around the FBO and found a five-gallon bucket and a small steel rod with which I created a make-shift fuel-draining system.

All in all, I drained about two gallons of water from the right fuel tank. I rocked the airplane around some and got about another half-gallon of water. I figured the fuel cap gasket had leaked water into the fuel tank during the previous week's rain.

This was where I learned to place a piece of Saran Wrap over the flush-mounted fuel caps on many different types of aircraft if they were to be left outside in the rain. Another lesson learned.

The return flight to Sand Springs four days later was uneventful, although a heck of a lot slower than the flight to Texas was. For fear of being criticized for one reason or another I did not think it was prudent to mention this event to the boys at the airport.

Chapter 5

Learning to Fly the Taylorcraft

As an aspiring teenage aviator, I often found life at work much more interesting and fun than a long and boring evening at night school that did not let out until midnight.

At work I was drilling rivets, fabricating skins, bucking rivets, installing engines, timing magnetos, rigging a flap system, helping do annual inspections, and reading maintenance manuals, and often times I got to fly a cross-country flight for company business. All of these activities were much more captivating than racing across town for a class that began at 5 p.m. to listen to an instructor talk about the things I had been doing all day, so needless to say, I was routinely late for class.

One such tardiness was the result of a trip I made with Boneyard Bobby in November Three Five Six Five Kilo (N3565K), one of the rental Piper Cherokees. We were on the hunt for serviceable parts we needed to finish the rebuild of a G model Bonanza.

After flying to a little town in southwest Arkansas, we were picked up by a gentleman who drove us to his farm, where his barn was stuffed full of aircraft parts, fuselages, wings, and a variety of components. Out back, he had a little grass strip and another little barn.

In front of that barn was this little airplane that kept smiling at me. I couldn't help myself, but I fell in love with that little airplane. It was as if she was laying there waiting for someone to come along and rub her belly.

She was all intact but she had some minor deficiencies. For one, she was upside-down (hence the belly-rub reference). It appeared that someone had flipped her over on landing. She still had a rope around her propeller where it appeared that someone had tied it to their trailer hitch to drag her off the little grass strip and up next to the barn.

There was something about the way that little Taylorcraft smiled at me, I just knew I had to have it.

I began to do a damage assessment to determine what it would take to get her flying again. The little T-Craft was constructed with steel tubing and covered with fabric, which was a construction process that was considerably different than the Cessnas and Pipers that I had been working on. From what I could tell, she suffered a bent propeller, bent engine mount, busted induction manifold spider, busted windshield, three bent wing struts, and a crushed vertical fin and rudder.

Evidently, I had spent a considerable amount of time out there with that little Taylorcraft because Robert came looking for me. It appeared that his business was done here, but I was not quite ready to go. "Do you think this is for sale?" I asked.

He replied that he was sure it was, but I would need to talk to The Man myself to confirm that and negotiate the conditions of the sale. With that said, he went back inside and left me to finish my assessment.

I finished inspecting the smiling little upside-down Taylorcraft and began to assess my current state of poverty. I thought that if I could sell my car, I might be able to pull off the purchase of this thing and maybe finance some of the necessary repairs.

I went inside to find Robert and The Man sitting in his office looking all business like, and the boss man said, "What's up, Turkey?"

"Well, I would like to talk to The Man about that little airplane out back."

"Okay, you have the floor," and with that he got up and left the room.

I was now on my own, entering into negotiations with someone who I perceived to be a shrewd negotiator.

"That little airplane outback by the barn, how much are you asking for it?"

"Three thousand dollars cash," was his reply.

I could tell that he saw the disappointment on my face as he knew that was way out of my price range.

"Would you like to make an offer?"

"I think I can come up with a thousand dollars, would that work?"

"I'll take twenty-five hundred bucks for it, and I will hold it for you for two weeks."

I pulled out my billfold and took a look inside. "I can give you a twenty-dollar non-refundable deposit to hold it for me for two weeks, but the best I can offer is fifteen hundred for it."

He smiled at me, reached his hand across the desk to shake my hand, and said, "SOLD."

My heart began racing and my mind went into overdrive. Either I just became the proud new owner of a wrecked airplane or I lost twenty bucks. Now, I had to figure a way to come up with $1,500.

I was kind of proud of myself as The Man drove us back to the airport.

During the flight home, Robert informed me that he had purchased some Bonanza parts and that he was going to send me and one of the other guys back with a truck and trailer in a few weeks to pick up the newly acquired Bonanza inventory.

As was more often the case than not, I was late getting to school that night-very late this time. Since I was one of only a handful of students who actually worked at an airport and, more importantly, on airplanes, my classmates always took great interest in my job.

They were really interested in the G Model Bonanza we were working on and the search for Bonanza parts as I described the day's adventure, but they were even more interested in my report about the T-Craft. Most knew of my financial situation, as their finances were fairly similar. I had a pretty nice car that I worked all through high school to pay for, but if I sold it to buy a wrecked airplane, how would I get back and forth to work and school?

Within a week, I had managed to pull off a magic trick. I now had a $200 Harley Davidson 350 Sprint motorcycle and $1,800 cash in hand. The first task at hand was to order up a new windshield from LP Aero Plastics for $75.

Next up was to travel to Nashville, Arkansas, to pick up my T-Craft, and all the newly acquired Bonanza parts.

The Man was there waiting when we arrived early Saturday morning and we sat down to close the deal on the little airplane. Robert had already paid for the Bonanza stuff we were there to pick up, but what I didn't know until now was that he had given The Man a $100 deposit for the T-Craft on my behalf.

I handed The Man $1,480 in cash and he handed me a signed Bill of Sale and $100. "You have a pretty good boss there, young man, he saw how interested in that airplane you were. He was going to see to it that you would be the next owner of that T-Craft even if you couldn't come up with all the money."

Wow. That statement left me speechless. I had no idea that the boss man thought enough of me to cover my six like that. I reckon that my hard work, dedication, and loyalty did not go unnoticed. It was kind of a proud moment for me.

Loading the Bonanza on the trailer was pretty easy, but the T-Craft was a different story. She was still smiling at me after we flipped her over upright, although we may have smacked the nose cowl up a bit, I could tell she was happy to be going to a new home. It did not take long to bust the wings and tail feathers off and load it on the trailer.

Even though I was still a teenager and had been working for Boneyard Bobby for only a year and a half, I had become fairly competent at assessing a damaged aircraft, and the steps necessary to begin executing repairs in a systematic manner. He seemed to take great pride in watching me develop as an aviator and mechanic and

31

would let me run with a project until I got stuck, at which time he would ride to the rescue and bail me out by providing me direction.

The first order of business for my T-Craft project was to sneak away at lunch time in the Cherokee and fly down to Okmulgee to drop the propeller off at Herman Fosters Prop shop for straightening.

The next order of business was to evaluate the engine. Robert was always a great mentor and teacher and he could tell that I was uncertain as to what to do with the engine. It was lunch time, and instead of running to town for lunch at straight up noon time, he began asking me what I thought I should do.

Your prop was bent, right? You think something else might have got bent as well? How about that crankshaft flange? That is the most expensive part of the engine, maybe we should check the run-out. And with that he instructed me to pull the spark plugs while he went to the tool cabinet to get a dial indicator.

After a five-minute lesson in checking the run-out on a crankshaft and getting satisfactory results Robert said, "If this were my engine, I think I would bust it down and take the crank to the shop for magnaflux inspection, just to be sure, then reassemble it with new bearings and rings." Then he went off to lunch.

I spent the rest of my lunch break removing the cylinders, magnetos, carburetor, and other knickknack parts, and cleaning a place in the corner of the hangar for all my little engine parts. The rest of the day went by painfully slow as I kept looking out at the tie-down spot where the wingless and now partially engine-less T-Craft sat patiently waiting for me.

When 4:30 rolled around, instead of jumping on that crappy motorcycle and racing off to school, I grabbed the engine hoist and pushed it out to the ramp, where I removed the remainder of the engine. By the time I wheeled it back to the hangar and mounted it on an engine stand it was 6 p.m. so it was off to school.

I spent the next day's lunch break further disassembling the engine and by the time everyone returned from lunch, the crankshaft, camshaft, and other steel parts were laid out neatly on the table. I knew there were a lot of engine shops in Tulsa on Sheridan Road, but had no idea what to do next or who to talk to about having a magnaflux inspection performed on these parts.

Upon arriving at work the following morning, I discovered all my parts missing, which greatly disappointed me. Being the youngest guy in the shop by at least ten years, somebody was always pranking me; even the two part-time flight instructors picked on me.

I was frustrated, but it was time to go to work on a Piper Cherokee rebuild project that we had been working on. When the boss man finally arrived at the shop, he informed me that my engine parts should be back within a week or so, which was a great relief.

I had recently completed a welding class at school and remembered all the recommended tube steel repairs laid out in the FAA publication AC 43.13, so my lunch break was spent at the bone yard looking for bent up engine mounts that were the right size that I could cut up and use to make a repair for my engine mount. I think Robert was kinda proud when he returned from lunch and saw the freshly repaired and painted engine mount hanging by a coat hanger. "Pretty good job on that mount, Turkey."

While waiting around for the steel engine parts to return from the shop, it was time to address the vertical fin and rudder damage. A quick slice with a pocket knife to peel about one-fourth of the fabric down the vertical fin revealed the damage that was nowhere near as bad as I had envisioned.

Simply bend the leading-edge tube back up to the top of the rear post, tack weld it in place, add a gusset for strength, clamp a pair of 2x4's around the tubes and tweak it slightly for proper alignment, and it was ready for fabric covering. The next day, lunch time was spent doing a similar repair to the rudder. Glue some new fabric on, throw in a few rib stitches and spray some silver dope on it and the tail repairs were complete. Installing the horizontal stabilizers and elevators was complete in no time at all.

The maintenance shop did not always work on the weekends, so my weekend duties were to man the gas pump and sign in and out the little rental fleet of airplanes, clean the office and shop, and any other chores the boss would come up with. With all my duties taken care of, I would spend the slow periods of the day loving on the little T-Craft.

The windshield had arrived and I removed it from the box and set it on the fuselage. It only took a few minutes to realize that this project was going to take some time because it would need to be carefully trimmed and fit, so I held off until Sunday for this task. By quitting time Sunday evening, I had managed to get the windshield installed, and with the help of one of our aircraft rental customers, I got the engine mount installed.

The following week, all my engine parts mysteriously reappeared, so with a little consultation from the boss man, I spent my next couple of lunch breaks assembling the little Continental engine. I stayed a little late after work to hang the engine and hook it all up. By the time I finished, I was an hour late to school, but all I needed was a propeller to run the engine.

The following day, after everyone had gone to lunch, I started noodling with the airplane. I wandered around the shop looking for a propeller that would fit on the T-Craft but there was not one laying around anywhere.

As I looked across the flight line, I spotted Jay's little Luscombe sitting out there. Jay was one of the freelance flight instructors. "Hey, that has a Continental A-65 on it; I'll just borrow that for a little while." In just a few short minutes, I had Jay's propeller on the T-Craft. Unfortunately, I had to remove it and re-install it because I had it clocked wrong the first time. Double check the oil, add a little gas, and I was ready to fire this li'l dumplin' up.

My experience with the little Continental A-65 was rather limited at the time, so learning how to start the engine was a lesson of trial and error. This updraft carburetor did not have an accelerator pump that would pump raw fuel into the induction system, so learning to pull the propeller through several blades with the throttle set at idle and listening to the air filter for the gurgling sound of fuel was an art that I was yet to learn.

I tugged and tugged on that propeller trying to get it to start with no luck. Adjusted the throttle some, gave it a few shots of prime, it popped and sputtered but quit. Gave it a little more throttle and went back to the front of the airplane.

I gave that propeller a mighty twist and the little Continental roared to life - at about half throttle. The airplane jumped the chocks and took off across the ramp, barely missing me as I dove out of the way of that meat cleaver.

Oh shit! I chased after the little wingless T-Craft and grabbed the tail just in time to steer it away from the flight school airplanes and the gas pump, and by the time it ran off the ramp into the grass, it had slowed down just enough for me to catch up with it.

I grabbed the throttle, pulled it to idle, and stood there by the door trying to catch my breath. That just scared the hell out of me. Well, as long as the engine was running, I might as well crawl inside and taxi it around a little.

I had never flown a trail dragger and had heard all these stories about how hard they can be to land, so I thought a little taxi practice was in order. The T-Craft had heel brakes that were going to take some getting used to, as was steering the airplane by the tail-wheel.

I was taxiing around the ramp as if I was out for a Sunday drive, and soon got bored with that so I taxied south down the parallel taxiway towards the end of the runway. I did a slow 360-degree turn looking for any traffic in the pattern and then slowly taxied onto runway Three Five.

I gently applied power while keeping her going straight down the runway, then I gave it full power and shoved the elevator full forward.

Wahoo! Dang she got squirrely, first she swerved right, I corrected with the rudder, oh no! I overcorrected, corrected the other way, she was now high centering herself and hopping sideways. I pulled the throttle back to idle as I departed the left side of the runway and circled the windsock.

Whew, that was a hell of a ride. I glanced back towards the office and hangar to see if the boss and crew had returned from lunch yet. No sign of anybody, and no cloud of white dust from the gravel road so I must have a little more time.

I powered up and slow taxied back up onto the runway and down to the turn-off, still looking for signs that it was time to go back to work. As I taxied back to the end of the runway, I tried to understand what I had done wrong to take such a ride. Determined that I could master a tail-wheel airplane, I lined it up on the runway and shoved the power in again.

She swerved left, she swerved right, she swerved left again, tail was in the air, she was trying to hop sideways, she swerved right, and then left. We were probably up to forty mph when at just about the same spot as last time she darted left off the runway and around the windsock we went, again. By the time I got the throttle to idle and we came to a stop, I was beginning to wonder about my airmanship skills.

Not to be discouraged, I looked back towards the hangar and saw no signs of life so I taxied back to try it again. Once again, she gave me a dance lesson with my feet on the rudder pedals and again, we ended up off the runway circling the windsock.

As I taxied back up onto the runway, I could see a cloud of dust coming from the road leading to the hangar and office indicating that the boss and crew were returning from lunch, so I turned north, taxied down the runway up to the shop, and shut down the airplane.

The first person to greet me was Jay. "Kev, you goofy son of a bitch, you can't fly that thing without any wings on it!" Crap, he had seen my last attempt and I would never hear the end of this.

"When did you go get your prop?" he asked as he looked across the ramp to discover that his Luscombe was missing a prop. "Why you son of a bitch!! That's my prop you almost bent!!"

He chased me around the hangar threatening me with bodily harm if he could ever catch me for what could have happened to his prop. I didn't even have time to recover from that confidence-shattering experience I had just subjected myself to before everyone on the airport was ragging on me.

With that ordeal behind me, I went back to work on the shop projects and finished off the day by taking wing strut measurements. There were a lot of broken up antique wing struts at the bone yard; I just needed to figure out what size I needed in order to repair three of the four struts for the T-Craft.

Still worried I could never fly a tail-dragger, I spent the following day's lunch period welding up scarf patches on the wing struts. That evening, the boss helped me stab the wings on the T-Craft, which suddenly wasn't so little anymore. Dang, she had a lot of wing area.

The following morning, Robert told me that Herman from the prop shop had called to say that my prop was ready and the bill was $75. He also told me that if I wanted to take the flight school Cherokee down there during my lunch break, well, that was okay with him.

With MY propeller installed, I spent the following day finishing up the wing installation and rigging the ailerons, and although she was ready to fly, I was not. Not with this crowd around. What if I really couldn't fly it? What if I wrecked it on my first try? My confidence had really been shaken during my previous off-runway excursions, and I needed to get my nerve back up to try it again.

A few days later, I opted to stay at the airport during lunch time. The wind was light out of the south and it looked like a pretty good day for flying. I looked across the ramp at the little Taylorcraft parked next to the hangar, and I swear she smiled at me.

I walked around the aircraft giving her a close pre-flight inspection as I untied her ropes. I pushed her over to the gas pump and topped off the main tank, and then pushed her over to an unoccupied tie-down and anchored the tail. I was not going to let her get away from me again.

I gave the propeller a couple of big spins to prime the engine and then turned the magnetos on and cracked the throttle just a little bit. She fired off on the first pull and chugged along at about 500 rpm. I was surprised how easy that was as I ducked under the left-wing strut to look in the cockpit to see if we had oil pressure and retard the throttle as far back as she would go before going back to untie the tail.

I hopped in the airplane and with some trepidation I began taxing out to Runway One Seven. With the mag check complete, I decided it was now or never. I lined up on the runway and slowly began adding power while having flashbacks of my last attempt at this.

Kev with his T-Craft at Eagles Nest Airport

Just a slight wobble left and right as the tail came up, but straight down the runway we went. When I could feel her get light on her feet, I gently pulled back on the yoke and we were airborne. Yaaahooo!! Would you get a load of this?

I climbed out just to the west of the airport and did a few stalls, then returned to see if I could land this thing. I got a little slow on my first attempt as I was trying to three-point land it and she kind of plopped down on the runway, causing a momentary directional control problem, but that was quickly corrected. Convinced that it was under control, I added power and flew back off the runway.

I spent the next thirty-five minutes in the traffic pattern making full stall three-point landings, wheel landings, and just generally buzzing the airport. Me and that little airplane were having a blast. Ripping down the runway on one wheel, slipping her in to land, we were having so much fun, that I did not even notice when the guys came back from lunch. The boss had to drive his truck out on to the runway just to get my attention.

"Lot different with the wings on it, huh, Kev?" Robert asked.

"Yes sir! I like it!"

Together, me and that little airplane have flown all over the country. From Oshkosh to Sun n' Fun, we landed in farmers' fields, dirt roads, beaches, river beds, from Florida to the Rocky Mountains, from the Texas Gulf Coast to the Canadian border. We even had a few close calls, and although I already had a pilot's certificate, she really taught me how to fly.

Chapter 6

Living on Tulsa Time

On a bright sunny February morning, Robert asked me to prepare Cherokee One Six Five Six Juliet (N1656J) for a cross-country trip. Check tire pressures, service up the oil if needed, top off the tanks, and generally spruce it up a bit. Happy to oblige, I proceeded with the assigned task.

With the cabin cleaned out, seat belts crossed, windows cleaned, tire pressures checked, the oil serviced up to seven quarts, I was in the process of topping off the fuel tanks when Jay showed up. He threw a bag in the cabin and walked around to the engine cowling to open it up to check the oil.

He explained that he was flying up to Ohio to pick up his ninety-two-year-old grandmother, who was on oxygen and could not fly on the airlines. Just about the time he finished saying all that he drew a deep gurgling breath and hurled up a big nasty loogie and spit it on the engine.

"Shit, Jay, what the hell did you do that for?"

"Just in case that sumbitch decides to quit on me, I'll be one up on it!"

"Dammit, Jay, no wonder you think airplanes are trying to kill you. Show them a little love and they will take care of you!"

After topping off the fuel tanks, I went to the office to file the fuel receipts and then returned to the shop to resume my work. Shortly thereafter, Jay climbed into the Cherokee and took off east bound for Ohio.

The following afternoon I went to the office to ask Robert a question and noticed that he was studying an aeronautical chart. Other than providing answers to my questions he did not say anything else, so back to the shop I went.

A few minutes later, with charts in hand, Robert came to me and said, "Hey, Turkey, need you to gather up all the tools you will need to remove an engine from a Cherokee, load up in Cherokee Nine Eight One Eight Two (N98182), and fly a rescue mission." Oh boy, another opportunity to bank some more flight time for my logbook.

My mission was to load up in Cherokee Nine Eight One Eight Two and fly to Pope Airport in Greenfield, Indiana, just east of Indianapolis. From the sounds of things, the engine on Five Six Juliet had a catastrophic failure and Jay was able to make a safe landing. I was to give Jay Cherokee One Eight Two so he could continue his trip back to Sand Springs with his ninety-two-year-old grandma and I was to stay behind and pull the engine off of Five Six Juliet and have it ready to load in the truck. Robert would meet me there with the truck just as soon as he could make the drive from Sand Springs.

Robert told me that I did not have time to run home and get an overnight bag, as he wanted me to launch right away and try to get there before dark. Oh, by the way, the little airport you are going to is a grass strip just east of Indianapolis and is covered in snow. Looking at the charts and the clock, I knew that with a fuel stop, there was no way I could get there before dark.

With nothing more than a light jacket and a toolbox, I took off northeast bound racing against the sunset. Prior to this trip, about the farthest north east that I had flown was to Joplin, Missouri, so this was going to be an adventure. I was hoping that I could make St. Louis before dark so I could see the famous Arch on the Mississippi River.

With the modest tailwind, the 300-mile trip to St. Louis went by rather quickly. While entering the traffic pattern at the St. Louis Downtown Airport for a fuel stop, I was able to see the famous St. Louis Arch. What a disappointment that was; it always seemed so much more glamourous in pictures and on television than it did in person.

After the quick fuel stop at the Downtown Airport and departing into the darkening sky, I was surprised to see how bright the snow-covered ground was. The remaining 200 miles seemed to go by rather quickly as the city lights of Indianapolis soon came into view. The next challenge was to find the little Pope Airport.

I intercepted the east-west highway coming out of Indianapolis just east of town and followed it to the little town of Greenfield. Finding the airport was a challenge as it did not have a rotating beacon, and if it had runway lights, they were buried in snow and not visible from the air.

Descending to about 1,500 feet and crisscrossing the highway for what seemed like an hour, I was ready to turn back and go to Indianapolis when just north of the highway, I spotted a square building with a single light pole on the northeast corner and what looked like a Cherokee parked underneath. According to my chart, the airport had a north-south and an east-west grass runway and was located just north of the highway.

Descending further, I flew north over what appeared to be the runway and noticed a considerable amount of wind drift coming from the west. Then I circled to the east and lined up on a westerly heading on what appeared to be the east-west runway. There was no clear definition of a runway on either the north-south runway or the east-west runway. All I was really sure of was that it looked really cold down there. After a few more passes to try to make out the runway and no idea what lay beneath the snow, I made up my mind to land on the shorter runway into the wind to the west.

The touchdown was smooth and the little Cherokee decelerated rapidly as it settled into the snow. I quickly realized that I could end up stuck out here so as soon as I was slow enough, I added power and executed a 180-degree turn to taxi back to where the other Cherokee was parked. It damn near took full power to plow through all the snow, but I kept her moving and eventually pulled up next to Five Six Juliet and shut down the engine.

Okay, so here I was, what's next? There was not a soul around. I had no idea where Jay was or how to find him. There was not even a pay phone, so I couldn't call Robert and I had spent all the money Robert gave me on fuel back in St. Louis.

After securing the airplane, I walked out to the highway and managed to hitch a ride in just a few short minutes. The driver dropped me off at the first hotel we came to, which was only a few miles down the road. Once inside, I tried to convince the front desk clerk to give me a room for the night and that somebody else would be paying for it. While pleading my case, up pops Jay and his grandmother on the television in the lobby. "Look, that's them right there on TV, those are the people that I am here to rescue. They will be paying for my room!"

Jay and his grandmother had made the evening news with their engine failure and emergency landing.

The desk clerk still wasn't sure about me but my story seemed to be lining up. Turned out, Jay and his grandma were staying in the same hotel and the desk clerk had loaned them his car so they could go into town to have dinner.

After explaining the entire story and giving several reassurances that Jay or my boss or somebody would be paying for the room, he relented and gave me a room key and pointed me in the direction of my room.

After about an hour or so, there was a knock at the door. It was Jay! He came bearing gifts in the form of a six-pack of Stroh's Fire Brewed Beer. Together, we sat down and reviewed the events of the day. I criticized him for spitting on the engine before his trip and gave him the "I told you so" speech. Even though he was happy to see me, he continued to scold me about landing at that little airport at night in the snow with no runway lights. He claimed that it could not have been my skills that got me here safely as much as it was just dumb blind beginner's luck.

After finishing off the beer, Jay got up and suggested that he would get us a ride to the airport in the morning and that I should be ready to go when he knocked on the door.

The following morning, we were greeted with overcast skies and the threat of more snow, so Jay was quite anxious to get underway. We looked at the tracks I had left in the east-west runway the night before and decided that the snow on that runway was too deep to attempt a take-off. After walking up and down the north-south runway, we found a pathway on the west side of the runway where the snow cover was fairly thin compared to the drifts on the east side of the runway.

Back at the airplane, we struggled to get One Eight Two turned around and Grandma and her luggage and oxygen bottle all loaded into the airplane. Jay climbed aboard and said, "With any luck, I'll see you back in Sand Springs." With that, he closed and latched the door and fired up the engine.

By the time Jay had the engine warmed up enough to perform a magneto check, I had the cowling removed from Five Six Juliet. I stopped to watch him taxi to the very south end of the runway. Without stopping he turned around, hit full power, and began his take-off run on the 2,100-foot runway.

Although he was not accelerating very fast, he left me in a white-out condition as he passed my location. All I could see was a white trail of snow progressing down the runway. I couldn't tell exactly where he broke ground, but he could not have been very high when he cleared the fence at the north end. He flew north for a little way and then did a 180-degree turn and buzzed down the runway southbound past my location as if to say "adios, sucker."

With Jay gone, I found myself all alone out in the bone-chilling cold standing in about a foot of snow with an engine that needed to be prepared for removal. All I had was a light jacket and no gloves.

Figuring that the fastest way out of the cold was to get the job done, I got busy. Trying hard not to drop any of the hardware in the snow, off came the propeller and the cowling, the oil cooler, and then the exhaust system.

It was not long before I was shivering so bad from the cold that I could barely hold a wrench on a bolt or tug on a ratchet, but still, I had to continue on with removal of the carburetor and induction air box, the wiring to the alternator and stater and magnetos, and the lower engine mount bolts. All that was left to remove the engine were the two top engine mount bolts.

With all that accomplished, I stabbed the cowling back in place with about four screws, stowed the tools in the airplane, and retreated back out to the highway to try and hitch a ride back to the hotel.

Arriving at the hotel, I discovered that when Jay checked out of his room, he also checked me out of mine. The new person behind the front desk was not going to let me back into my room unless I could pay for it in advance. I used the lobby phone to place a collect call to Robert's wife to see if she had any information for me but she had not heard from Robert since he left Tulsa.

I guess I fell asleep in the lobby chair because I was awakened by Robert shaking me. "Get up, Turkey, we have work to do!"

"Shit, how the hell did you get here so fast? My feet have not even thawed out yet!"

Robert had driven all night and the truck was nice and warm for the ride back out to the airport. I briefed him on Jay's departure and what was remaining to drop the engine off the Cherokee. Thinking he would be happy with my perseverance at getting the job done under such adverse conditions, instead he began to chew me out for making such a bad decision as to land here at night. Hero to zero in less than three seconds, but what was I supposed to do?

It only took about thirty minutes to get the engine off the Cherokee and in the back of the truck and secure Five Six Juliet. Somehow, Robert managed to get in touch with the airport manager to make arrangements for short-term parking. With all that accomplished, we were back in the truck heading westbound toward home.

"Think we can stop somewhere to get something to eat?"

"Why, didn't you have breakfast this morning?"

"No, there was no food at the hotel and I don't have any money, spent it all on gas. I have not eaten since before I left Sand Springs."

Sitting in some greasy spoon we found along the way Robert informed me that we had another mission. We would be stopping at a farm near St. Louis to look at a Cessna 172. He didn't offer much in the way of details, but did say that if he liked the airplane, we would be bringing it home with us. Since we did not have a trailer that meant a few more hours of flight time for my logbook.

Being out in the cold and shivering uncontrollably must take a lot out of you because the next thing I knew we were pulling up to a farm house somewhere outside of St. Louis. We were greeted by a gentleman who appeared to be owner of the place. He got in his truck and we followed him down a snow-covered pathway to a barn. As we got out of the trucks, Robert instructed me to grab a screwdriver and be ready to pull some panels and remove the engine cowling.

Inside the barn was a pretty little 1968 Cessna 172 by the name of November Eight Four Nine Nine Lima (N8499L). At first glance she appeared to be in pretty good shape. The sheet metal was all straight and the original Cessna paint scheme in Italian gold was in pretty decent shape.

After some small talk Robert instructed me to remove the engine cowling and a few inspection panels while he sat down to review the logbooks. After he reviewed the logbooks and gave the airplane a brief inspection, we opened the barn doors and pulled the airplane out into the snow to run the engine.

Several attempts to start the engine yielded nothing more than a battery that was getting weaker by the minute. The engine showed no signs of life, so we pushed her back into the barn and pulled the doors closed. After some more discussions, Robert sent me out to the truck to snatch the magnetos off of the Cherokee engine with instructions to install them on the Cessna's engine.

It was pretty apparent that the Cessna owner was uncomfortable with a kid working on his engine but Robert assured him that everything would be alright. With the old magnetos removed and the Cherokee magnetos installed and timed, Robert began playing with the removed magnetos.

One mag was completely dead and the other only had a weak orange spark. Once again, we opened the barn doors and pushed the Cessna out into the snow for another attempt. Even with a weak battery, this time, she fired right up. After letting the engine warm up, Robert climbed in and took the seat next to me. We ran the engine up and did a mag check, a full power static rpm check, and played with the radios to see that they appeared to work. With that, we shut her down and pushed her back in the barn.

Once inside with the doors closed, I began reinstalling the inspection panels and the engine cowling while Robert carried on discussions with the farmer dude. With the airplane all back together, I checked to see that the airplane had about half a tank of fuel onboard.

After all the discussions took place that were way above my pay grade, Robert handed me a little pink piece of paper and told me to keep it with me at all times and not to lose it. It was a Special Flight Permit that had been issued by the FAA, otherwise known as a Ferry Permit. When or where he got it, I had no clue but I took his words seriously.

About this time another truck pulled up to the barn with two big burly dudes inside. The farmer introduced them as his boys, and they were going to help us push the airplane through the snow onto their sod runway for departure. The snow cover was not near as deep as it was at Pope airfield, but there was still plenty of snow just the same.

"You see that tree line down there?"

"Yes sir."

"You see the break in the trees? Well, you take off aiming right for that break and fly between them trees and you will be just fine. Don't go too far to the right, there is a culvert over there, if you hit that you will wreck the airplane."

"Yes sir."

With Robert and the three farmers pushing on the wing struts and me in the cockpit with the engine running at full power, we managed to get the airplane out to a location where they decided was right and pointed the airplane towards the break in the trees. I pulled the power back to idle to study the environment, and when I looked to my left, Robert gave me the launch signal as if I was flying off an aircraft carrier. (Robert had been stationed on an aircraft carrier during the Vietnam War.)

On his signal, I applied full power, but the little ol' Nine Nine Lima did not move. In a split second, I had two guys on each wing strut pushing me forward. After about thirty to forty feet I began to out run my ground support crew and was on my own plowing through the snow creating a white-out condition.

It became rapidly apparent that attempting to do a typical soft field take-off was not going to work in this case, as it felt like the airplane was just plowing into the snow and not getting on top of it or gaining any airspeed. I released the up-elevator pressure and began pushing forward and pulling back on the yoke in a rhythm that seemed to match my progress.

It was as if I was bouncing the airplane and each time I pulled up, I could feel her accelerate a little more, but not enough to get airborne. The air speed indicator finally came alive and began creeping towards a sustainable speed with each bounce, but I was rapidly approaching the fence. It would sure be nice if there was another 1,000 feet of runway here.

Timing. Timing was going to be the issue here. If I could just get her to bounce a little higher and time it just right, I could bounce her right between the trees and over the fence. Already well past the abort decision point, I had better get this right, otherwise there would be four strands of barbed wire fence wrapped around the propeller and no telling what kind of other collateral damage.

Instinctively, not trained, not taught, but instinctively, I reached over to the flap switch and went from ten-degree flaps to twenty-degree flaps. I only had room for one more bounce, it was do or die time. Timing it just so, I gave her full up elevator and she broke ground, not with enough flying speed, but the reduced drag from the snow allowed some acceleration. At risk of busting off the nose gear, I pushed the nose over and bounced off the snow-covered ground up and over the fence. Barely maintaining flying speed just above the ground on the other side of the fence, the airplane began to accelerate.

Whew, that was a close one. As the airplane accelerated, I slowly retracted the flaps and climbed a few hundred feet and reversed course. After the customary fly-by it was time to set a course for the St. Louis Downtown Airport. During the thirty-minute flight, I wondered what Robert saw that inspired his confidence in me. I was just nineteen years old and happy to have his confidence and would probably kill myself before I could ever let him down.

I arrived at the St. Louis Downtown Airport just before dark and set up for what should have been a really smooth landing, except that the airplane pulled hard right on touch down. I struggled to maintain directional control by rolling in full left aileron and rudder until it became apparent that I was going to take out a few runway lights. After narrowly missing a runway light I added full power and went around for another try.

As I flew around the pattern, I wondered if I might have a flat tire. It didn't feel like a flat tire, though-wait a second, I bet the wheel pants are packed with snow, sludge, and ice. That had to be it, but what could I do about it?

Touching down lightly on the left side of the runway, the airplane began to swerve hard right again so I added power just enough to get airborne and then, at risk of breaking something, I stalled the airplane and dropped her onto the runway from about ten feet, bounced once, and then did it again. Not sure if I had cleared any ice from the wheel pants and landing gear, I bounced her one more time just for good measure and then went around.

49

Once again, I lined her up on the left side of the runway and this time, she rolled right on smooth and straight as an arrow. As I rolled down the runway to the turn-off, I spotted several clumps of ice and sludge that must have broken loose on my previous landing attempts. After getting out of the airplane, I was greeted by a line service technician, who took my fuel order and made a few comments about my unusual arrival attempts.

After about forty-five minutes, Robert showed up and paid the fuel bill and asked how the airplane was doing. I described my landing issue and he just laughed and told me that I did a good job. I suggested that if we ever come off the snow again, we should first remove the wheel pants. He asked if I thought I could make it back to Sand Springs tonight or if I needed a break and a hotel room.

After we discussed our options, he told me that I did not need to show up for work tomorrow, but to call his wife and let her know that I made it home safely. I climbed back in the Cessna and made an uneventful three-and-a-half-hour night flight back to Sand Springs.

All said and done with, I only missed two nights of school, but chalked up another great adventure.

Chapter 7

Turn Out the Lights – The Party's Over

By January of 1976 I had graduated from Spartan School of Aeronautics with my Airframe and Powerplant Mechanics Certificate and I had my Private Pilot Certificate with over 250 flight hours logged, so I began asking the officials at Spartan about their promise to help me out with my advanced flight training as they had promised. Unfortunately, their flight school was still booked solid and did not have any openings for at least another year or so.

GRADUATES, JANUARY 1976 - SPARTAN SCHOOL OF AERONAUTICS, TULSA, OKLAHOMA

With that revelation, my first instinct was to flee Oklahoma and move back to Texas, but I was really engaged with work and having fun doing it. I was also now able to go on many more road trips with Robert without fear of missing school, and he had just given me my first pay raise since I started working for him.

With an abundance of leisure time, I found myself a steady girlfriend who I really did like, and I actually began having a social life with several of my former classmates and airport friends. There was Jay in his Luscombe, David in his Taylorcraft, Joel in his Cessna 140,

Mark in his Ercoupe, John in his little Cessna 150, and me in my trusty Taylorcraft.

We would get together on Sunday afternoons for a day of flying adventures. John and Mark were the only ones with a radio, so most of our communications were by hand signals. We were all over the skies of northeastern Oklahoma flying in formation, landing in farmers' fields, chasing each other from one airport to the next, and just having an all-around good time.

Working for Robert became more interesting, and my responsibilities increased exponentially. On one road trip, we picked up three 1970's vintage Cessna 150's. I was impressed as all three of these Cessnas would be relatively easy to repair compared to other aircraft we had repaired in the past.

On the ride home, Robert explained that as we finished rebuilding each of the aircraft, we would put them in service with the flight school, and then we would sell off the '60s vintage Cessna's. The newer aircraft would increase the value of the flight school. In just a few short months, we went from a fleet of 1967 and 1968 model Cessna 150s to a fleet of 1972 to 1974 model Cessna 150s. The newer Cessna's had a slightly wider cabin area and a few more modern features.

Just before going home one evening after work, Robert pulled me aside and suggested that I bring an overnight bag to work with me in the morning. He said that he was in negotiations with someone about something and was close to making a deal. Evidently, he closed the deal that evening.

The following morning, he instructed me to pack a toolbox and load it into a recently completed Cessna 150, November One Five One One Quebec (N1511Q). He had already packed up the logbooks and loaded them in the airplane. My mission was to fly out to Thomas, Oklahoma, disassemble a Cessna 182 Skylane and have it ready to load on a trailer when he arrived the following day. We would be trading One One Quebec even for the Skylane. The Skylane was a larger four-passenger airplane with a lot more capabilities than either the Cessna 150 or 172, or any of the Cherokee's that we had.

It took a little over two hours to make the flight, which was pretty good time considering the head wind and the crosswind that I had to contend with on landing. My first impression was that this little town was just one dust storm away from being blown off the map.

After visiting with the elderly airport welcoming committee, I showed them One One Quebec and the logbooks. Afterwards, they offered to take me to the hotel. They were somewhat surprised when I asked to see the Skylane, and even more surprised when I asked if they had a ladder and a pair of saw horses that I could borrow.

Looking over the Skylane, it appeared that someone had made a hard landing which wrinkled the firewall a bit and misaligned the nose gear. It also appeared that after the landing incident, rather than attempt to repair the damaged firewall and belly skin, somebody decided to install a STOL Kit (Short Take Off & Landing) on the airplane. They never finished the STOL Kit installation, as the cuffed wing leading edge skins still had clecos holding them partially in place.

The locals thought I must have been kidding when I stated that I would be removing the wings and tail feathers today and have the airplane ready to load on a trailer when Robert arrived the following day. They laughed at me and said that it would take them at least three days to get that airplane trailer ready, and "they" knew what they were doing.

I said, "Fine, then what you are saying is that someone will be around here in about hour and a half to help me drop the wings and lay them on the sawhorses. I will only need about ten minutes of your time."

"Sure, sonny, we will be around, you just come find us, and if you have those wings ready to drop, why we'll be happy to help you." There was a considerable amount of snickering amongst them as they walked back to the office.

I must confess, I was snickering too at these good ol' boys here in Bubbaville. Evidently, they underestimated me. They didn't know that I knew how to field strip a Cessna and load it on a trailer. I was way too young to know how to do this type of work. I should have bet them a case of beer.

Shortly after they left me to my work, they came back out to the hangar to inform me that they were going to lunch and would be back in about an hour. By then, I already had the access panels removed and the flap and aileron cables disconnected and pulled through the wings to the fuselage.

When they returned from lunch, I was sitting on the front porch to the office drinking a soda pop from the vending machine. "What's the matter, boy? You give up already?"

"No sir, just waiting on you guys to give me a hand dropping the wings and setting them on sawhorses."

Of course, they didn't believe me, but while they were gone, I had disconnected the electrical connectors to the wings, the fuel lines, the pitot tube line, and the fresh air ducts, and punched out all the wing bolts. The only thing holding the wings in place were the screw drivers that I stabbed in place of each wing bolt to temporarily hold the wings in place.

"Those wings better be ready, don't make us waste our time standing around watching you try to figure out what to do next!"

"The two of you get hold of that wing tip and lift up slightly while I remove the wing strut."

I removed the strut and laid it on the floor under the airplane.

"Now hold what you got, while I pull these two screwdrivers from the wing attach fittings. Okay, now, slowly take a step back with the wing, I've got the inboard end. Okay now, let's carry it over to the saw horses and set it down."

"Damn boy, you made that look easy. Is the other wing ready to come off just like that?"

"Yes sir, should be just as easy. Same process, lift up on the wing tip while I get the strut out of the way, then we pull the wing just like before." With both wings now lying on saw horses, they asked me if I was looking for a job. "No thank you, sir, I have a job, and I kinda like it, can I use the phone?"

After a brief consultation over the phone with Robert, I was back in the hangar removing the rudder and elevators. With the rudder and elevators removed, I disconnected the navigation antennae and the beacon light wires and loosened all the attaching hardware. Not wanting to drop or damage any of the parts, I recruited the help of the same two guys for the removal of the remaining tail feathers. The guys were happy to help out, and in short order, my day's work was done.

After securing my tools back in the box and laying out all the aircraft parts and hardware for loading on the trailer, I asked if they would take me into town and drop me off at the hotel. During the mile-and-a-half ride, they pointed out a little burger stand that was just a block away from the hotel and suggested I should try it out for dinner.

After checking into my room, I called Robert to brief him on the status of the Cessna and he said that he should be here between ten and eleven the following morning. With that, I was off to the burger joint. I could feel my arteries hardening as I placed my order, and this place did not disappoint. The only thing better would be a couple of ice-cold beers to wash down that juicy cholesterol burger I had just consumed.

There was a little convenience store across the street from the burger joint, so I headed that way in hopes of quenching my thirst. Outside the convenience store, three long-haired guys were loitering at the corner of the building.

As I passed their location, they all looked at me. I nodded my head as if to say howdy, as I opened the door and went inside. When I grabbed a six-pack of beer from the cooler, the thought never occurred to me that in Oklahoma, I was still too young to buy beer until the man behind the counter asked for my ID. Leaving the store empty-handed, I paused when one of the long-haired guys said, "What's the matter, cowboy? The man won't sell you beer?"

"No, reckon Oklahoma still thinks I'm too young to drink beer."

"We'll buy the beer for you if you will buy enough for us, we're old enough."

"Well, okay. Here, this should be enough for a twelve-pack, and I get at least three," I said as I handed him a ten-dollar bill.

I just wanted to get a couple of beers and head back to my hotel, but the locals were insistent that we walk down the street to a nearby field. One of them started a fire in a well-used fire pit while I and one of the others busted opened the twelve-pack. We began the usual conversation/interrogation, who are you? where are you from? what are you doing here?

While I was explaining my mission, one of them pulled out a little baggie and took a sample of its contents and passed it on. The next guy did the same, and then passed the baggie to me. "What's this?"

"These are peyote buttons, eat a couple, you will like them."

"Oh heck, I can't do that, it's illegal, and I am a pilot. I can't be caught doing drugs, it would ruin my career."

"These are not drugs, this is part of our religion. Come on, you are sharing your beer with us, do us the honor and let us share our peyote with you. Give it a try, it will release your spirit!"

I tried one and it tasted like dirt and I had to wash it down with beer, but they insisted that I needed several more for the spiritual experience. Yup, it became a spiritual experience alright. Before long I was sitting on a stump mesmerized by the fire while they were all standing around the fire, with their backs arched and their arms outstretched chanting at the stars.

"Hey, guys, is that a cop car over there?"

"Yes, but don't worry about him, he watches us every night. He can't do anything to us, we are American Indians, this is our religion, it's legal for us to do this."

"Well, what about this gringo? It's probably not legal for me?"

Still not quite sure how the rest of the evening went, I was not feeling my best when I woke up the following morning with Robert banging on the door to my hotel room. He was quick to pick up on the face paint and my lethargic mood and began an interrogation. I was shocked when I looked in the mirror, as I had no recollection of how or when that white and black paint got on my face. It made for some fun conversation between Robert and the good ol' boys at the airport afterwards.

Admittedly, I was not at my best when it came time to load the Skylane on the trailer. I even asked Robert to check all my tie-downs to verify I didn't miss anything. The truck ride back to was relaxed but Robert wasted no time in telling everyone at Sand Springs of my "spiritual experience" with the Indians in western Oklahoma. He provided everyone who came to the airport more ammunition to taunt and pick on me, and I reckon I was okay with that as I had become accustomed to it.

As soon as we unloaded the Skylane, we began the reassembly. First, all the tail feathers were bolted back on and the elevator and rudder cables were rigged. Then we completed the cuffed leading-edge installation and the stall fence installation on the wings for the STOL kit and installed the wings on the aircraft. With the flaps and ailerons rigged and the wing installation complete, we removed the engine and began the firewall repairs.

As repairs on the Skylane progressed, it became apparent to me that the business model for Lot Aero Flying Service was changing slightly. More and more of our shop projects were flyable aircraft that needed refurbishment and avionics upgrades, and the flight school aircraft were being sold off one at a time and not being replaced.

We began flying out and picking up flyable airplanes and ferrying them to Mena, Arkansas, for paint and interior refurbishment. It was fun building flight time in a variety of different types of aircraft and a heck of a lot better than cutting skins and banging rivets all day.

Although I could not put my finger on it, I got the sense that there was something going on in the background that Robert was not telling me about. The flight instructors were not coming around much anymore as both had taken on other full-time jobs. All but one of the flight school airplanes had been sold or traded off, and for some reason, we began parking airplanes at Riverside Airport.

One morning while I was working on a Cessna 182 firewall repair, Robert came to me and said that we had a problem. The City of Sand Springs had given the airport management contract to someone else and we were going to have to move. He knew the deal with the city was up for renewal, and submitted his proposal, but he did not think there was any competition. Unfortunately, there was, and they won the contract and we had thirty days to vacate the airport. I suspect Robert thought this was a possibility, which explained why more and more, we were parking airplanes at Riverside and not getting too involved in extensive rebuild projects. To me, this was just wrong, but it was reality.

We had long since moved the sheet metal shop from Harvey Young Airport and consolidated the entire operation at the Sand Springs Airport. Harvey Young was a beehive of activity and there was no space available there. All the hangars at Riverside were full. We suddenly became an FBO without a facility or a hangar.

My first thought was that this was my cue to flee the scene and move back to Texas, but doing so would leave Robert in a bind without any help. We had the 182 that was close to completion, the Cessna 172 that I flew out of the snow-covered field in Missouri, an old tuna tank Cessna 310 that once belonged to astronaut John Glenn, and a Mooney. The 310 and the Mooney were tied down at Riverside Airport. In addition, we had the main hangar that we worked out of that was full of tools and equipment and several T-hangars that needed to be cleaned out. Besides me, all we had was a moonlighter who worked for a tire shop. He only came out once or twice a week to help out.

I moved my T-Craft to Eagles Nest, which was a little grass strip airport about five miles west of Sand Springs. It was owned by the Chief Pilot for Williams Companies. He was a real nice guy and let me keep the T-Craft in a covered parking spot for free. He said he enjoyed watching me and my misfit friends fly in and out of his airport, telling me we brought back fond memories of his days as a young aviator.

I got the sense that Robert was at a loss as to Lot Aero Flying Service's next move. We spent part of each day cleaning out hangars and carrying stuff off to the boneyard and the other part of the day finishing up the 182 and the annual inspection on the 172. On our last official day at Sand Springs, I ferried the 172 over to Riverside Airport and tied it down outside next to the Cessna 310 and the Mooney. Robert picked me up and we went back to Sand Springs and hung the engine on the 182 and pulled it out of the hangar and tied it down outside.

The following day was a sad day for Robert and me, as this was the end of an era, more so for him than me. He had been there long before I arrived, but this place was where I got my real start in aviation. We returned to Sand Springs and, using the tailgate of the pickup truck as a work bench, we completed the engine installation on the ramp.

I am pretty sure that watching the new airport operator bring in truckloads of his furniture and moving himself into the facility that held such fond memories kind of set Robert off just a little bit. Although we had fulfilled our obligations to be out of the offices and hangars, we were welcome to stay on the ramp as long as we wanted, but Robert insisted that we fly the 182 out of there that day.

We ran the engine a couple of times, made a few adjustments, and then installed the engine cowling. I was instructed to ferry the 182 over to Eagle's Nest, where he would pick me up and take me to my car. That was the last time either of us set foot on the Sand Springs Municipal Airport.

The following morning, Robert dropped me off at Eagles Nest Airport. I was to ferry the Skylane over to Riverside Airport. Eagles Nest was a grass airstrip, and he was afraid that the forecast rain showers would soak the runway and the Skylane would be stranded there for an extended period of time until the runway dried out.

The sky was overcast, and the ground and the airplane were already moist from the humidity. By the time I finished the pre-flight inspection of the airplane, my boots were soaking wet.

The big 470 cu in Continental engine fires right up with a rhythm that lopes along as if she has a racing cam in it just waiting to be unleashed. Like a big block Chevy engine at the starting line waiting for a green light on the light tree.

With the magnetos checked, the propeller cycled through a few times, the flaps set at 10 degrees and all the before take-off checklist items completed, I pulled onto the runway and shoved the throttle to the firewall. The mighty Continental engine roared to full power and the airplane began a rapid acceleration down the runway. Just about the time that I was going to raise the nose for take-off, the big Continental engine choked and quit.

"Shit!" I pulled the throttle back to idle and got on the brakes. Even with the engine shut down the airplane seemed to accelerate as I applied the brakes. She was sliding on top of the wet grass. Quickly I raised the flaps to get the weight of the airplane on the wheels, but that seemed to have no effect.

As the northern airport boundary fence and Shell Creek Road grew closer and closer, my mind had flash backs of all the work we had put into repairing the firewall and nose gear structure. Although I did not mind the work, I was not interested in doing it again.

I began a series of frantic S-turns going down the runway. Left rudder to the left side of the runway, then right rudder to the right side of the runway, then back to the left, then back to the right before finally coming to a stop perpendicular to the runway with my right-wing tip over the fence. Whew! That was close.

My first thought was the engine failure must have been caused by the collapse of the duct in the induction manifold when I hit full power.

Robert had made it a point to be sure I understood to confirm the duct was in good condition and how to properly install it so that it would not collapse from the vacuum created by the big engine and starve the engine for air.

After regaining my composure, from that experience, I reached for the ignition and re-started the engine and taxied back to the south end of the runway for another engine run. Performing a magneto check at 1,700 rpm yielded no anomalies, so I ran the engine up to full power and it ran just fine for just a couple of seconds and then began to stumble again just like on the take-off run. Applying carburetor heat seemed to make the problem worse for a few seconds and then it cleared right up and ran fine.

I realized the humidity in the air and on the ground combined with the temperature drop was causing ice to form in the venturi of the carburetor and restricting airflow, causing the engine to quit.

With a certain amount of apprehension, I lined up on the runway, selected ten-degrees flaps, and applied full carb heat. As I pushed the throttle all the way in, and holding the brakes, the airplane began sliding on the wet grass but was maintaining power.

Releasing the brakes, I noticed vapor trails coming off the propeller tips as the Skylane accelerated down the runway. It was cool looking and reinforced my theory about carburetor ice being the culprit for the engine failure. Although I had to scud run and request a Special VFR clearance to get into Riverside Airport, the flight was uneventful.

I stuck around Tulsa with Robert for a couple of months, helping to clean up loose ends and looking for my exit. Unexpectedly, on the day he sold the Cessna 172 he sat me down over lunch and explained the facts of life to me. He described how his wife has been on his ass a lot lately regarding financial security for their family and their young daughter. As a result, he had applied for and accepted a job at the American Airlines maintenance facility at Tulsa International Airport.

He handed me what was to be my last paycheck from Lot Aero Flying Service and thanked me for my dedication and loyalty. He said that he knew my heart was in Texas, and he reached into his pocket and pulled out a wad of hundred-dollar bills. "Here is some extra traveling money, Turkey. Let's keep in touch."

I was truly grateful for the opportunities and experience I gained from working for Robert. And although he was my boss, I considered him to be my best friend. I never once dreaded going to work. Every day was an adventure that I cherish to this day.

The following morning, I began going through the possible scenarios in my head regarding my girlfriend. I really did like her and we had great fun together. Should I ask this gal to marry me and haul her off to Texas? Should I just have one more fling with her and tell her adios? What if she didn't want to move to Texas? I wondered if I could get a job at American Airlines with Robert and stick around Tulsa. Maybe I should just tell her what I was faced with and see what she thought. I really did like this gal.

As I was pondering my dilemma and organizing my things for an eventual move, my phone rang. It was my girlfriend calling to invite me over for dinner. She said that she had someone really important that she wanted me to meet. Regardless of what the evening brought, I would still need to move within a week, whether it be to Texas or an apartment somewhere in Sand Springs or Tulsa, so I continued organizing my things.

Later that day I went out to Eagle's Nest and flew the T-Craft around for a while before going to my girlfriend's place. Upon knocking on her door later that evening, I was greeted by a guy who handed me a cold beer and introduced himself as her husband. Oh shit!

Just a minor detail here, right? Apparently, he was in the Army and was stationed in Fort Hood, Texas, and was home for three days on leave. The gal I had been dating for the last six months had placed me in a really awkward situation, as she never gave me any indication that she was married.

I was really uncomfortable throughout most of the night as I kept expecting someone to bring up the romantic affair that we had been having for the past six months. Not a word was said. He was a really nice guy and we had a pretty good evening. I offered to take him flying in the T-Craft the following day and he accepted. As I was saying good night and promised to call in the morning, my girlfriend walked me to the door and in front of her husband, gave me a big hug with a full on deep wet juicy kiss. I struggled a little to pull away, but she just held me tighter. It was really awkward for me as I glanced over at her husband, who just smiled and nodded.

The following day, as promised, I called and took her husband flying. We flew all over northern Oklahoma. We flew for a solid four hours, making stops at a variety of interesting little airports. During the entire day, not one word was mentioned regarding me and his wife, about our relationship, how we met, how long we had known each other, how long we had been sleeping together, nothing. Just a couple of good ol' boys flying around on a Sunday afternoon.

After the flying was done, he thanked me for the day's adventure and stated that he would be leaving in the morning for Fort Hood. Then he went on his way. As I drove home that evening, I had visions of an armored tank division and his platoon coming after me with the intent of inflicting serious bodily harm. It suddenly became clear to me what I needed to do next.

Chapter 8

Welcome Home

There was this maintenance shop at Red Bird Airport in Dallas called Modern Aero that always fascinated me as a kid. I would ride by there on my bicycle and just stop to watch the airplanes coming and going. The flight line was always littered with big twin Cessnas, Beechcraft Bonanzas, and the typical Cessna and Piper trainer type airplanes. You could hear rivet guns going off in the back hangar and the smell of fresh paint was always in the air. It was like Lot Aero Flying Service, only on a much larger scale.

I called Flight Service and got a weather briefing for the following day with the intention of flying the T-Craft to Texas to look for a job and an airport to call home for the T-Craft. As much as I wanted to, there was no way I could continue seeing my girlfriend now that I knew she was a married woman. Her husband was a really nice guy who was spending time away from home serving our country. It just wouldn't be right.

Within a week, I had flown the T-Craft to Texas, secured a job at Modern Aero, and returned to Sand Springs to get my truck and other belongings.

Working at Modern Aero took some getting used to. I was the youngest in the shop by decades. Most everyone was retired from their union jobs at the defense contractor LTV, and it seemed that I had to stop work just to keep up with these guys. Aside from a couple of road trips to repair stranded airplanes I was growing bored with this place fast.

I made several inquiries about a discount rate at the flight school side of the operation to earn my Commercial and Instrument Ratings and possibly expand my duties, but it was made clear to me that all I was going to do at this company was bend tin and bang rivets. And by the way, there would be no employee discounted rates for aircraft rental or flight training.

My goal was to become an airline pilot and I did not see how bending tin in the back shop was going to help me achieve that goal. With that in mind, I began surfing through the yellow pages looking for other aviation companies in the area that might be a better fit for me.

The first place I went to was this FAA Part 141 flight school at Dallas Love Field. Their Director of Maintenance had just been called back to his jet aircraft maintenance job at Cooper Airmotive, where he had been on furlough.

Getting the job was not easy, as the owner of the flight school was an airline pilot who flew for one of the major airlines. He didn't feel that I was old enough or had the experience necessary to take care of a fleet of little Cessnas and Pipers that were constantly flying and training returning Vietnam veterans under the GI Bill.

This guy was the first real airline pilot that I had ever met and I was not impressed. If he was an example of the way all airline pilots are, I may need to change my career goals. Instead of being compassionate about my goals and dreams of becoming an airline pilot and my willingness to bust my ass to get there, he continuously looked over his glasses and down his nose at me, discrediting my experience in such a condescending fashion that my first instinct was to simply walk out.

He used every excuse in the book why he would not hire me. I was too young, I had not had my mechanics certificate long enough to qualify to be Director of Maintenance, I didn't have the experience to keep fourteen airplanes flying. They had people in the past who were much older and more experienced and could not keep up with the demand.

At a few points during his interview process, I had to contain myself to keep from laughing in his face. All I saw was a simple task of keeping a few little airplanes ready for duty and he was making it out to be some huge monumental ordeal.

After giving me all the reasons why he would not hire me, for some unknown reason he decided to give me a tour of "HIS" operation.

We looked at the classrooms and the Link Trainer, and then finally the maintenance office. He was especially proud to point out that they were an "approved" Cessna Flight Center and were required to maintain a substantial spare parts inventory. They did not have a parts department, or anyone to manage their inventory; that too was the responsibility of the Director of Maintenance.

He described the continuous problems they were having with nose wheel shimmy on the Cessna's and in particular an aircraft by the tail number of November Seven Zero Four Echo Hotel (N704EH). He expressed to me how upset he was that all those "highly experienced mechanics" who had worked for him in the past spent thousands of dollars replacing the shimmy dampers but still no one could seem to fix the shimmy problem, and he was certain that I could do no better.

Having concluded the condescending interview and being rejected for the job, I exited the office and went to my car, but for some reason, I decided that somebody needed to teach this prick a lesson. Instead of getting into my car and leaving, I popped the trunk and grabbed a couple of 7/16 wrenches and a pair of dykes and headed to the maintenance office.

I grabbed a brand-new set of torque links that I had spotted during my tour, a couple of shims, and a couple of cotter pins and headed out to the flight line. Just as I expected, the torque links on that poor little Cessna November Seven Zero Four Echo Hotel (N704EH) were as sloppy as I had ever seen.

Not wanting to be seen, I quickly pulled two cotter pins and the top and bottom bolts and removed the torque links as an assembly. In no time flat I had installed the new torque links, shimmed them for a proper fit, and installed new cotter pins. I realized that I had one more trip to make, so I gathered up my tools and the removed parts and hustled back to the car.

I threw my tools in the car and went into the shop, where I left the old parts in the bin that I got the new ones from and began looking for a grease gun. Back out to the airplane, I applied a few quick squirts of grease to the fittings on the torque links and ran around to the tail of the airplane and pushed down on the tail to verify that the nose gear strut would still extend properly.

Back to the shop I went and with the grease gun returned to its original location, total time for this project was well under ten minutes. Feeling pretty proud of myself, I walked back in the office to find Mr. Airline Captain sitting at his desk acting all important and said, "You might want to go out and check the nose wheel shimmy on Echo Hotel, I don't think you will have any more problems with it." As I turned to walk away, he began asking questions, which I completely ignored. I just continued walking out the door, got in my car, and left.

By the time I got home that evening, there were six messages on my answering machine from Mr. Airline Captain insisting that he may have misjudged me and that I should give him another chance to hire me, what did you do to fix the shimmy problem? They had three more Cessnas with a shimmy problem, how soon could I start?

Based on my first encounter with Mr. Airline Captain, I really did not want to work for him, but feeling like I might have something to offer, I made him a deal. He had a flight school that needed aircraft maintenance and I needed my Commercial, Multi-Engine, and Instrument Ratings.

He would write me a check every two weeks for my efforts and give me a discount on my advanced flight training and in return, I would keep the entire fleet in the air. Despite this guy's attitude, my goal was still to be an airline pilot and I needed more flight time and ratings just to qualify to send in applications. This was just the place to get those ratings.

We agreed on the deal and I proceeded to bust my ass to keep the fleet flying. The nuts-and-bolts part of the job was easy. Packing wheel bearings, changing brake linings, compression checks, cylinder changes, oil changes, and inspecting the airframes were simple tasks that I had already become well accustomed to. It was all the other administrative duties that I had to learn on the fly.

It was sourcing parts like spark plugs, brake linings, and cylinder repairs that I had to learn. Researching and complying with Airworthiness Directives and manufacturers Service Bulletins and making logbook entries. In addition to becoming the youngest Director of Maintenance in the region, I had to get a waiver from the FAA, which brought about my first serious encounter with that organization.

Enter Tom Germino, my Principal Maintenance Inspector from the FAA. For the first several months he scrutinized everything I did and every logbook entry I made. He also came out and rented our aircraft from time to time to fly out and conduct base inspections of other operators in North Texas.

We had a love hate relationship. I hated to see him pull up in his little G-Car, and I loved to see him get in the car and go away after his visit. But I learned a lot from Tom, like crossing the t's and dotting the i's in logbook entries, detailed Airworthiness Directive compliance records, and accurate aircraft equipment list revisions and weight and balance in the Airplane Flight Manual. He taught me about conformity and compliance issues that would serve me well into the future.

The flight school was so busy with the GI Bill vets from Vietnam that I could hardly find time for my own flight training. I was performing 100-hour inspections on every aircraft in the fleet twice a month and about the only flying I was getting was the occasional new cylinder break-in flight. I would schedule a flight with an instructor, only to be bumped from the schedule by a retail customer.

Finally, our Piper Apache had a slight break in its schedule and I jumped on it. In less than a week and seven hours of flight time, I earned my Multi-Engine rating. The flight school did not miss a beat due to my time off for training. I only had to stay late one day to catch up on my work, but that was a piece of cake.

Next on my list was to get my Commercial Pilots Certificate. During the course of the last few years, I had earned most of the requirements and hours necessary for the rating, I just needed to complete a three-legged long cross-country flight with each leg 200 nautical miles in length and a little practice on the flight maneuvers, then a logbook sign-off from an instructor and I would be good to go take a check ride.

The flight school aircraft were booked solid, so I managed to rent a Beechcraft T-34 to finish off my cross-country requirements. The T-34 was painted up in the "Fly Navy" colors, and was a pretty fun airplane to fly. I planned to fly from Dallas Love Field to Galveston Saturday afternoon after work and spend the night with a friend and then on to New Orleans for the second leg and then back to Dallas Love Field the following day. For company, I asked my younger brother if he wanted to ride along.

We got off to a late start due to some additional maintenance needed on a flight school airplane, but we were underway about an hour before dark. About halfway to Galveston I began to smell a nauseous odor. I had smelled that odor before but I could not place it. It was bad enough for me to roll the canopy back a couple of inches for some fresh air.

We arrived in Galveston well after dark and I called my friend who had agreed to pick us up. He complained that it was getting late and he didn't want to drive that far. He suggested that we fly to Houston Hobby and he would meet us there.

Before departing Galveston, I needed to find someone to sign and date my logbook to prove that I in fact flew to Galveston on this date. The only person we could find on the airport was a mechanic working for PHI Helicopters. I got him to sign my logbook and went back to the airplane for the short trip up to Houston. Unfortunately, the airplane wouldn't start. After a brief investigation, I discovered the source of the odor on the previous flight. It was battery acid that had boiled out of the battery due to a voltage regulator issue.

We found an empty Coke bottle and filled it with water from a garden hose attached to the back of the PHI Hangar and serviced the battery. We went back inside the hangar to ask the mechanic if he could give us a jump start. He was busy and didn't have time, so as we walked back to the aircraft, I spotted a ground power unit.

We pushed it over to the T-34 and in the dark somehow figured out how to connect it to the airplane and get it started. I crawled into the cockpit and the engine fired right off. My brother disconnected the power cart and with all his might managed to push it clear of the airplane so we could taxi out. He climbed in the back seat and off we went.

We made it to Houston Hobby and met up with my friend, who wanted to stay up all night and party. By now, it was very late, and I was beat. One beer and I was knocked out.

The following morning, I woke to check the weather in New Orleans only to find some really nasty weather complete with tornados and hail was heading that way. I had not planned on that, so it was time to change the plan if I was going to be back at work on Monday morning as expected.

Consulting with Flight Service and my aeronautical chart, I felt Hondo, Texas, would be a good alternative. The weather was forecast to be good and it met the mileage requirements for the long Commercial Cross-Country flight, both from Houston and back to Dallas. The only question remained was if the airplane would start.

With the aircraft all fueled up, I climbed in and tried to start it. Well crap, nothing, it would not even pull the battery relay. We went back into the FBO and asked for a ground power unit to start the aircraft and were informed that it would cost fifteen dollars. Fifteen bucks? For a cart start? I couldn't afford that. I wouldn't have enough money to buy gas at the next stop.

As we walked back out to the airplane, we spotted their GPU and devised a plan to hi-jack it just as we had done the night before to get the airplane started. We grabbed the GPU and pushed it all the way across their ramp to the airplane. My brother connected the power plug to the airplane while I wrangled with getting it started. I jumped in the cockpit and fired up the engine and got busy with the radio getting a taxi clearance while my brother unplugged the GPU and shoved it out of the way.

I reckon the FBO was a little upset with us as we saw a couple of the line guys running out to the GPU as we taxied off the ramp. My brother informed me that he didn't have time to shut it down, so he just unplugged it and left it running.

The flight to Hondo was uneventful but one thing that I failed to notice during my pre-flight planning was that Hondo was an auxiliary training facility for Randolph Air Force Base, which was near San Antonio. Nonetheless, the tower directed us to the gas pump after landing where we were greeted by a handful of Air Force personnel.

After gassing up the airplane, we informed them that we were going to need a jump start. Well, that started it. Here we were in a T-34 with stars and bars and "Fly Navy" painted on the side at an auxiliary Air Force base. In spite of all their comments and criticism about Navy maintenance and the jabs we were taking they confessed that they did not have a power cart, and they were convinced that I had no business flying such a cool airplane while they were flying the Air Force version of a Cessna 172, which is called a T-41 Mescalero.

In spite of all that, they tried their best to take over the situation and help out. The T-34 has a 24-volt electric system powered by a generator. With the engine running, the generator would run all the avionics, flaps, and landing gear but it would not charge the battery. They pulled their trucks up close to the airplane and tried jumping the airplane off of two trucks with three pairs of jumper cables. They made more sparks than a Fourth of July celebration trying to find the right combination of connections.

After an hour or so in the hot south Texas sun, I had finally had enough. "Okay guys, this is not working. Pull your trucks out of the way, we are going to hand prop this thing."

"Oh heck no, there is no way!" "That has an eight to one compression ratio, there is no way!" "That's too dangerous!" "Leave it to the Navy to come up with an idea like that!" "It'll never work!"

"I am on a mission that needs to be completed today, one way or another!"

My brother had been flying with me in the T-Craft and had become pretty good at hand propping it, so I figured what the heck. I needed to get back to North Texas.

I verified the magneto switch was off and rotated the propeller a few times to position it properly and then asked the guys to move back. I briefed my brother on the procedure and crawled into the cockpit. Setting the brakes and switching the magneto switch to the ON position and setting the mixture and throttle, I called out "Hot and brakes."

With that, my brother reached up and gave that propeller a mighty spin. The engine popped, coughed, sputtered, and then roared to life, much to the amazement of all the Air Force guys who were by now scratching their heads. As my brother climbed into the back seat, I looked to my left at the Air Force guys and gave them a salute, to which they replied by coming to attention and saluting back.

The flight back to Dallas was uneventful and I had just completed the final requirement for my Commercial Pilot check ride. Within a week, I had my check ride scheduled, but had to postpone it for a few days as the airplane I scheduled the check ride in came due for a 100-hour inspection, which I had to perform.

With the Commercial and Multi-Engine pilot's certificate in my pocket, it was time to go after the Instrument rating. It was tough getting on the schedule for that. My flights were scheduled early in the morning and late at night, and occasionally one of the instrument instructors would give up their lunch break to fly with me. Eventually, I was very close to having all the necessary requirements for the Instrument rating in my logbook. Just a few more hours and I would be ready for another check ride.

Then one day, at 6 a.m. I got a call from one of the flight instructors stating that the battery was dead in the airplane he had scheduled with a student. After a quick discussion about the schedule of the other 172's in the fleet, I suggested that he take a different airplane and make a note on the schedule of the change of planes so the other instructors would know. There were several scheduled flights for

7 a.m. so I had time to get to the airport and get the battery swapped out in time.

Arriving at the airport, I simply removed the battery from the airplane that was down for a cylinder change and replaced the dead battery. I then took that battery to the shop and put it on charge. I jumped back in the truck and left so that I could be at the cylinder shop when they opened to pick up the cylinder that I had dropped off the day before.

After picking up the freshly repaired cylinder I stopped by Van Dussen to pick up a few more needed gaskets, brake pads and other supplies and then headed back to the shop to install the cylinder so it would be ready for a test flight by noon and back on the schedule by mid-afternoon.

It was probably 8:45 or so when I arrived back at the shop, where I was greeted by Mr. Airline Captain. Apparently, he was here for another one of his inspirational drive-bys. He only appeared once or twice a month, but it seemed like he would spend part of his time following me around as I performed my job telling me what a lousy job I was doing. That was a bogus argument, as the truth was in the number of hours the aircraft were flying.

Today would be no different. He had no clue what had transpired during the previous weeks or the previous day. All he knew was there was an airplane down for maintenance, and who the hell did I think I was to show up to work at 8:45!

I kind of ignored him as I went to the office to check in with our dispatcher and let her know that I was here and see if there were any new issues that needed my attention. I informed her about the morning's battery issue and that I had picked up the cylinder from the shop and should have it installed by noon followed by a test hop and it would be back on the schedule by early afternoon.

I turned to head back out to the truck and Mr. Airline Captain began yelling at me. It was pretty embarrassing as there were a lot of people around. He followed me out to the truck yelling at me the entire way. When I got to the truck I turned and asked him if he had any idea how many hours the fleet had flown that month, or where he was at 6:45 this morning while I was dealing with a dead battery issue.

He did not want to hear anything I had to say. He just continued with his rant. I began unloading the cylinder and supplies from the truck and carried them into the shop. I don't think that he even realized that he was getting in the way of progress.

In the shop, I tried to focus on preparing the new piston, rings, cylinder, and valve tappets for installation on the aircraft when finally, I had enough. "Instead of coming up here once or twice a month to browbeat everyone, perhaps you should take a look at the flight logs and the records first and then perhaps thank everyone for the great job they're doing."

With that, I thought he was going to blow a gasket or have a heart attack. His face got all red and he began yelling at me at the top of his lungs. It was embarrassing as there was a classroom right next door, and I was sure all the students were impressed with his ungrateful animation.

I said, "Mr. Airline Captain, the only thing around here you own is the name above the door. You are so busy building a house and flying for the airline that you have no idea of what takes place around here and you do not appreciate the work any of us do for you. Screw you, I quit!"

With that, I packed up my tools and went inside the office to say goodbye to our lovely dispatcher and left without ever looking back. That evening there was a message on the answering machine from Mr. Airline Captain suggesting that he may have overreacted and in fact the fleet had been flying a record number of hours, I had been doing a great job, and by the way can you come back and install that cylinder?

It was too late, as once again I had surfed through the yellow pages and found a few possible opportunities. I was already scheduled to interview for a Director of Maintenance position for a little night check hauling outfit the following day at the Mesquite Hudson Airport.

Chapter 9

Frost Bite

The morning after I left the flight school, I drove out to the Mesquite Hudson Airport, where I met a guy who presented himself as the Director of Operations for this little FAA Part 135 Certified Air Carrier charter company.

This little charter company flew high-performance single- and twin-engine aircraft around Texas, Oklahoma, New Mexico, Arkansas, and Louisiana, picking up and delivering canceled bank checks for the Federal Reserve Bank, undeveloped film for Fox Photo, and biomedical samples for several hospitals and labs.

Although the Director of Operations was not very forthcoming with details about the company, he repeatedly asked if I knew how to "Return an Aircraft to Service," as in signing off logbooks after maintenance. He also asked my thoughts on setting up a maintenance operation at the Mesquite airport.

As our discussions evolved, it was revealed that they had over a dozen aircraft and they had absolutely no maintenance personnel or capabilities. Most of the local flight operations were conducted from Dallas Love Field so logistically speaking it made more sense to set up shop closer to where the main operations were taking place.

He asked about my credentials and ratings. I informed him that I held an Airframe and Powerplant Mechanics Certificate and was a commercial multi-engine rated pilot with nearly all the requirements met for the instrument rating. He said not to worry about the instrument rating, they would help me out with that if it all worked out. He was speaking my language.

He then directed my attention across the ramp to a very nice new-looking Piper Lance and asked if I had ever flown one. When I replied no, he suggested that I go climb in the left seat and familiarize myself with it and he would be with me in a few minutes.

Man, this thing was nice. November One Zero Four Zero Hotel (N1040H) was a pretty new aircraft and had these fancy new digital avionics with flip-flop frequency selector button, autopilot, and club seating in the back. As I was reviewing the check-list and the limitations section of the Flight Manual, the Director of Operations climbed in and said, "Let's go, take me to Addison Airport, I have something to show you."

I reckon I did a decent job of flying the Lance because when we got to Addison, he directed me to taxi to a T-hangar. While fumbling for keys to the hangar, he asked if I had ever flown a Twin Comanche. "No." "Well, here is your chance, we need to get this to Love Field because it has a flight at six p.m. Take it to the Cooper Airmotive north ramp and tie it down, I will be along shortly to pick you up."

I was glad that there was no one around to witness my first flight in the Twin Comanche. The take-off was a little hectic as I tried to keep the aircraft on the ground until I had reached Vmc on the air-speed indicator (minimum controllable airspeed with one engine inoperative), but she would not stay on the ground. I went part of the way down the runway on the nose wheel with the main wheels in the air. I learned later on to just let her fly off the runway and keep it close to the ground until it accelerates and then climb out. Once airborne, the Twin Comanche was fun to fly. Roll and pitch was really responsive, and the little fuel-injected 160 HP Lycoming engines and big Hartzell propellers seemed to provide plenty of power.

Arriving on the designated ramp at Love Field, I was directed to a parking space by the lineman. As I secured the Twin Comanche in its tie-down spot, my mind could not help but wonder what else was in store for me today. I waited around for the Director of Operations, expecting him to arrive in N1040H, but when he arrived, he was in his car.

As we drove to an off-airport office complex, he began to brief me on the operation. The daily flights and the routes, the number of aircraft they had operational, and the number of aircraft they had that were broken down at various locations. It was quite an impressive fleet with three Piper Lances, three Twin Comanches, a turbo charged Piper

Aztec, a Piper 250 Comanche, a Piper Turbo Arrow, two Beechcraft Barons, a Beechcraft Travel Air, a Beechcraft Bonanza, and a Mooney.

Once at the office, I was introduced to the owner of the company. Together, we sat down to discuss the status of the company, current route structure, upcoming bids for new routes, and their lack of any maintenance support. They would simply fly an aircraft until it broke down, leave it where it broke, and then get another one. We discussed the need for some basic tools such as aircraft jacks for performing landing gear retraction tests and other knick knacks commonly found in a maintenance shop.

Because the main location for the Federal Reserve cargo drop-offs and pick-ups were at Love Field, I suggested that we establish the maintenance base at Love Field, perhaps in the recently abandoned terminal building at one of the gates. I knew there was a lot of space available on the backside of the terminal from the flight school that I had just left.

We discussed my desire to finish up my instrument rating with the ultimate goal of becoming an airline pilot and my willingness to work my ass off to achieve those goals. We discussed the reasonably good relationship I had with the FAA and that I thought I could keep the fleet flying.

A salary was proposed that I promptly rejected, knowing full well that I was worth much more than the initial offer. They made another offer. I was young and eager and probably settled for much less than I should have gotten, but they agreed to help me finish my Instrument Rating, so I accepted the job and agreed to start the following day.

My alligator mouth may have just overloaded my hummingbird ass.

On the drive back to the Love Field, the Director of Operations handed me a pager and suggested that I keep it on me at all times. That pager would be his means of contacting me. I suggested that my first order of business, aside from finding a place to set up shop, would be to locate all the aircraft logbooks and establish an aircraft maintenance status board and begin planning the routine inspections while taking care of the immediate aircraft maintenance needs first.

When we arrived at Love Field, we walked across the ramp, but instead of climbing in the Twin Comanche, we went to a Beechcraft Baron and began to untie the ropes and perform a pre-flight inspection. This Baron was a very nice airplane and not your stereotypical freighter. It had a King KFC 200 Flight Director complete with autopilot and all the whistles and bells. It was a fun flight back to Mesquite Hudson Airport. Upon parting ways, I was advised to be ready to get busy in the morning, there was a lot to do.

Wow, what a day! Yesterday, I walked off a job and today I flew three different high-performance airplanes, got a new job making a lot more money, and these people really did not even know me. They didn't even ask for copies of any of my FAA Certificates.

Flying high performance complex aircraft instead of a bunch of trainers is a lot more valuable in the pilot's logbook. This is the kind of flying time I needed in my logbook and this was the kind of job I was looking for when I initially came home from Tulsa.

The following morning, I went to the FAA's office at Love Field to talk to the station chief. I informed him that I had accepted the Director of Maintenance position. His reaction caught me by surprise, as he stated that they had been "playing cops and robbers with that organization ever since they were issued their FAA Part 135 Air Carrier Certificate."

That statement did not sit very well with me so I asked if I could visit with their Principal Maintenance Inspector. With all the interested parties gathered in the room, we sat down to discuss their areas of concern.

They were happy to hear that the company hired someone to see to their maintenance needs, but they would not identify any specific issues or concerns regarding the company. In general, they were concerned that there was no one place where they could review the aircraft and logbooks to verify compliance with the required maintenance and inspections. They hinted at the thought that some of the aircraft may be operating without required maintenance. I could tell they had other concerns, but they would not specify.

With very little to go on, I asked that they give me three months to see if I could get my arms around the operation and bring their maintenance up to standards. If I did not think I could bring the maintenance side of the company into compliance, I would let them know and promptly resign. They promised to give me three months and expressed their confidence after they heard of my job performance at the flight school from my former Principal Maintenance Inspector.

My pager went off as I was leaving the FAA office and I went back inside to use the phone. I was instructed to meet the Director of Operations on the south side of the terminal building next to the Air-Go hangar. Air-Go was a large cargo operator operating DC-3's, Convairs, and YS-11's out of Love Field.

Rounding the corner towards the Air-Go hangar, I spotted the car belonging to the Director of Operations and pulled up alongside him. He had been to the airport manager's office and just leased some ramp and shop space earlier in the morning. He also came up with a white dry eraser board. He told me that he would have a desk and some shelving delivered later that day. I was impressed as things seemed to be moving right along, and this was just day one.

Within just a few short days the shop began to take shape. I had a telephone, a desk, a couple of accounts set up at the local aviation parts supply companies, and some shelving for parts and supplies. I had drilled into the concrete ramp and secured anchors for twelve aircraft, and I began working on the maintenance status board.

It was shocking as each aircraft's maintenance status became apparent. Every single airplane was out of date on one thing or another. Pitot-Static Transponder correlation test, 100-hour inspections, oil changes, weight & balance, you name it, something was due on every single airplane.

I called the Director of Operations and asked him to come by the shop. When he arrived, we discussed the status of the fleet and devised a logical plan to rotate some of the aircraft through the shop to knock out the easy stuff first, and then move on to the aircraft with bigger outstanding issues that would take more time to complete.

The first couple of months were chaotic and kept me really busy. As the fleet's maintenance status began to improve, I began to fly out on the freight runs to recover aircraft that had been stranded due to one mechanical deficiency or another. All the pilots were really good guys and all were Certified Instrument Flight Instructors. They would let me do all the flying and get actual IFR experience and shoot instrument approaches. They would sign off my logbook, and in return, I promised to do my best to keep them in safe and reliable aircraft.

Most all of the maintenance work was performed outside on the ramp at Love Field, but we still had the little T-hangar at Addison that I would occasionally use if it looked like we would be having bad weather for an extended period of time or if an aircraft needed to be on jacks for a few days.

One morning, I went to the FAA office to fill out the paperwork to get a Special Flight Permit (Ferry Permit) for a Turbo Arrow that was stranded in Abilene and was confronted by my Principal Maintenance Inspector. He expressed his desire to come by the shop for a visit. I told him that he could come by anytime, just so long as it was not an official base inspection.

He suggested that he was available right now and would like to follow me over to the shop just to take a look around at how things were shaping up. I agreed but told him that I could not spend more than about ten to twenty minutes with him as I was on my way to Abilene to try and ferry a Turbo Arrow back to Love Field.

As soon as we got to the shop, he could tell that there had been some drastic improvements to the maintenance operation. He studied the Status Board (which was incomplete) and made a note of the cabinet with all the logbooks and then suggested that it might be time for a base inspection. I asked for two more weeks, to which he agreed as he left the shop.

By now, I had pretty much figured out how many flight hours each route took and could shuffle aircraft from one route to the other in order to cycle one to the home base for a scheduled maintenance event or to repair a discrepancy. The job was getting easier and less stressful and I was beginning to do more flying and training towards my Instrument rating.

I made it out to Abilene to take a look at the Turbo Arrow. This was the first time I had seen this airplane. After noodling around under the cowling and starting the engine a few times, I discovered that the right magneto wouldn't fire the spark plugs. I decided to remove it and take a closer look at it.

Sure enough, the points were burned up. Fortunately, Abilene Aero had a set of points and a condenser that I was able to charge to our fuel bill. After replacing the points and condenser, reinstalling the magneto, and timing it to the engine, the magneto check was satisfactory. With the cowling reinstalled, the flight back to Love Field was uneventful.

Two weeks later at 8 a.m., my Principal Maintenance Inspector and another Inspector from the FAA arrived at the shop armed with a bag of doughnuts. I told them that I would love to sit and chat, but had an airplane on the ramp that needed my loving in order to depart by 2 p.m. I offered them my desk, making sure they knew where to find the logbooks, maintenance manuals, and the aircraft status board. They got down to business and I went to work on my project.

I was pretty confident they would be happy with the results of their inspection. Every aircraft that was actively flying a scheduled run was current with inspections and identified on the status board with a green arrow pointing up. Airworthiness Directives, and routine inspections, and maintenance were all up to date. All the aircraft on the ramp at Love Field were either almost ready for duty or waiting their turn for an inspection or parts to complete a maintenance event, and identified on that status board with a red arrow pointing down. A very simple and easy to understand system.

As the day progressed, I would go in and out of the shop several times to get another tool or a part and would stop to answer a question or two. Around noon time, I heard a car horn honking and looked up from under the cowling to see the FAA boys waving at me as they drove away.

I didn't think much of it at the time, but about a week later the Director of Operations called instructing me to meet him Friday evening at the Brookhaven Country Club. When I asked why, he simply said, "Just be there." I really did not want to go as I had better things to do on Friday night, mainly playing with my newly found little redheaded girlfriend.

Reluctantly, after work, I put on my cleanest dirty shirt and headed over to Brookhaven.

Upon arrival at the country club, I was surprised to find the owner of the company, all the office staff, the Director of Operations, and most of the pilots. "Oh, I get it, it's a company party, why didn't you just say so, I would have brought my girlfriend."

"No, Kev, it is a surprise party, for you! We just received a letter from the FAA giving our maintenance operation a clean bill of health. It's the first time we ever got a clean bill of health from the FAA for anything, and we would like to say thank you! In addition, if you ever want to take your girlfriend to the beach or anywhere else on the weekend, feel free to take any one of the airplanes at the company's expense, you have earned it!"

Well now dang it, somebody should have brought some ice cream to go along with that humble pie they just fed me. I had no idea. I figured the FAA guys would have come by the shop or at least called me to let me know the results of their Base Inspection. Instead, they sent a formal letter to the official company address, which was the off-airport office. Those folks kept the letter and the results of the FAA inspection a secret from me until now.

Still, I could not see the significance of spending money on a party at a country club, considering that I was constantly being told how broke the company was when I asked for more specialty tools and support equipment for the shop. And, although it was a generous offer to let me use the airplanes, I didn't think it was appropriate to tell them that I was working seven days a week and did not have time for a vacation.

I guess everyone had a pretty good time. The office folks socialized with the office folks, the pilots socialized with each other, and aside from an occasional comment or two, I spent most of the time pretty much to myself. I was somewhat out of my element; after all, my natural habitat was the airport.

The company had a daily route they called the East Run. The flight departed Dallas Love Field and went to Fort Smith, Arkansas, stopped to pick up freight, then proceeded to Texarkana to pick up more freight, and then flew back to Dallas Love Field. The flight would generally leave around 6 p.m. and return around midnight. I would routinely fly that route with an Instrument Instructor until I met the qualifications for my Instrument Check ride.

With the Instrument Rating written test passed and the flight time requirements established, I went back to the flight school to visit with their dispatcher to see if I could get on the schedule for a practice check ride and then a formal Instrument Rating check ride. That pretty little dispatcher and I had always gotten along well, and she said that she would make it happen somehow without Mr. Airline Captain finding out.

Within a week I had passed the Instrument Rating check-ride and was a Commercial, Multi-Engine, Instrument rated pilot with an Airframe & Powerplant Mechanics Certificate. That officially allowed me to fly any of the freight runs provided the weather was VFR, as I did not yet have enough hours to qualify for IFR Part 135 flying.

They offered me the East Run a couple of times a week if I felt up to it. Working on the fleet aircraft all day and then flying until midnight made for a long day, but I managed to pull it off a few times a week. There were still other aircraft flying the western freight runs with occasional mechanical breakdowns in remote locations that would need my attention as well, so I was getting a considerable amount of flight time.

Usually, a pilot would brief me over the phone what the nature of the mechanical failure was and I would drop what I was doing, gather tools and take a guess at what parts were needed, load them into a spare aircraft, and fly to the location of the breakdown. I would help the pilot of the stranded aircraft transfer the cargo to my aircraft, and off he would go to finish his route. Meanwhile, I would stay behind to repair his aircraft and then fly it home.

The Director of Maintenance job was much more difficult than simply slinging wrenches and flying the aircraft; that was the easy part. The administrative and logistics side was just as challenging. Logbook entries needed to be made for all the maintenance performed. Every two weeks the FAA sent out paper copies of the Bi-Weekly Airworthiness Directive revisions that needed to be properly filed and maintained.

All the different aircraft and engine manufacturers' maintenance and parts manuals had the same revision requirements. Forecasting and scheduling outside services such as pitot-static instrument tests and transponder correlation tests and propeller inspections mandated by Airworthiness Directives. Replacement of life limited items such as engine mount bushings and fuel and oil hoses. Ordering and maintaining an inventory of engine oil, filters, brake pads, spark plugs. It was a lot of work and responsibility for one person.

While performing some of the admin tasks one evening, I got a call from the pilot flying the East Run in the Comanche. He was broken down in Fort Smith, Arkansas. He described the breakdown as a mechanical failure of the starter ring gear. The steel starter ring gear is press fit onto the aluminum flywheel that mounts to the crankshaft right behind the propeller. It has a pulley groove on the back side for the belt that drives the generator. The starter ring gear is what the starter engages into to spin the engine during start. With the steel ring gear separated from the flywheel, there was no way that aircraft was going anywhere.

84

There was a spare flywheel on the shelf in the shop, but it came off the Travel Air, which had Lycoming O-360s on it and the Comanche had a Lycoming O-540. I knew the bolt holes would line up but was not sure if it would match up with the tooth count on the starter. At that point, it didn't matter, we had a stranded pilot on a revenue freight run and even if he could hand prop that 250 hp Lycoming, that unsecured steel ring gear would destroy the aircraft.

I grabbed a tool box, the starter ring gear, and a five-gallon bucket and loaded up Twin Comanche November Seven Three Two Three Yankee (N7323Y) and launched for Fort Smith. Although the weather in Fort Smith was clear, a snowstorm had just blown through, leaving about six inches of snow on the ground, and it was bitterly cold there.

The flight to Fort Smith seemed to go by rather quick for a 200-mile trip. Upon my arrival, the Comanche pilot was happy to see me and described the events leading up to the failure. Together we examined the starter ring gear. After the brief evaluation, we needed to get him on his way as he was already behind schedule. He had been stuck out here in the cold for the last two hours. We got my tools and equipment out of Two Three Yankee and loaded his freight onboard and in short order, he was on his way to Texarkana for the next leg of his route.

As the sound of the little Lycoming engines on Two Three Yankee faded into the crisp cold night air, it was replaced by the eerie rattle of the nearby hangar doors caused by the wind. The FBO was closed and airport was essentially abandoned at this time of night. The single light pole in the parking lot next to the FBO and the hangar was the only source of light. With the entire airport covered in snow, the windchill index in the teens, and me being way underdressed, the chill was rapidly overcoming me.

The only way out of the cold for me was to fix the Comanche and fly it home. I didn't have money for a hotel, much less a cab ride, so it was time to get busy.

The first order of business was to get the cowling off and then remove the propeller and loosen the generator to free the drive belt.

85

Things were moving along pretty well, and although it was hard to see as my flashlight batteries were rapidly dying, I was making good progress. With the prop sitting on the five-gallon bucket, I cleaned up the oil that was draining out of the crankshaft and installed the replacement flywheel in position making sure the generator drive belt was in its groove.

Next came the propeller. It was a real pain getting all the bolts run down, properly torqued, and safety wired. By now my hands were covered in oil and nearing the frostbite stage, but the finish line was near. For some reason, I then grabbed the top cowling and installed it. One more chore and the bottom cowling could be installed.

Finally, down to pulling the drive belt down over the generator pulley, I discovered a problem. At first it appeared that the drive belt had slipped off the flywheel pulley, but it was hard to tell as I had already installed the top cowling and the flashlight was almost dead. After a few minutes of struggling with the drive belt, the problem became apparent. The diameter of the pulley on the new flywheel was about a third the size of the old pulley. This difference in size meant that the generator belt tension adjustment slide was too short to get any belt tension.

As my enthusiasm began to diminish, I crawled into the airplane to get out of the cold wind and think about my options. The belt tensioner slide was about an inch too short of obtaining a proper belt tension. At this point, whatever I could come up with only had to last long enough for the two-hour flight back to Love Field.

Thinking to myself, I wondered what my mentor Robert Lotero would do in this situation. He would find a way to get the job done and get the airplane home. Ransacking my tool box yielded nothing that could be used as a substitute or an extension for the slide tensioner. Time to think outside the box and brave the cold and explore the airport.

Wandering around the airport in snow up past my ankles, I looked everywhere. In the trash cans, around the hangars, everywhere that looked like a pile of rubble, but turned up nothing. Behind one of the hangars, I discovered a pair of deteriorating vintage pickup trucks in various states of corrosion and disrepair. Hoping to find a generator tension arm on one of the engines, I made my way through the snow drifts to the engine compartment only to find no hood or engine in either truck. Searching the truck beds and the cabs thinking there may have been parts of the engine left behind yielded no results either.

Frustrated, I began to turn away when I notice the inside door panel was missing from the left door. There was no window in the door, but the scissor slide mechanism that operates the window was still in place. Ah-ha, that looks just like what I need to rig this generator up for the one-time flight back to Dallas. After a quick trip to the ramp to gather some tools, I was kneeling down in the snow drift disassembling the window drive mechanism. It was not exactly the perfect part, but I knew I could make it work.

My jeans were soaking wet from kneeling down in the snow, and the bitter cold wind was only making it worse as I made my way back to the Comanche to begin rigging up the window slide onto the generator tension slide. In just a few short minutes, I had the proper generator drive belt tension. Adding a couple of additional wraps of safety wire just for good measure, I was ready to install the lower cowling. The thought of firing up the engine and having cabin heat kept me moving at a pretty good pace.

With the tools all stowed in the aircraft, I did one more walk-around to ensure that I had not overlooked anything before climbing back into the cockpit. The engine fired right up and as I sat there letting it warm up, I began dialing in the avionics for the trip home. It took quite a bit of power to break the Comanche free from the snow to begin taxiing to the runway, but what was unexpected was that the instrument panel lights got really bright. They went back to normal when the throttle was returned to idle.

At the end of the runway, the power setting required to perform the magneto check and cycle the propeller produced an extremely loud noise coming through the cockpit speaker and brought the instrument lights up so bright, I thought they were going to blow.

Pulling onto the runway and applying take-off power again brought the instruments lights up so bright it was difficult to see out the windshield and the noise coming from the radio was unbearable. The weather was VFR for the entire route of flight so after clearing 2,000 feet I turned off all the lights, the radios, and the master switch and continued climbing to a cruise altitude of 6,500 feet. With the cabin heat on full hot, it felt really good to warm up and thaw out as I climbed into the dark night sky.

Arriving into the DFW Metroplex was a bit tricky. After turning the master switch and the radio on, it was necessary to pull the engine power back to idle in order to communicate with ATC; otherwise, neither of us could understand each other with the generator-induced interference over the radio.

Lining up for final approach to runway 31R and selecting gear down, I noticed that the landing gear extended really fast. A quick flip of the nav light and landing light switches lit the airplane up pretty good. The landing and taxi to the shop was uneventful, but came with a suggestion from the tower controller to have the radio checked out before trying to fly again.

Well, okay, but it was not the radio's fault, as the smaller pulley wheel on the flywheel was turning the generator much faster than it was designed to turn. The following Monday, I obtained the proper replacement flywheel and installed it and everything was back to normal with the old Comanche.

Obtaining a proper debrief from the pilot flying the Comanche when the failure occurred, he disclosed that during engine start in Fort Smith, the engine kicked back, thus separating the starter ring gear from the flywheel.

Chapter 10

A Christmas Story

On Christmas Day, I was running around town with one of my old high school buddies, who by now had moved off to Houston and gotten married. I had not seen him in about three years so upon discovering what I had accomplished with my FAA Ratings, he really enjoyed parading me around in front of his parents and bragging about all I had done since our high school days.

After all, his parents never expected either of us to amount to much, but here he was running around with his buddy who by now was a FAA Certified Aircraft Mechanic and a Commercial Pilot. I tried to down play all the fuss, but I knew that he took great pride in my accomplishments, and to some extent, so did his parents.

As the day grew on, the inevitable question came up. "Hey, Kev, why don't you fly me and the wife back to Houston tonight?" Christmas fell on a Monday and both of them had to be back at work on Tuesday morning. Although they had airline tickets for the ride home, they thought it would be cool to have me fly them home.

I did the best I could at holding them off, but they both continued to insist that I fly them home. At the time, all the reserve aircraft in the charter fleet were down for scheduled maintenance events or waiting for parts, which would not arrive until the middle of next week considering the Christmas holidays and all. It seemed that all my excuses and explanations fell on deaf ears. Finally giving in, I made a phone call to the owner of the little avionics shop next door.

He had a little Cessna 175 that he kept insisting I go fly in my spare time to help him break in the new cylinders that he had recently installed on the engine. Neither one of us ever had much time to take care of our personal equipment as we were so busy taking care of our respective jobs.

After a quick briefing on the telephone, it was all set. The 175 has a geared Continental GO-300 engine and he provided me with the power settings that he wanted me to use during this cylinder break-in period.

My buddy and his new wife were all excited. They would get home around 9:30 p.m. instead of 7 a.m., they could cash in their airline tickets, and I was going to get stuck with the gas bill for the airplane. What's not to like about a deal like that?

We arrived at Love Field just after dark and I began by getting a weather briefing which revealed that we would have clear skies all night and a headwind of about thirty knots for the trip down. After a thorough pre-flight inspection and a brief cockpit familiarization, we were ready to go.

It was nights like this that really made me appreciate my ability to fly an airplane. With the wife sitting next to me and my buddy in the back seat, we launched into a crystal-clear star-filled sky. As we climbed to our cruising altitude of 7,500 feet the impressive array of lights of the DFW Metroplex began to captivate my passengers' attention. Off to the west was Ft. Worth and all the mid-cities and on the other side was the dark outline of the lakes just east of town.

There was not a ripple in the sky, and smooth steady purr of that little Continental engine was just what was needed to put the wife's slight apprehension to rest.

After leveling off at 7,500 feet and making the cruise power setting adjustments, we made a quick ground speed check and determined that for once, it appeared that Flight Service was correct with their winds aloft prediction and our trip to Houston would be just over two hours.

After passing the southern outskirts of the Metroplex, Interstate 45 made its definition apparent on the ground below as a solid ribbon of red and white lights. The red lights were the southbound tail lights and the white lights were the northbound headlights of the cars traveling between Dallas and Houston.

Happy to be up here at 7,500 feet and not down there, I began looking for something to pass the time. I began tuning the Automatic

Direction Finder (ADF). The ADF is basically an AM radio that you can listen to and it has a needle that will point to the radio station you select.

The strongest signal I could find was coming from a Dallas radio station that was playing the Cheech and Chong Christmas story. Although the quality of the overhead speaker was marginal, we could all still hear the Christmas story fairly well and were laughing along with it as we made our way southeast towards our destination. My buddy pulled out some barbecue beef sandwiches that his mom made for the trip and passed them around. She knew we had been eating turkey for the last couple of days and thought this would be a nice change.

About halfway through my sandwich, I noticed the warm glow of the Houston area lights beginning to make their appearance on the horizon ahead of us. The cabin heater was working well and everyone was comfortable. Suddenly, and completely without warning, the engine chugged and shuddered violently three times and within a fraction of a second, it completely quit.

Except for Cheech and Chong on the radio, all was completely silent in the dimly lit cabin of that little Cessna. Instinctively, I pitched the nose of the aircraft up and rolled into a left bank, performing a maneuver that is called a Chandelle. A Chandelle is basically a maneuver where you trade your airspeed for altitude and roll out going the opposite direction at approximately your best glide speed.

After executing the Chandelle, I shut down the ADF, rolled in full nose-up trim, dialed up the emergency beacon code of 7700 on the transponder, and set 121.5 into the communication radio - all this while desperately trying to fend off the wife, who had suddenly become hysterical and had her hands all over me. Normally, I would be flattered by all the attention I was getting but I had a serious situation to deal with.

Had it not been for her seatbelt, she would have been in my lap, but as it was, she was screaming at the top of her lungs, grabbing and clawing at me and the control yoke, interfering with my efforts to address the situation at hand.

I knew that we had passed Corsicana some time ago, but just how far away we were was unclear. Considering that our thirty-knot headwind was now a thirty-knot tailwind, we were going to need all the help we could get if we were to reach the airport. I told the wife that she needed to help me find the airport beacon.

"Look out the windshield! You will see a light down there; it will be green and then white." Finally, she was back in her seat with her hands on the glareshield peering out into the darkness. After what seemed like an eternity, I finally spotted it. "Look there it is, it is going to flash white now…flashing green now…flashing white now."

"I see it! I see it!" she screams.

"Great, now keep your eyes on it, do not lose sight of that beacon, that is where we are going to try and land!"

With her attention drawn away from me, her claws firmly implanted in the glare shield, and her face in the windshield, I glanced at the altimeter, which read just under 8,000 feet, and grabbed the microphone.

"Mayday, Mayday, this is Cessna Seven One Nine Zero Mike we're about twenty miles south of Corsicana with an engine failure, Mayday, Mayday, Cessna Seven One Nine Zero Mike is about twenty miles south of Corsicana with an engine failure, we are going to try to make it to Corsicana, but if it looks like we cannot make it, look for us on Interstate 45." And with that I turned off the radio; it was time for me to do some of that serious pilot stuff.

Up until that point, my buddy thought I was just messing with him and his new bride by shutting off the engine, but with that radio transmission, he knew this was a real life-or-death ordeal. To his credit, he behaved really well and did not say a single word throughout the entire affair.

Concentrating on making a safe outcome from the situation, I aligned the nose of the airplane approximately half way between the Interstate and the airport beacon. With all the Dallas–Houston Christmas traffic on Interstate 45, the interstate looked like a red and white ribbon for as far as the eye could see, and the thought of landing amongst all those cars was not too appealing.

With the elevator trim set to the full nose up position and the engine not running, the airplane established itself at an airspeed which resulted in the best glide speed, allowing me to concentrate on other tasks at hand.

With the help of the thirty-knot tailwind, we were moving right along. It was beginning to look like we might make it to the airport. A slight heading adjustment set us up for a left downwind traffic pattern entry for Runway One Four, it looks like we might be a little high, but we can fix that.

At mid field on downwind, I pulled in a notch of flaps; judging altitude and distance while turning base, I added another notch of flaps. After turning on the landing light on and seeing that prop stopped in an almost vertical position, I decided I did not need that distraction and turned the light back off.

Turning on to final approach, this was looking good, but we were not there yet. Application of full flaps too soon would have us landing short of the runway. It became a waiting game for the ground to come up and meet us. Once across the runway threshold, in went full flaps.

The tires never squealed or chirped, we did not bounce, we were on the runway center line and without any application of the brakes, we rolled to a stop on the runway centerline, just abeam the little terminal building which was approximately seventy-five to a hundred yards away. Perhaps this was the best landing of my life.

My buddy leaned forward and popped open the right cabin door and because the wife's seat was all the way forward, he was able to jump out of the airplane. In all his excitement to be on the ground, he was not paying attention to the flaps, which were still fully extended, and he promptly smacked his forehead with the right flap, which resulted in him lying flat out on the runway.

As the wife unfastened her seat belt, I retracted the flaps. She exited the aircraft and she and her hubby began dancing on the runway and whooping and hollering. It was all I could do to just sit there, until they came around to the left side of the airplane and opened the door.

They tried to pull me out of the airplane to celebrate with them but my seatbelt had me securely in place. Leaving the navigation lights and beacon on and looking around to see what else I should do to secure the airplane, I tried to step out onto the runway.

As I did, my knees gave way underneath me and I went into a pretty severe shiver. I could not stand up and could not stop the shakes, so there I sat, leaning up against the left main landing gear while my buddy and his wife celebrated on the runway like it was their wedding day. It was the first time he had said anything since the engine failed.

A few minutes after they calmed down, the pay phone over at the terminal building began to ring, breaking the silence of the crisp night air. It rang and rang and rang and just would not stop ringing. It became a nuisance so the wife decided to go answer it. Several minutes went by and she returned to report that there must be another airplane out there in trouble.

"What? Why do you say that?"

"The guy on the phone was looking for an airplane with engine trouble, I told him that we were the only ones here and we have not seen anybody else!"

"Geez, woman, did it even occur to you that they may be looking for us! I declared Mayday on the radio, that was probably Flight Service and they are trying to find us to make sure we are okay!"

Just then the phone began to ring again. "Now go back over there and tell them that we are the people they are looking for and we are all okay, we made it down safely with no damage to the airplane and no injuries." As she ran back across the field to answer the phone again, I crawled over by the wing strut and tried to pull myself up, only to find that my knees still would not support me.

While I was still hanging onto the wing strut, the wife, who was now out of breath, returned from her phone call and advised me that the guy insisted on talking to the pilot. "Tell them I can't make it to the phone right now, get their number and I will call them later." Dutifully, she ran off while my buddy and I made light of the situation and expressed our feelings about being alive.

It must have been a mistake to have her tell Flight Service that the pilot could not make it to the phone, because the first thing they thought was that the pilot was injured. The wife returned with confusing statements about injuries and why the pilot couldn't come to the phone and all kinds of nonsense that I could not understand.

I mustered up my strength and determination and stumbled across the field to the telephone. As I approached the terminal building, I noticed a trash can at the corner of the building, so I went and grabbed it and dragged it over to the telephone with me.

It must have made a hell of a racket over the telephone, because as I sat down on the trash can lid and picked up the phone receiver the trash can lid collapsed and I nearly fell all the way into the trash can, yelping as I went.

The Flight Service guy on the other end of the line was startled and wanted to know what all the noise was about, so I told him that I could not stand up and needed something to sit on. Curiosity got the better of him as he was thinking I was injured, so I described all the events to him, assuring him that during the engine failure and throughout our return to earth, I had remained calm, cool, and collected, but just as soon as the airplane stopped on the runway, I began shaking. Satisfied with that explanation he said he understood and took down some details such as my name and our departure point and intended destination, but while doing so, I noticed a car pulling onto the runway.

I told the gentleman at Flight Service that I had to go; a Texas State Trooper had just arrived. I hung up the phone and by the time I got back to the runway, the Trooper was wrapping a tow chain around the nose gear on the airplane.

"Whoa there, bubba, what the hell do think you are doing?"

"You the pilot?"

"Yes sir, I am."

"Well, we got to get this airplane off the runway."

"Not like that we aren't!"

I went to the airplane and retrieved the tow bar, and while the wife rode in the car with the State Trooper, my buddy and I sat in the trunk of the patrol car with the lid open and held on to the tow bar as he pulled us over to the ramp and to a tie-down spot.

With the airplane secure, the trooper pulled out his note pad and began asking all the typical questions you would expect and while he was busy with me, my buddy went over to the pay phone and called his dad to ask him to come down to Corsicana and drive us back to Dallas.

I dreaded his dad's arrival. My buddy's dad was a gruff old World War II vet who never held back any of his criticism of my buddy or me. Just as I expected, he did not disappoint. His relentless ranting and raving made that ride back to Dallas one of the longest car rides of my life.

The following day, the avionics shop owner and I flew down to Corsicana with tools in hand to investigate the catastrophic engine failure. Upon removing the top engine cowl, it was obvious that the number four-cylinder head was partially separated from the barrel and the crankcase was busted at the number four-cylinder base. Further investigation revealed that the little valve keepers had failed on the number four-cylinder intake valve, which allowed the valve to be sucked into the cylinder, destroying the piston and bending the connecting rod.

I took the piston and the bent up intake valve and made a little trophy complete with a plaque that simply said "Christmas Night 1977" and gave it to my friend a few months later.

Chapter 11

Duck at 2,000

It was a late Sunday afternoon and I had been working all weekend in a T-hangar at Addison Airport on one of the Twin Comanches, November Seven Five Six Six Yankee (N7566Y). I was about to take it down off jacks when this gentleman driving one of those fancy BMWs pulled up to the hangar.

"I am so glad to find a mechanic working today. My name is Ray and you've got to help me with a magneto problem on my Cessna 402!" He greeted me in such a fashion that I almost felt obligated to help him out with his problem.

"I am sorry, sir, but I don't have time. I need to finish up here and ferry this airplane down to Love Field. Wish I could help you out, but I have other obligations."

My mind was going into overdrive as I made my comments. Here I was, by myself, at Addison Airport with my car and an airplane. I still needed to do engine runs and leak checks before I could put the engine cowlings back on, then I needed to make logbook entries before I was finished. The airplane needed to be at Love Field for a 4 a.m. departure and I had no idea how I was going to get back to Addison to get my car. Maybe this was an opportunity to solve my immediate transportation problem, and this just might be a flying job opportunity.

The man was insistent that I help him out with his magneto problem as he had a charter trip first thing in the morning. He even offered to fly the Twin Comanche to Love Field for me. He seemed reasonably startled when I informed him that he was not going to cheat me out of a half hour of multi-engine flight time in exchange for me working on his airplane. It just wasn't going to happen; I needed that flight time.

As far as pilot career advancements went, the general consensus was that complex multi-engine flight time in IFR conditions all added up to moving one step closer to the Airline Transport Pilot Certificate and that coveted airline interview, and at this point I needed all the flight time I could get.

Another problem with helping this guy out was I knew we were going to need magneto parts and there was no place to get them on a late Sunday afternoon.

It soon became clear that he would not accept no for an answer. He patiently waited around until I had all the cowlings back on the Twin Comanche and made my logbook entries and stowed the logbooks, and then we drove across the airport to his airplane.

We hopped up into the cockpit and fired up the engines, and although both engines seemed to start okay, the problem became obvious when he advanced the throttle on the right engine to do a magneto check. The engine did not accelerate smoothly, it sort of stumbled. He pulled it back to idle and advanced the left engine throttle, which responded smoothly. A quick magneto check of the left engine yielded a satisfactory 50 to 75 rpm drop on both mags.

He brought the right engine up again, and it stumbled on the way up to 1,700 rpm. After allowing the engine to stabilize for a few seconds, he switched the left magneto off and the response was an immediate 500 to 700 rpm drop. With the left magneto back on, he switched the right magneto off and got just about the same results as before. Based upon my initial observation, my first instinct was that he had a busted cylinder head.

We shut down the engines and with the sun rapidly setting in the west, I removed the cowling for the right engine. With a flashlight and a mirror, I began looking for obvious signs of cylinder failure, but the engine looked clean. None of the obvious tell-tale signs of cylinder head failure were present, so I turned my attention to the magnetos.

Thinking to myself that having two magnetos fail at the same time was very unusual and I was wasting my time but, I proceeded to remove the cover for the points and condensers on the left magneto. Oh wow, get a load of those points. They were severely burned and pitted.

Let me check the other magneto. Pulling the cover off the right magneto revealed the same problem.

After discussing my findings with Ray, I suggested that at the very least we should rustle up a set of points and condensers for both mags. He jumped in his BMW and drove to a payphone to make some phone calls. While he was gone, I removed both magnetos and sat down on my little two-step ladder to inspect the magnetos closer.

With a flashlight between my shoulder and chin, I began probing the points. It was clear that one side had a large burnt build-up and the other side had a corresponding crater. I hate working in the dark on components that have such little screws, but I removed the points and condensers from both magnetos anyway.

When Ray returned from his phone calls, he found me crawling around the ramp on my hands and knees with my flashlight looking for one of the screws that secured the points in the magneto. He was proud to inform me that he had managed to get in touch with the owner of a local well-respected twin Cessna maintenance shop, who agreed to come out to the airport to sell us some parts for the magnetos.

With tools and magnetos in hand, we drove over to the Cessna maintenance hangar. As we sat out in the parking lot waiting for the shop owner to arrive, Ray began to inquire as to what I was doing and who I worked for. He asked what my ratings were and was surprised to find out that I was a pilot with commercial, multi-engine, and instrument ratings as well as a certified airframe and powerplant mechanic. I was the Director of Maintenance and a utility pilot for the little FAR Part 135 cargo operator flying nightly freight runs for the Federal Reserve Bank, and various other customers.

He asked if I had any flight time in a 400 series Cessna, to which I replied no. He asked what kind of twins I had been flying. At this point, I was wondering if this might just be an impromptu job interview, I replied that I had time in Piper Apaches, Aztecs, Twin Comanches, Cessna 310s, and Beechcraft Barons.

When the owner of the Cessna maintenance shop, arrived, he was surprised to see me. He asked why Ray called me instead of him. After all, his shop had been doing all the major maintenance and inspections on Ray's aircraft for several years already. Ray explained that it was Sunday afternoon, and he didn't think they would come out, and besides, I was already there. The shop owner said that it was okay as he had known me for a while and considered me to be a knowledgeable and capable mechanic.

Oh cool, if this was a job interview that comment would certainly help. Together we looked over the magnetos and agreed that they both needed points and a condenser. He promptly headed back to the parts room and a few short minutes later he returned with the parts necessary to fix both mags.

He took one mag, I took the other, and while standing at the reception counter of his office, we reassembled the magnetos with new points and condensers and sparked them out to check for proper operation. A few minutes of small talk and we were ready to head back to the airplane and install the magnetos. We thanked him for coming out and saving the day and as we turned to head out the door, he stopped us and said, "Hey, wait a minute." He headed back to the stock room and returned with a pair of gaskets, "I think you might need these."

"Thank you, sir, yes, we will. Good catch," to which he replied "I just didn't want to get all the way home, only to have to come back out just to sell you a dollar's worth of gaskets!"

Back at the aircraft and under rapidly dying flashlight batteries, I manage to get both magnetos installed and timed to the engine. With me standing out at the wingtip, Ray climbed in and fired up the engine. After a few minutes of warm-up time, he advanced the throttle and right there I knew he was good to go. He did a mag check and even though he was under the dim glow of the cockpit lights, I could see him give me a thumbs-up.

After shutting down the engine, I climbed back up on my ladder to inspect my work one last time before installing the cowling. Ray climbed out of the airplane and said, "How about I follow you down to Love Field in this so you can deliver your Twin Comanche, and I will bring you back to get your car?"

"Sounds like a great idea, Ray, I would really appreciate that, thank you." After I installed the cowling and gathered up my tools, Ray drove me back to the Twin Comanche. I told him that I would be parking on the Cooper Airmotive ramp over on Love Field Drive between runways 13L and 13R. He said he would just follow me and try not to overtake me enroute.

With all my tools stowed back in the car, I jumped in the Twin Comanche and taxied out. Ray waited until I taxied past his location, advised ground control that he was ready to taxi, and began to follow me. Normally, after the maintenance event that I just performed, I would depart and fly out east of town for forty-five minutes to an hour or so, not only to just check out the aircraft and its systems, but as one of the only benefits of the job, that being a little more multi-engine flight time in my logbook.

Since it was getting late and I had someone following me, I decided to just head straight to Love Field. After departing Runway One Five at Addison and contacting Love Tower, I made a slight right turn for a modified base leg entry for runway One Three Left at Love Field.

After pulling into the tie-down spot I jumped out and began to tie the airplane down. Ray pulled up on the ramp in front of me in the big Cessna 402 and shut down the left engine. I hadn't noticed, but Ray had also set the parking brake, left his seat, gone to the back of the cabin, and opened the door for me. By the time I finished tying down the Twin Comanche and got over to the 402, he had climbed back into the cockpit and into the co-pilot's seat.

After closing the cabin door and climbing into the pilot's seat, I thanked him for the opportunity to fly his airplane. As we taxied out, he briefed me on the initial power settings and speeds to use and suggested an initial heading of Zero-Three-Zero degrees after take-off and climb to 2,000 feet. Shortly, we had a clearance from Love Tower and were on our way down Runway One Three Left.

Acceleration was reasonably impressive. The elevator forces were a little heavier than I expected, but a quick spin of the trim wheel and it lightened up it nicely. Once airborne, a gentle tug on the landing gear selector handle and you could feel the additional drag impose its will on the aircraft as the big inboard gear doors opened, but as the landing gear retraction cycle completed itself and the gear retracted fully, you could feel the airplane accelerate as it became much more aerodynamic and streamlined.

As I grew more comfortable with the airplane, I began to admire the vast glow of lights from the Metroplex below with that big wing tip fuel tank in the foreground and the steady roar of the big Continental engines that were propelling us through the sky. The warm orange glow from the turbo chargers through the louvers on the cowling was a little alarming at first. I had seen that at night with the cowlings off doing engine runs, but didn't realize it was this visible in flight from the cockpit.

Thinking that this might be the airmanship portion of an impromptu job interview, I gently banked the airplane twenty degrees to the right and then rolled back to the left just to get a better feel of the roll control and then began to level off at 2,000 feet.

As the airspeed indicator increased through 160 knots, I turned my head left to see if I could spot Addison Airport when suddenly KABOOOM, SMACK, WHOOOSH!

Something bounced off the back of my head, and suddenly my grip on the control yoke was now all slippery and slimy. Each time I tried to look forward my face was hit with a cold blast of air. Eventually, I found a position with my head all the way against the side window where I could actually look around the cockpit.

Under the dim glow of what was left of the cockpit lighting, I could see that the windshield was busted out. The glare shield was bent up and deformed and the compass was hanging by a wire. I couldn't tell what the slimy substance was, but it was on the right side of my face and the back of my head was all wet. My jacket was covered with some sort of gristle.

My mind began racing as to what happened. Could we have just had a mid-air collision? Did the combustion heater, which was mounted in the nose, just blow up? As I pondered what might have happened, I realized that Ray had not said a word.

Still leaning as far left in the cockpit as I could, I looked over at Ray. He was slumped over against the right side window and not moving. I grabbed his arm and began to shake him, looking for some sort of a response. Finally, he slowly turned to look at me, only to reveal that his face was all cut up and bloody. Even though there was not much light in the cockpit, I could tell that whatever we hit messed Ray up pretty good. He then slumped forward against the yoke. I wrestled him off the yoke and kind of shoved him back against the right window.

This was not exactly how I envisioned my first Cessna 400 Series flight to go, but I knew that I had to get us on the ground and get Ray some help. As I rolled the big twin Cessna left towards Addison, I scanned the skies and ground for any signs of traffic in the vicinity

Through all the noise of the cockpit I managed to call Addison. "Addison Tower, this is Twin Cessna Four Zero One Mike Papa, we are out over Garland at 2,000 feet...we have a problem and need to return for landing."

"Roger One Mike Papa, winds are calm, runway of your choice, cleared to land. Will you be needing any assistance?"

"Roger Tower, understand Mike Papa is cleared to land, we'll take Runway 33, and I think we might need an ambulance."

"Roger Mike Papa, we'll get to work on that for you."

Although we were only about ten miles away from Addison Airport, it seemed like it took an eternity to get there and with no clue as to the extent of the damage to the airplane there was no certainty the landing gear would even come down. While enroute, I continued to try to assess the damage and determine what had happened.

I was guessing as I squeezed the power back to about 25 inches of manifold pressure, and then on back to 20 inches. The airplane was beginning to slow down. I had no idea what any of the airspeed limitations were for this airplane.

I eased the power back to 18 inches of manifold pressure, shoved the propeller levers full forward, and put the gear handle in the down position. I could feel the drag of the landing gear as I glanced over to see that Ray wasn't going to be any help.

The cockpit had an eerie feel to it, the dim blue cockpit lighting, the slimy organic substance that covered me, and the slippery feel of my grip on the control yoke, the loud wind noise, the busted-up glare shield, and a guy in the co-pilot seat who may be dead for all I knew.

I slapped the flap lever for another notch of flaps as I approached short final and established what felt like a comfortable approach speed and maintained that all the way until touchdown. I pulled off the runway and fast taxied back to the airport terminal building, where I was greeted by a line service kid. I got out of the seat and went back to open the cabin door and asked, "Have you seen an ambulance?"

I got out of the airplane and walked around to the nose section to see if I could determine what had happened, but on the dimly lit ramp, all I could see was the windshield busted out. As I walked around towards the back of the airplane, I could hear a siren off in the distance.

I crawled back into the airplane to check on Ray and the line service kid followed me in with a flashlight. Best I could tell, Ray was alive but unconscious. It wasn't until I turned to exit the cabin that the line service kid's flashlight revealed feathers and duck parts all over the cockpit and the cabin. A large portion of a duck was implanted on the little coat hanger rack at the aft bulkhead by the cabin door. There was blood, gristle, goo, and feathers all over the cockpit, the cabin, and me.

The ambulance finally arrived, and the paramedics removed Ray from the cockpit and carried him away to the hospital. With the ambulance now gone, the line service kid announced that he was closing down and going home.

The aftermath was somewhat surreal. There I was on the dimly lit ramp, all by myself, with this busted up airplane that belonged to somebody that I really didn't know, who was now enroute to some hospital somewhere, I was all covered in blood, and my car was on the other side of the airport. Just goes to prove that no good deed goes unpunished.

At least Six Six Yankee was in position for its scheduled departure.

Chapter 12

The Great Awakening

As time went by, I was doing a pretty good job at keeping the charter fleet up and running and, as time allowed, retrieving the aircraft that had been left behind at some distant airport for one reason or another.

When a currently flying aircraft broke down, I was on it immediately. I made multiple trips to rescue one aircraft or another. One such trip had me travel to Amarillo to change the center cylinder on the left engine of a Baron in a bone-chilling 35-degree, thirty-knot wind. Start to finish, I completed that task in six hours and flew the aircraft home that evening.

When it came to the aircraft that had been abandoned, or left behind for one mechanical deficiency or another, it seemed that nobody could recall what the problem was or why they simply left it behind. It was kind of a crap shoot as to what tools and supplies to take to try to recover an aircraft from a remote location, but it was always an adventure.

One of the Twin Comanches, which I had never seen before, had been left in San Angelo for an undisclosed reason. Armed with tools and a spare battery, I hopped on one of the scheduled runs and went to ferry the aircraft back to Love Field. On the flight home, the right engine quit and I was unable to restart it, so I made a single engine landing at Love Field. Upon getting back to the shop and taking a closer look, I discovered that the engine failure was due to an improperly rigged fuel selector valve.

The fuel selector lever would point to the fuel tank that you wanted to draw fuel from, but the selector valve was mis-clocked so it was essentially shutting the fuel off to the engine. The fuel selector valve has detents so that when turning the fuel selector lever from one tank to the other, you are supposed to be able to feel the detent and know that your fuel selector valve is in the proper position. Turned out, the pushrod controlling the valve was bent and the top of the selector valve was covered with crud and fuzz balls from the carpet so that the detents could not be felt. A little bit of cleaning and re-rigging had that airplane back in service in no time. It appeared that was the only reason they left the aircraft out there.

Another example was the Mooney. Someone thought that the Annual Inspection was overdue, but for some unknown reason, the logbooks were in the airplane, and the airplane was in Big Springs. I obtained a Ferry Permit from the FAA, gathered up some tools and a spare battery, and caught a scheduled flight out to retrieve the aircraft.

After I spent some time with the aircraft and looked it over, it was time for an engine run. That was when the problem disclosed itself. Both brake pedals went to the floor - crap, this thing had no brakes. After looking at the brake reservoir and seeing it completely empty of fluid, I began to look around the airport for somebody who might have some MIL 5606 hydraulic fluid. Unfortunately, the place was a ghost town. Not a soul to be found anywhere.

Not to be discouraged, I placed chocks under all three wheels and fired up the engine. It seemed to run just fine, had good oil pressure, the magnetos checked out, and the propeller cycled okay. The fuel tanks were full, so I began to weigh my options. In the air, not having brakes is not an issue and getting out of here should not be a problem. The real concern was landing at Love Field. Both airports had runways that were plenty long, and if anything went wrong, I could simply pull the mixture control out and shut down the engine, steer the aircraft into the path of least resistance, and coast to a stop.

Perhaps it wasn't such a good idea, but I launched anyway. The flight to Love Field was uneventful, but it was rather nerve-racking taxiing around Love Field with all the Southwest Airlines 737s taxiing around at forty knots and me not being able to stop if need be.

All the aircraft we operated were leased from individual owners, several of whom I had never met, but over the course of time, I had become acquainted with a few of them and I felt an obligation to take care of their aircraft as if they were mine. One such owner was Captain Carl. Carl was seniority number One at Braniff International Airways, flying Fat Albert (the orange Boeing 747SP) to Hawaii and back a few times a month.

Captain Carl owned a Twin Comanche that we were operating. One day he came by the shop to introduce himself to me. "There are mechanics that work on airplanes, and there are mechanics that fix airplanes, which one are you?" he asked in a commanding voice.

"I reckon you will just have to wait and see, and then let me know," was my reply.

Needless to say, I took a great deal of pride in being able to tell him and the other aircraft owners that their aircraft was out flying or giving them a progress report for an ongoing maintenance event such as an Annual or 100-Hour Inspection. Captain Carl was the kind of person I was hoping to meet and perhaps get a little guidance from as to how to land an airline job, so I always went a little above and beyond the call of duty when looking after his airplane.

In the mix of all the adventures and maintenance activities, I began to notice some anomalies with some of the aircraft times. It was difficult to pinpoint at first, as I initially thought that I had simply misread the tach time and made a few mistakes when making the logbook entries. But going back through the flight logs revealed that somebody had been putting a substantial number of flight hours on several of the aircraft, and they were not logging the time.

This discovery was pissing me off, as I would finish a 100-hour inspection on Thursday afternoon and by Monday the aircraft already had thirty hours on it. We did not fly any routes on the weekend, and generally, the aircraft in question had not even been assigned a route. It was usually an aircraft that we had designated as backup airplane for the week.

I was guessing that since I had been given authorization to fly the company aircraft for personal reasons, maybe the pilots had been given that same authorization. If so, they should have at least logged the time in the flight logs. The issue bothered me so much that I went to the office to discuss it with the Director of Operations and the owner of the company.

Upon presenting my dilemma, they immediately accused me of flying all those hours. "WHAT? Just when the hell do you think I have had the time to fly ninety hours? I put my heart and soul into keeping the maintenance status of the fleet current and the only flying I have done is documented flying the scheduled runs and retrieving broken airplanes!"

The conversation did not go as expected, which began raising red flags for me. Everybody in the company knew damn well what I was doing at all times, and they knew that I did not have time to be joy riding around in the airplanes.

One thing struck me as kind of odd shortly after that meeting, was when I was on a flight to Amarillo with one of the pilots in the Turbo Aztec. After leveling off at altitude, he said that he wanted to manage my power settings for a little while. I was fine with that, but was extremely surprised when he pulled the power and the fuel mixture back, and when I say back, I mean way back.

Those big fuel-thirsty Lycoming TSIO-540's normally burn twelve to fourteen gallons per hour per engine and the aircraft would cruise around 140 miles per hour, but he had them pulled back to where they were only burning seven gallons per hour per engine. With a 200-gallon fuel capacity, that would mean that the aircraft could stay in the air for fourteen hours; although it was only going 105 miles per hour, that was some thrifty fuel burn.

I didn't think much of it until the following week when it was pointed out to me that the Aztec was due another 100-hour inspection. It had only been three weeks since the last inspection; there was something fishy going on here.

During the course of this inspection, I found some remnants of what appeared to be red duct tape on the side of the airplane and upon closer inspection, I could see glue residue. After studying this for a few minutes, I realized that someone had temporarily changed the aircraft registration number with matching red duct tape.

I continued on with my inspection and with the aircraft up on jacks, I climbed on board to perform the landing gear retraction test. As I did, the seat back came unlatched and flipped forward. An aeronautical chart fell out onto the floor. I didn't pay much attention to it as it was beginning to get dark and I was working with drop lights, so I continued with the task at hand. After cycling the landing gear a few times and getting in and out of the airplane a few times, I noticed a few other items in the back of the airplane. One such item was one of those seven-gallon steel gas cans. Looking further, I found a 30-30 Winchester rifle wrapped in a blanket laying in the aft cabin. What a surprise.

I grabbed the aeronautical chart and took it to the office to have a look at it. It was a World Aeronautical Chart which covered mostly Mexico. There were hand-drawn instrument approaches on the chart drawn from remote NDB Radio Beacons to remote nondescript locations in Mexico. This seemed pretty suspicious to me, but I still had work to do so it was back out to the airplane I went. As I finished up the aircraft and let her down off jacks, my suspicions were getting the better of me. Mexican aeronautical charts, extra gas cans, a rifle?

The following Monday, I went to the office to explain to the boss what I had found, and as if my questions were anticipated, the boss pulled out a very poorly doctored document that he claimed was a lie detector test report. It was made to appear that the lie detector report exonerated the boss and the company of any knowledge of any drug smuggling activities.

I was now more suspicious than ever. Why would an innocent person waste their time and money taking a lie detector test just because their Director of Maintenance raised a few questions? That document was the original cut, copy, paste, and copy again in the crudest sense. It was plain to see how it had been made with the copy machine.

My mind was racing in all different directions as I left the office, but once again I had a lot of work to do. To ease my mind, I buried myself in my work. Concentrating on a discrepancy or performing an inspection always helped take my mind to another place.

As the week went by, when a pilot would show up to begin their scheduled flight, I would ask about them flying extra time on an airplane, or if they noticed any discrepancies with the flight logs. Although no one would admit to any extra flying, a few of them acknowledged seeing the flight time discrepancies, but did not think much of it.

Arriving at the airport the following Monday, I was greeted by a swarm of DEA Agents. The Aztec was sitting on the ramp with a flat nose tire, there was a tree branch sticking out of the left flap, the left engine cowling was smashed, the right propeller was bent, and the tail number had been modified by using red and white duct tape. And, as before, there was a rifle and seven seven-gallon gas cans in the cabin.

The DEA agents were sealing the Aztec with their Red Seizure tape. Other agents were taking pictures of the other aircraft on the ramp and commenting about chasing that one a few weeks ago, and yet another one just recently.

The agents interrogated me as to my association and involvement with the aircraft on the ramp. After explaining that I was the Director of Maintenance for the FAA Certified Part 135 Air Carrier that operates these aircraft, they told me that they were confident I was not involved in any illicit activities. They admitted to having the entire operation under surveillance for some time now and they knew I was not involved in any wrong doing. They suggested that trouble was in the air for the Certificate holder and I should distance myself from the company as bad things were about to happen.

I wanted no part of this. I needed to get as far away from this situation as fast as possible. Any hint or implication of my involvement in whatever they were up to would most certainly ruin any chance of an airline career.

With that, I gathered up my tools, loaded them in the car, and headed to the FAA Office. I informed my Principal Maintenance Inspector that I was resigning my position as Director of Maintenance.

I went home and called all the aircraft owners that I had established relationships with to let them know that I was no longer working for the company, what had transpired that prompted me to walk away, and how to contact me if they needed any assistance with their airplanes.

This company had been a big disappointment for me. I was hoping the job would last long enough for me to earn 1,500 flight hours and my Airline Transport Pilot certificate. Sometimes things just do not work out, but there was no time to worry about it now, I needed to wrangle up another job. I had around 900 hours in my logbook along with a Commercial, Multi-Engine, and Instrument rating so it seemed like a good idea to find a type writer and sit down and put together a resume.

After hacking out what I thought was a pretty good-looking resume, complete with a misspelled word or two, it was time to go knock on some doors to see if I could land a job as a co-pilot mechanic. The first place I thought of was Air-Go.

Air-Go was a cargo company operating a variety of unique aircraft like the YS-11, Convairs, and DC-3s. I figured a place like that would always be on the lookout for a good co-pilot mechanic, but the grumpy old boys running that place would not even give me the time of day. They made me feel unworthy of even walking on their oil-soaked hangar floor. "Go away, kid, go bother someone else!"

My next stop was Falcon Airways at Addison Airport. Those folks were also a cargo company operating DC-3s and Carvairs. The Carvair was a highly modified DC-4 referred to as ATL-98 that was designed to ferry cars across the English Channel. I always admired those pilots flying for Falcon, as I would routinely see them coming home with one engine shut down and the propeller feathered. I figured that an outfit with that many round engines and old airplanes would certainly be interested in someone with my skills and ambition, but I struck out there as well.

Since none of the legacy aircraft operators seemed interested in my services, I turned my attention to the corporate jet operators. Love Field was abuzz with those sexy private jets, and although I knew my chances were slim, I started knocking on their doors.

I spent the following few days papering Love Field with my resume. Every nook and cranny of the airport was covered in search of the Chief Pilot for this company or that company. I managed to meet some interesting people and have some good conversations but was not able to secure a job. I was, however, provided with several leads.

In hindsight, I think most of those leads were a setup, as the Chief Pilots were probably all calling each other to tell them about this kid looking for a pilot job and they just sent him their way. Most of these folks appeared to have been vets from the recent Vietnam War, and as a civilian, I was clearly an outsider to their club.

I finally wandered into a little place that I thought for sure would have a place for me. They had a DC-3, an old Convair, and a pair of Learjet 36s. It was a well-known semiconductor manufacturer. Those boys dished it out. I had never been so humiliated in my life. "I would rather be broke down in Greenland with a co-pilot that has a Bachelor Degree than one with an A&P!" quipped one of the gentlemen. "How much Learjet experience do you have?" asked the other.

After having eaten a healthy dose of humble pie, it was clear to me that I should be looking into some of the charter companies instead of the corporate jet operators. After surveying the airport, my choices were Western Jet, Alpha Aviation, and Jet Fleet.

There was never anyone around to talk to at Western Jet. Alpha Aviation had a King Air and a Learjet, but they were not interested in a 900-hour pilot. By far, the busiest place at Love Field was Jet Fleet. The place was always a beehive of corporate jet activity. If a flying job was in the cards for me, it would be here.

Chapter 13

Jet Fleet

After parking my car in the overcrowded Jet Fleet parking lot, I found my way to the door to the maintenance shop and with some trepidation I walked in. Rock and roll music blared from a little radio on my left in an area that appeared to be the sheet metal fabrication shop. Off to my right was the distant sound of country music all interrupted by the sound of a hydraulic mule circulating the life blood through a Falcon 20 as the landing gear began cycling up and down.

The hangar was stuffed full of Learjets, Cessna Citations, and Falcons. The ramp outside was full of yet more aircraft. Across the way somebody yelled, "Clear for power? Power coming on!" I could almost hear the snickers and "who is that kid" from the mechanics as I walked across the hangar floor looking for someone to talk to about a job.

"Through those doors, all the way down the hall and up the stairs, should be a gal at her desk, she can help you."

"Thank you," I replied, and off I went. One thing that struck me as odd was the laughter coming from all the offices and the avionics lab as I progressed down the hallway. This kinda seemed like a happy work place.

Once upstairs, I presented my resume and announced that I was here seeking a co-pilot job. This was quite a contrast from the experience downstairs. People upstairs were all dressed in very professional business attire, which made me slightly uncomfortable. I was promptly provided with an application and shown a chair to use while filling it out.

I filled out the application seeking a pilot job and upon turning in my application the lady informed me that they did not have any positions available, but she would keep my resume and application on file. I thanked her for her time and proceeded back down the stairs and hallway and back into the maintenance shop.

As I got closer to the hangar door, I stopped to watch the guys doing the gear retraction test on that Falcon 20 when a voice behind me said, "Hey, what are you doing here?"

"Looking for a job," I replied to a guy with a goat-tee and a blonde afro hairdo.

"Can you do sheet metal work?"

"Yeah, sure, used to work in a little shop where we rebuilt wrecked Cessnas, Pipers, and Beechcraft."

He walked over to me, handed me a rivet, and asked, "What kind of rivet is that?"

"Well, that would be a 426AD number 4, it takes a number 30 drill bit and a copper-colored cleco," I replied.

"Did you fill out an application?"

"Sure did, for a pilot position."

"What did they say?"

"That y'all aren't hiring."

"You want to work in the shop?"

"Sure, why not?"

"Wait right here."

A few minutes later he returned and asked me when I could start and I replied that I could start whenever they needed me to start. He instructed me to be there in the morning at 8 a.m. with my tool box.

When I was hired, I knew absolutely nothing about the company, and although it was not the flying job I had hoped for, it was a step towards learning a new class of aircraft. And besides, most all of my previous flying opportunities began in the maintenance shop anyway.

At the top of the food chain was Bert George, president of the maintenance department, and then there was Bill Henderson in charge of the avionics department. The name plate on Bill's desk was inscribed "Bill Henderson – slightly left of Attila the Hun."

On the other side of the hall was an office that housed the quality assurance and inspection department and next to them was the parts department, led by Gary Green and Al Neighbors, along with all their supporting staff.

Further down the hall and closer to the shop was Doug, who was in charge of the shop, and Stan as the shop foreman. On down the food chain from there were the aircraft crew chiefs and then the all-around everyday aircraft technicians.

Stan would assign a crew chief to an incoming aircraft along with a crew of technicians necessary to accomplish what ever task the aircraft required. The crew chief would ram rod the project through the shop and keep Stan informed of progress, and either requesting more or releasing mechanics from that particular project based on need.

Jet Fleet was a culture shock for me. I became one of about twenty-five guys marching to the tune of the time clock, and it took some getting used to. Although the aircraft were different and more complex, everywhere else I had worked consisted of only a few people and my responsibilities were much greater and broader in scope than at Jet Fleet.

It was no longer my responsibility to research logbooks and Airworthiness Directives and make logbook entries, chase parts, or schedule airplanes in and out. There were other people in the organization for all those logistics. All I had to do was learn Jet Fleet's FAA Approved Repair Station manual, follow their procedures, and work on and learn these sexy jet airplanes.

The guys on the shop floor were a rough and tumble mixed bag of Vietnam vets and civilian rednecks whose ages ranged from the early twenties to the mid-thirties with a diverse experience base. It was a great bunch of guys to work with, but at times they could also be crude and ruthless. It was the kind of place that would cause the modern-day woosified social justice warriors' heads to explode. There were no snowflakes here.

If you screwed something up or said something stupid, you could count on being ridiculed, and if that bothered you, it would only get worse. You might even earn a nickname. Thin-skinned people did not last very long at all. They seemed to just slither out the door never to be seen or heard from again.

Tool boxes were decorated with the latest battery or tool manufacturer calendar that featured a new semi-naked girl for each month of the year. There was no such thing as sensitivity training, nor was there a need for it in those days; if there was, the Jet Fleet maintenance department would have never existed. You had to man up to survive.

For the first couple of months, I was kept in the sheet metal department working on a special project. We installed the first of several modifications to the Cessna Citations with what was to become known as a Freon System Air Conditioner. We struggled with the first couple of air conditioner installations as the prints were not exactly perfect, parts that had been provided didn't fit properly and so on, but with each passing day, we eventually got all the details dialed in so that air conditioning kits could be sold and installed under a Supplemental Type Certificate.

They could tell that I wanted to peel away from the sheet metal shop and dive into the big inspections going on in the hangar. I wanted to learn how to perform hot section inspections on the Pratt & Whitney JT-15, the General Electric CJ-610, and the CF-700 turbine engines that were on the aircraft in the shop. I wanted to learn the cabin pressurization systems, how to perform landing gear tests, and do all the inspections.

Eventually, I was assigned to a crew working on Citations. It was great, all I had to do was follow someone else's lead, do what I was told, and work on airplanes, learning something new every day. I excelled, earning a substantial pay raise in fairly short order. It was not long before I was assigned my own aircraft and after a few successful maintenance events, I was promoted to crew chief.

We worked hard and it seemed that most everyone took pride in their knowledge of the aircraft and their work at Jet Fleet. We worked hard to complete inspections within the flat rate times that the manufacturer published. We prided ourselves on striving to be the best maintenance shop in the country. Of course, there were those who were simply riding the time clock for the paycheck and never went above and beyond the call of duty.

It took me a while to comprehend the significance of Jet Fleet to the rest of the world. This was the era when private jet transportation was just becoming vogue, and Jet Fleet was the leader in the industry. At the time, Jet Fleet was the largest jet charter company in the country and you just never knew who you might run into in the lobby. We flew just about every rock and roll band there ever was, a lot of big business people, movie stars, celebrities, and even the slimy politicians.

In the maintenance shop, we were a factory-authorized service centers for Learjet, Falcon, Cessna Citation, and a slew of different avionics manufacturers. Tech reps from the manufacturers were always in the facility. We were seeing maintenance issues come up that the manufacturers never anticipated or saw before and we were constantly devising appropriate repairs and modifications.

We also played hard. We had this thing we called beer ball. Basically, it was a game of softball with plenty of cold beer being consumed during the games. What was even more fun was that Bert, Bill, and all the folks in the parts department showed up to cheer us on. It was truly one of the finest examples of team building I had ever seen.

Thursday evenings were reserved for romancing the babes at one of the local honkytonk night clubs where notables such as Asleep at the Wheel and Ray Wiley Hubbard would entertain the crowd. The City

Dump was another interesting watering hole that attracted a mixed bag of patrons such as the local motorcycle gang, some left over hippies, and the Jet Fleet crowd.

For the first time in my life, I was part of a large organization. A family of aviators with a nationwide reputation. Jet Fleet was regularly highlighted in aviation trade publications and our leaders were highly regarded in the industry.

I had been satisfying my quest for more flight time by driving to the drop-zones at Aero Country Airport or the Seagoville Airport on Saturdays and Sundays and flying the jump plane for the skydivers.

I was becoming comfortable in my new role and did not want to do anything wrong to screw it up, so when a few of the aircraft owners from the old charter company contacted me for help with their aircraft, I went to Doug to ask if it was okay. He asked what type of aircraft I was talking about and when I told him it was Twin Comanches, Barons, and Bonanzas, he said it was okay with him as long as it was not anything that Jet Fleet worked on. As long as it did not interfere with my work at Jet Fleet, I could go work on those "pee-poppers" all I wanted.

So, my moonlighting career began. At first it was a simple oil change after work. Then it was a couple of annual inspections that I performed on the weekends. Then a local aircraft dealer noticed me and asked if I could fix a few discrepancies on an aircraft he was trying to sell. It just kinda snowballed from there. I could have quit Jet Fleet and done just fine financially, but I knew there was still much to learn about the aircraft that I worked on there. Besides, they had sent me to several formal schools for training on those aircraft, and I felt like I owed it to them to stick around.

In the hallway leading to the offices, on the "Wall of Shame" as we called it, was an individual picture of each one of the Jet Fleet maintenance technicians along with a brief description of our job title, our FAA certificates, and the formal training schools we had been to.

For me, that "Wall of Shame" was a certain source of pride. My mug shot had the caption:

Kevin Lacey
Airframe & Powerplant Mechanic
Commercial, Multiengine, & Instrument Rated Pilot
Cessna Citation School
Learjet School
Fan Jet Falcon School
Pratt & Whitney JT-15

Our maintenance customers were all the time loitering around in the hallway in the area of our mug shots and pretty soon I began getting clandestine phone calls from local aircraft operators looking for someone to help them out with maintenance on their aircraft. You know, outside of Jet Fleet, as in moonlighting. Just as I had hoped, the casual mention of a possible co-pilot/mechanic position almost always came up.

It didn't take long for me to have a few local Cessna Citations and a Falcon to take care of. I didn't really see it as moonlighting in as much as I saw these opportunities as possible co-pilot mechanic jobs. Jet Fleet did not see it that way, so they fired me. Interestingly, I had become a Citation flight control rigging specialist and Jet Fleet had a string of Citations scheduled for a maintenance event that required flight control cable rigging, so after a few weeks had passed, they called and offered me my job back, with a pay raise.

The following several months, I did my best to stay out of trouble. I kept my moonlighting strictly to the little "pee-poppers" and I made sure that everyone knew what I was working on. It was interesting to discover that almost nobody in the shop at Jet Fleet knew how to install and time a magneto to an engine, but then again, jet engines do not have magnetos.

Everything was moving right along until one evening, as I was riding home on my motorcycle, my world came to a complete halt. I was run over by a car full of illegal aliens from Mexico. I was busted up pretty good.

I was diagnosed with a concussion, multiple contusions on my head, separated shoulder, broken ribs, multiple compound fractures on my left leg, and torn lateral and co-lateral ligaments on my right knee. Needless to say, I was in considerable pain. The first couple of weeks went by in a blur as I was constantly medicated with Demerol.

Finally, one evening two of the guys from Jet Fleet came to my hospital room to see me. It was good to have some company, but they did not like the hospital room environment. One of them left the room and returned a few minutes later with a wheelchair.

"What the hell are you gonna do with that thing?"

"We are going for a ride, Kev!"

"Where did you get that wheel chair?"

"We stole it from some little old lady down the hall, now shut up and let's see if we can get you into this thing!"

They rolled me off the bed and into the wheelchair, making a tangled mess out of the two IV bags and the hoses that were plugged into me. When all that got straightened out and me wearing a stylish backless hospital gown, off we went. Going down the hall, they hustled me past the nurses' station and into the elevator.

Down the elevator, out the door, across the street, and into the parking garage elevator we went. When we got to the top floor, the doors opened to a round of applause and cheers. About half the Jet Fleet maintenance crew were up there sitting on the tailgates of their trucks drinking beer, and there was plenty to go around!

We sat up there on the top of that parking garage and watched the sun go down, telling stories of things happening at the shop, drinking beer, and carrying on. I had the best time that evening, that is, right up until it was time for everyone to leave. In typical Jet Fleet fashion, they put me in the elevator and went down to the bottom floor, pushed me across the street, and said, "Adios sucker," and left me there by the door to find my own way.

I had no idea what floor my room was on or where I was. This was a big hospital and it was the first time I had been out of my room. The effects of the Demerol were wearing off and it was apparent that the Budweiser was not strong enough to ease the pain, but I had to find my room.

I toured the part of the hospital where they had all the newborn kids and wandered into and out of multiple different treating rooms. I found the emergency room where they pointed me to an elevator that took me to the ICU. Fortunately, a pretty young nurse saw me rolling around looking lost and offered to help. She decoded my hospital-issued wrist band and proceeded to take me to my room. As we passed the nurses' station, my nurse spotted me and began scolding me as she joined up with the other gal to push me down the hall. Together, they got me back into my bed and got the IVs hooked back up.

As time went by, the hospital began to reduce the painkillers and I was spending more time awake than asleep. My room was situated such that with the wind out of the north, I could briefly see aircraft on final approach to Love Field and with the wind from the south, I could briefly see the departures. I began to reflect on my current position in life compared to what my goals and dreams were.

As I lay there each day, I realized that I had lost focus of my dream of flying for the airlines, and although I loved working with the people at Jet Fleet, I had become complacent and content with my current life and wasn't flying much anymore except for the occasional test flight of a little "pee-popper" that I had worked on. I needed to get out of the hospital, get healed up, and start doing some flying to get the hours needed for my Airline Transport Pilot Certificate.

Soon after I was discharged from the hospital, reality set in. Even though I had pretty good insurance I still had hospital bills that amounted to over $10,000 that I had to pay. I was shocked and very uncomfortable, as I had never been in debt before. To make matters worse, I was looking at several more months of rehabilitation and physical therapy before I could even go back to work.

After several months, the doctors finally released me to return to work for light duty. Although it was good to get out of my apartment, it was frustrating returning to work. After all, I had a cast on both legs and was hobbling around on crutches. We had an extensive hard copy technical library and the only assignment they would give me was to sit around and insert the revisions into the maintenance manuals. It was a great opportunity to study the maintenance manuals, but I needed more physical activity.

As I regained my strength and mobility, I would occasionally sneak out of the library and find something to do on the shop floor. Unfortunately, I would get caught, reprimanded, and sent back to the library. I reckon it isn't in my DNA to sit in an office all day.

It was eight months since the crash when the doctors took off my last cast. That was a long rehabilitation period and I had a lot of lost time to make up for. I began notifying moonlight airplane maintenance customers that I was back on my feet and available to take care of their aircraft maintenance needs. Pretty soon, I was chipping away at that hospital bill.

While I was all busted up in the hospital, one of my Jet Fleet co-workers accepted the Director of Maintenance position at a major flight department in Monterrey, Mexico. Their fleet consisted of Citations and Falcons. One evening he gave me a call and invited me to go to Monterrey and work full time with him.

I really wasn't interested in moving to Mexico full time, but he did have an upcoming maintenance project on a Citation that I was interested in. He offered me a daily rate that was about four times what I was making at Jet Fleet. Thinking that would go a long way towards paying off my hospital bills, I put in for a week's leave of absence and headed for Monterrey.

I did not realize the working conditions or the lack of support and equipment in Monterrey. Every bit of the inspection on that Citation was a struggle. Tooling and parts support was nonexistent. Everything we needed had to come from the U.S. All in all, it took a month to complete the inspection and get a test flight accomplished. At the end of the inspection, they paid me half of what they owed me and promised to send me the balance due within a week.

Upon returning to Jet Fleet, I didn't even get to my toolbox before I was called upon the carpet. They confronted me with faxed pages of parts orders from Mexico and copies of my parts requisitions from similar inspections that I had performed at Jet Fleet. The paperwork was identical. The handwriting, the parts ordered, and even the order in which the parts were listed.

They had taken a copy of my standard parts order form that I had been using for that particular maintenance event and faxed it to Jet Fleet to order the parts needed in Mexico. The folks in the parts department recognized my handwriting. Although management at Jet Fleet thoroughly understood that I was trying to dig myself out of the hospital debt, they could not allow me to moonlight on what was once their maintenance customer's airplane.

Welcome to the world of self-unemployment.

Chapter 14

Target Practice

It was a little nerve-racking walking out the door at Jet Fleet for the last time not knowing what the future held, but before long my moonlighting had turned into a full-time job. I had two local Cessna Citations to take care of and several little airplane dealers that kept me pretty busy with their needs.

Although I began doing a few aircraft deliveries for one of the aircraft dealers, others claimed that pilots were a dime a dozen and I was much more valuable to them in the shop fixing up their sales inventory. While swinging wrenches put food on the table and paid the rent, I really wanted to be out flying and building my hours.

One morning I walked into an airplane dealer's office to drop off an invoice only to find him engaged in a heated discussion with a representative from one of the local banks. The banker was reasonably upset as he had several outstanding aircraft loans on aircraft that the dealer had sold and arranged the financing for through the bank. The banker wanted these non-performing assets recovered.

The dealer was explaining that he had been sending pilots out to bring some of the airplanes home, but they were not very successful for one reason or another. They were not able to locate some of the aircraft while others had mechanical deficiencies. He claimed to have spent a lot of money trying to recover several airplanes for the bank, but had been unsuccessful.

As the banker was leaving, I stopped him and handed him my business card and suggested that I might be able to help him with his problems. He looked at my card and said "Thank you" and left the premises. Upon seeing this, the airplane dealer began scolding me. "Just who do you think you are interfering in my business?"

I was not very pleased with this airplane peddler trying to pigeon hole me into the maintenance shop, a role that I did not choose, but there was a need to maintain a relationship with him because of the volume of aircraft that passed through his hands. I apologized for my apparent indiscretion and reminded him that he did not own me and I would not be happy unless I was doing a certain amount of flying.

About two hours later, my pager went off with a phone number that I didn't recognize. I found a telephone in the lobby of the FBO and returned the call. It was the banker and he wanted to meet with me for lunch.

At lunch, he presented me with an impressive portfolio of non-performing assets, or airplanes that were in default, that he needed help with. He seemed impressed when I showed him my credentials and described my experience level. We discussed our relationships with the aircraft dealer. He had a couple of aircraft in his inventory that he suggested I could use in my search and recovery efforts.

Next thing I knew, I was involved in an airplane repo derby. I was grabbing two to three airplanes a week. Some were simple no-brainers where the owner would meet me and turn over the keys and logbooks and I would fly away, while others were more challenging. Some aircraft owners would challenge me with "you can have the airplane if you can find it!" Other aircraft had mechanical deficiencies that had to be addressed before flying away.

One of my assignments was to hunt down and recover a Cessna 172 that was reported to be on a private airstrip somewhere close to Tulsa, Oklahoma.

I still had a few friends up there from my days at Spartan School of Aeronautics and Lot Aero Flying Service, so I made a few phone calls. One of my old flight instructors, Jay, who used to own a Luscombe, was now flying a Cessna Conquest for a charter company. He informed me that he had long since sold his Luscombe and was pretty much out of the loop with respect to little private airplanes in the area.

I called my old boss Robert, knowing that although he took a job at the American Airlines maintenance base, he would somehow always be involved with little airplane maintenance. We had a great chat, and my suspicions were right about his general aviation involvement, but he had not seen this particular aircraft.

My next call was to my other former flight instructor, Stan. "That tail number sounds familiar, Kev, stand by a minute while I get my logbook. Yes, looks like I did about three hours with the new owner. I checked him out in the airplane about a year and a half ago. Last time I flew with him, he was keeping it over at that crop-duster strip north of town. Why are you asking?"

"Between us, and please keep this confidential, the bank has requested that I repo the airplane for them."

"Oh, I wouldn't go there if I was you, Kev. I hear the owner of that place is one crazy son of a bitch! He's an old crop duster and he is likely to shoot you if he catches you. I do not want to read about you in the newspaper!"

Well, at least I had a place to start looking, next problem was finding a ride. The logistics of this kind of operation could be a nightmare sometimes. I could fly up commercial and get a rental car and drive to the airport out in the country, but once I got the airplane, I had to leave the car behind. I could always get one of my friends in Tulsa to help with ground support, but none of them wanted anything to do with this airplane or that airport.

As I sat there in the FBO pondering my options, a local pilot walked in and asked me what I was up to today. When I told him that I needed to get to a little airstrip outside of Tulsa to pick up an airplane he said, "hell, I'll take you up there in the 170 if you pay for the gas."

He had a pretty nice little Cessna 170 and it was a really nice day for flying. I had flown with him a few times in the past, so I grabbed my little bag of tricks and accepted his offer. The flight up was uneventful and pleasant.

As we neared our destination, I began to brief him on what we were doing. If we spotted the airplane, we would land, pull up next to it, I would jump out and begin working the lock and ignition switch, while he ran around and got the tie-down ropes. I would check the gas and oil and pre-flight as much as I could. Once I got the engine started, I'd haul ass and get outta there. I would meet him at Tulsa Riverside and we would gas the airplanes up and head back to Texas.

It appeared that he was not expecting all that. Maybe he was thinking that we were going to sit down and have a cup of coffee before beginning our return trip, but his demeanor changed and he began sweating profusely.

We had a hard time finding the airport as the winter effects on the surrounding vegetation had turned everything brown. We flew up and down the little river twice before spotting a couple of airplanes tied down along what appeared to be a northeast-southwest-oriented runway with a building of some sort on the northeast corner.

We landed to the southwest and rolled down the runway and pulled off right in front of the Cessna 172 November Eight Four Two Six Uniform (N8426U). I was out of the airplane with my bag and pick keys before he was able to shut down the engine on the 170.

By the time he got out of the airplane, I had the door opened and a key that fit the ignition all ready to go. I quickly began untying the tie-down rope on the left wing as my partner-in-crime got the right-wing tie-down. I looked the airplane over as I went around to the tail to get the tail tie-down rope. Moving up the right side of the aircraft towards the cowling, I suggested that he saddle up the 170 and flee the scene. We would meet back up at Riverside Airport.

With that said, he gladly jumped in the 170 and fled the scene. As he departed, I climbed up on the right-wing strut to look in the fuel tank to determine how much fuel was onboard. Out of the corner of my eye, I noticed some movement on the porch of the building on the northeast corner of the airport. It was hard to make out, but it looked like someone was up there with a broom in their hand sweeping the porch.

I didn't think much of it as I climbed off the strut to check the engine oil. Satisfied this gal was safe to fly, I climbed aboard and fired up the engine. Oil pressure came right up. One more glance at the porch and it appeared that whoever was up there was now out in front of the building still holding that broom, watching me.

I took my time as I taxied to the southwest end of the runway to give the engine time to warm up. The magnetos checked good and everything seemed normal so I spun her around and shoved the throttle in. Rolling down the runway, the airplane accelerated rather quickly in the cool December air and in no time I was airborne.

As I passed the building at the northeast corner, it appeared that whoever that was on the porch was pointing his broom at me. I sensed something wasn't right, as Stan's words echoed in my head. I got to tree-top level and turned southbound and stayed low until I was a few miles away.

Landing at Riverside a few minutes later, I found my buddy and his 170 on the ramp. He had just finished fueling up and had instructed the line service guy to bill me for the fuel. He waived at me as he fired up the 170 and taxied out. What? No time for a de-brief?

After climbing out of the airplane and stepping out to talk to the line service guy, I noticed two holes in the fuselage just in front of the horizontal stabilizer. Holly shit! That was not a broom that son of a bitch had, that was a rifle - and he shot at me! My nerves were a little rattled, and my first thought was to call Stan to tell him what happened, but I decided to just continue on with the mission. Not much I could do about it now anyway except to gas up and head for Texas.

The airplane flew great and the only thing it needed was a few nickel and dime patches to cover up the bullet holes and some touch-up paint.

Somehow or another the banker came up with the logbooks and after all four of the patches had been installed, they asked me to do a demo flight with a potential new buyer.

Their potential new buyer was none other than the Police Chief of Lacy Lakeview, Texas.

He was a really nice guy and completely understood my explanation of the bullet hole patches. After the test flight, he handed over a check for the asking price of the airplane and flew away.

Next up was a Beechcraft B-55 Baron that was in Mineral Wells that had a flat nose tire and a dead battery. I grabbed an air tank and went and bought a new battery, jumped into one of the bank-owned airplanes, and had the Baron back home in less than four hours. Then there was a Cherokee 235 that I snatched from Waco, Texas. With each recovery, it was becoming more and more difficult to find someone to ferry an airplane home for me.

I was instructed to deliver all the aircraft I recovered to the aircraft dealer that had sold the aircraft in the first place. That brought about a little friction between me and the dealer, as he felt like he should be in charge of the recoveries. He really was upset that I was working directly for the bank.

The dealer had airplanes that needed a little attention in the maintenance shop and he was upset that I was not always at his disposal.

Chapter 15

Meet Johnny Law

With several recent successes, I was rapidly becoming the number one go-to guy for my new found banker. After recovering all the aircraft in the first batch of files, they handed me several more file folders. Each file folder contained all the necessary documents for a legal repossession along with a letter appointing me as having their Power of Attorney, and several handwritten notes for each aircraft.

One file they handed me was on a Piper Cherokee 180 November Nine One Three One Juliet (N9131J). The file folder had all the required documents with handwritten notes. The last known whereabouts of the aircraft and defaulted party was out in Midland, Texas, which was about 250 miles west.

Because I only got paid when I completed an assignment and I was cash strapped at the time, a trip out west without verification that the aircraft was there did not make financial sense to me. I grabbed my trusty AC-U-KWIK directory of airports and began making phone calls. My angle was to pretend to be a long-lost friend of the airplane owner hoping to track him down for a reunion during my future visit to Midland.

After several phone calls, I got a hit. Unfortunately, my aircraft was not there. It turned out that my aircraft and its owner had packed up and fled the oil patch in search of greener pastures. The FBO operator in Midland was very helpful in that he informed me that the owner of the Cherokee did finally manage to earn his private pilot certificate just before he left Midland. He wasn't really sure but he thought he may have landed a job somewhere near San Antonio.

Happy that I had not bought an airline ticket and gone to Midland, I began looking at the aeronautical chart of San Antonio in an attempt to identify the type of airport the owner of this

Cherokee might be comfortable at. Based on the information provided by the FBO operator in Midland, it had to be an uncontrolled field because he really didn't like to talk on the radio.

That information was a great help as it narrowed my search to just a few airports. After a few minutes of thought, I devised a new strategy for my next phone call campaign. Now, I would be his former flight instructor from West Texas with a plan to pass through San Antonio and would like to stop by and see how my former student was getting along.

The first few airports I called yielded no information at all, but then I called the West Side Airpark. This place sounded like the kind of place I would want to park my airplane. The good ol' boy on the phone was friendly and informed me that yes indeed my Cherokee 180 was on the field.

He also informed me that the owner along with several other airport tenants usually came out every Saturday morning for coffee and then would spend the rest of the day flying around. At the end of the day, they would sit around and have a beer or three, tell a few stories, and then go home.

I asked the airport operator not to mention that I had called and spoil my planned surprise visit. After explaining that my new plan was to show up Saturday morning, surprise the Cherokee owner, and maybe spend the day with his newfound aviating friends, he agreed not to say a word.

As I hung up the phone, my mind began to wander into the world of logistics. If I hopped on Southwest Airlines and ran down there, I could rent a car to hunt down the Cherokee, but what did I do with the car after I flew away in the airplane? Just leave it there? West Side Airpark was thirty miles away from the big airport.

There was a Cessna 172 sitting on the ramp that I had previously swiped for the same bank, so a quick call to them secured authorization to use it. Now all I needed was another pilot to fly down there with me and bring the Cessna back, which was becoming a seemingly impossible task these days.

Although there were a lot of unemployed pilots running around, not many were interested in flying a repo mission. They all seem to think that their names would end up in some FAA database somewhere and that might inhibit their potential career opportunities. Me, I didn't care, I was still trying to get the necessary flight hours I was told I had to have and put food on the table at the same time.

I decided to go wander through the FBO to see who might be hanging around when I spotted a young pilot named Steve. Although I had seen him around several times, I never really talked to him much. I introduced myself to him and asked him what he was up to.

Steve was passing out resumes hoping to find a job. He was a well-mannered young man, very clean cut, naive, with a polished and proper vocabulary, probably the exact image my mom had hoped I would turn into.

When I asked him if he would like to add about four more hours of 172 time to his logbook he replied, "How much will it cost me?" Boy oh boy, there is one born every minute, I was ready to pay him a hundred bucks or so, but I simply replied that I wouldn't charge him anything.

All we needed to do was fly to a little airport just outside San Antonio, pick up a Cherokee, fly over to San Antonio International to fuel up the airplanes, and head back to Dallas.

As we walked across the ramp, I could tell that he was curious that, along with my flight bag, I was also carrying a pair of binoculars, but he never said a word. After a quick pre-flight, we hopped into the 172 and began our journey.

We had a high overcast with fairly strong winds and balmy temperatures. The flight progressed along fairly well with only some occasional small talk, but as we got closer to our destination and began our descent, I rearranged my side of the cockpit with my binoculars on the glare shield and a little bag of goodies in my lap.

Now, about this time, ol' Steve begins to get a little suspicious about the true nature of our trip, and begins to make some rather nervous inquiries. I had to confess that we were repossessing the Cherokee and reassured him that everything would be okay.

Looking through my trusty binoculars as we circled the airport, I spotted the Cherokee! Outstanding, this was going to be easy. The Cherokee is tied down in an open T-Hangar on the front row facing the runway. The FBO was on the opposite side of the runway and slightly west of the Cherokee.

As we flew the traffic pattern in preparation for landing, I devised our plan and explained it to Steve, who was now becoming reluctant to have any part of this operation. We would park the 172 in such a way that would obstruct the view from the FBO but leave room to taxi the Cherokee straight out. Steve's role would be to begin with the left wing tie-down rope and work his way around the airplane, inspecting and untying the tie-downs and removing the pitot cover as he went. I would jump out and check the engine for oil, check fuel quantity on the right wing, and attempt to get inside the aircraft and get the engine running.

The landing was uneventful and just as planned, we taxied right up to a spot that blocked the view from the FBO. Before Steve completely stopped the 172 I had grabbed all my gear, jumped out, and ran towards the Cherokee.

I immediately got the two latches on the cowling undone and pulled the oil dipstick. There was plenty of oil, and it was pretty clean - that was a good sign. A quick cursory look around and the cowling was latched. A peek inside the right fuel cap revealed a full tank of fuel on that side so I ran around, hopped up onto the wing, and began working to unlock the door.

Then I noticed that Steve was just standing there watching me. As I yelled at him to get busy with his job of untying the airplane, the lock I was working on gave way and the door popped open. Quickly I gathered my gear and threw it in the back seat and dove into the pilot's seat and began working on the ignition switch. Ha - The first key I tried worked and before Steve could get around the airplane and get the last tie-down rope undone, I had the engine running.

As he came around the left wing to get the tie-down rope and pitot cover off, I yelled at him through the little side window to saddle up the 172 and meet me at San Antonio International at the FBO.

As I taxied away, I looked back to see Steve standing there with a tie-down rope in one hand and a pitot tube cover in the other watching me in total disbelief. I motioned to him to hurry up and then focused my attention on getting airborne. Total time from touchdown in the 172 to take-off in the Cherokee was less than ten minutes.

The short flight to San Antonio was uneventful and the little Cherokee performed very well. The landing was smooth, and although I should have known better, I was already congratulating myself for a job well done and thinking what I was going to say when I called the banker dude to tell him that I had the airplane and would have it back in Dallas in about two and a half hours. After all, I had only received this assignment this morning.

As I taxied to the ramp, I was greeted by a line service technician who had a pair of chocks slung over his shoulder and a marshaling wand in each hand guiding me to my parking place. Suddenly he did something completely unexpected. He didn't give me the crossed wand stop sign or anything; he just dropped the chocks and ran back toward the FBO, occasionally looking over his shoulder as he went.

It wasn't until I stopped and shut down the engine that I realized why he ran away. It appears that an entourage of unmarked cars, San Antonio police cars, and airport police cars had followed me down the taxiway to the ramp.

I never saw them until I shut down the engine and they surrounded me and jumped out of their vehicles with their guns drawn. "Get out of the plane," they yelled. They had me and the little Cherokee surrounded. The guys closest to me were all wearing business suits and pointing pistols at me, while the guys on the outer perimeter were local uniformed police officers who also had their gun sights set on me.

I exited the airplane and just as I stepped on to the tarmac, I was grabbed by two suit-wearing guys who promptly pushed me face down on the wing of the Cherokee. As they were fitting me with a pair of handcuffs, I tried to reassure them that everything is okay "Easy, guys, I ain't doing anything wrong here!"

Just about the time they stood me up to begin their interrogation, I saw Steve in the 172 taxi up with the line service technician waving him clear over to the other side of the ramp. As he taxied by, we made eye contact and I could tell that what he saw scared the crap out of him.

After a few minutes of explaining to the FBI that I was simply repossessing the airplane for the bank, they began to lighten up a bit.

"Hey, if it's a repossession, then you must have some paperwork?"

"Well, yes sir, as a matter of fact, I do, it's in my flight bag on the floor behind the seat."

One agent wandered over, peered through the window, and confirmed to the other agent that there was in fact a flight bag looking thing on the floor behind the seat. After a brief consultation with each other they decided that I should be the one to retrieve my flight bag from the airplane.

Thinking these guys were becoming somewhat relaxed with my story, I asked "How about undoing these handcuffs?"

To which they replied "You are not off the hook just yet."

"Well, how the hell do you expect me to get that flight bag out of there with my hands tied behind my back?"

"That's your problem!"

So, with my hands tied behind my back, I stepped up on the wing of the airplane and proceeded to open the door up with my foot, and I used my knee to push it open enough for the latch to catch and hold the door open. I turned back towards the cabin and attempted to move the seat back forward with my knee, while trying to spin around and stoop down low enough to grab my flight bag.

Evidently, the door catch was defective, because just when I was semi off balance reaching down for the bag, the door came swinging closed and knocked me over into the back seat. So now I was on my back half in and half out of the airplane and my hands were cuffed behind my back. I struggled for a while to inch my way back up to a sitting position and was finally able to grab the handle of the flight bag.

I was pretty sure all the cops and agents were getting a kick out of this. I couldn't hear what they were saying, but they were all grinning. As I stood up on the wing holding the bag behind me, I noticed a fuel truck was now over there with Steve fueling up the 172.

After stepping down off the wing and walking out towards the wing tip, I placed the flight bag on the ramp in front of the agents and told them to have at it.

Well now, they weren't going to have any of that either. I had to kneel down on the ramp and from behind my back, open both latches, and pop open my flight bag. I stood up and said, "Okay, boys, that is as far as this little game is going. There is a manila file folder in that bag, you get it out! I am done with these games. This is getting a little ridiculous!"

As we stood out by the wing tip, the agents began going over the contents of the file folder and I looked up to see Steve taxiing out in the 172. I was not sure where he was going, but one thing was clear, he didn't want anything to do with what I was involved in.

After a moment or so one of the feds approached me with a key and began to undo the handcuffs while telling me what a cool gig I had. The other fed went over to the local police to explain to them that everything was in order and I was simply performing a repossession.

"Wow, what a cool job, you former military?"

"You must be pretty good, the guy that called it in said you were only on the airport for about three minutes."

I gathered up my belongings, put them back in my flight bag, put it back in the airplane, and then proceeded over to the FBO. Admittedly, there was a slight spring in my step as I passed the few corporate jets on the ramp and walked into the FBO, knowing that everybody inside had been watching the activity through the window.

First order of business was a trip to the men's room to take care of some long overdue business. With that task out of the way it was time to call my client and let him know that his airplane was in my care, custody, and control.

I used the phone in the flight planning room and had just gotten my client on the line when I sensed a presence behind me. My free hand was grabbed and I was spun around to come face to face with a local policeman. "Can I call you right back? I have an issue I need to take care of right away."

With that, I hung up the phone and was promptly handcuffed again. "Okay, what now?"

"You are now being arrested for trespassing," was the cop's reply.

"How the hell do you figure that?" I asked.

It appeared that the cops had been talking to the owner of the airport, the same guy I had talked to earlier in the day when I discovered where the Cherokee was. "The owner of the airport told us you trespassed on a private airport to get the airplane and he is going to press charges."

Lucky for me, we were in the flight planning room that had a full-size aeronautical chart pasted on the wall.

"Officer, let me show you something here, you see that little purple dot right there, the one I am pointing to with my nose?"

"Yes."

"You see what the letters are right next to it? P-V-T."

"Yes"

"Okay now, that means that airport is private, do you understand?"

"Yes."

"Okay now look at the airport that I am pointing to with my nose. Do you see the letters P-V-T?"

"No."

"Ok then, you can look over here at the legend on the map and see that I took the airplane from a 'public use' airport. You see that?"

"Yes."

"Okay, sir, so what is the problem?"

"Well, now I do not see a problem, I'll be right back." He left me alone in the FBO to go consult with his superiors.

With my hands still cuffed behind my back and all the eyes upon me, I wandered over to the counter to place a fuel order. Reluctant to talk to me, the gal promptly and professionally informed me that "the gentleman in the 172 said that you would be paying his fuel bill as well, is that correct, sir?"

Well, that figured. "Yes, ma'am, I'll pick up his fuel bill as well."

The cop came back inside the building from his conference with the airport owner and the other cops outside and as he unlocked my handcuffs, he thanked me for cooperating with their investigation and told me to have a nice day.

Although everyone in the lobby - pilots, FBO employees, and waiting passengers - had been watching my every move since I arrived on the ramp, not one person would look me in the eye as I walked over to the flight planning room to call my client back.

After a brief conversation with my client, I was enroute back to Dallas. The trip was uneventful except for the temporary outburst of laughter as I reviewed in my mind the events of the day. The look on Steve's face with those pie plate eyes as he taxied by and saw me in handcuffs with all the cops was priceless.

I arrived back at Love Field well after dark and taxied right up and parked next to the 172. Looked like Steve made it back okay. Funny thing though, I never saw him again.

Chapter 16

Viva Las Vegas

During all this repo madness, I was still performing the maintenance on my two Cessna Citations, hoping that someday I might be considered for a pilot position. The aircraft were easy to take care of and aside from the routine inspections there was an occasional discrepancy or a tire change to take care of.

I was in the planning stages for the Phase 1 through 5 Inspections on a Citation 550 that I was going to begin in a couple of weeks when I got a page from Hal, the chief pilot. He wanted me to come out and take a look at the potty. Every time somebody hit the "Flush" button, it would blow the circuit breaker.

He was disappointed when I informed him that it would be a few days before I could get to it. He asked why so long. "I am leaving in the morning to deliver a Comanche 400 to Virginia."

"Oh, okay, well then call me when you get back to Texas."

Upon returning to Texas, I called Hal, to inform him that I would be out in the morning to take a look at the potty. He was happy to hear that as he had a flight the following day and promised to meet me at the hangar.

While I was troubleshooting the problem with the potty, Hal kept asking questions regarding my Comanche delivery trip. The weather had been pretty crappy, did I have an instrument rating? Of course, I had previously briefed him on all my certificates and ratings, but apparently, he forgot. He seemed to perk up when I told him about all the schools I had been to, and particularly when I mentioned all the Citation schools I had been to.

After I found the problem with the potty and executed a repair, we sat down to discuss his flight schedule and the amount of time I would need to perform the Phase 5 Inspection. He had three more flights to do, then he would schedule the aircraft down for two weeks for the inspection.

A few weeks later Hal called to tell me that the aircraft was back home in the hangar and gave me a couple of discrepancies that needed some attention. He told me to call him if I needed anything, otherwise he would see me in a couple of weeks.

I notified my banker friend that I would not be available for a few weeks and then got busy with the inspections on the Citation.

Aside from the discrepancies Hal gave me and a couple noted during the inspection, everything went quite well. I recruited an avionics specialist to trouble shoot and repair the avionics discrepancy and rounded up a couple of friends to help with the bigger tasks such as jacking the aircraft and performing the landing gear checks.

Hal came by the hangar to check on progress, and was surprised to see that the airplane was going back together. It looked like the inspection was going to be completed within the time frame I had quoted him. He was satisfied with the description of the repairs for his discrepancies and the parts I ordered to repair the discrepancies discovered during the inspection.

A few days later, I called Hal to tell him the airplane was ready for a test flight. He was happy to hear that and said he would meet me at the hangar in the morning.

By the time he arrived the following morning, I had the airplane pulled out, 300 gallons of fuel loaded onboard, and a ground power cart plugged in. We began briefing what I wanted to see during the test flight with respect to the avionics repairs, engine performance, and flight control rigging. During this briefing, I really wanted both pilots to be briefed at the same time and kept stalling until his other pilot arrived.

Finally, Hal said, "I will start her up, you pull the plug and close the hangar door and hop in."

"What? What about your co-pilot?"

"He can't make it today, it's just me and you."

Oh, hell yes!!

With both engines running, the ground power cart disconnected and stowed, hangar door closed, I hopped in, closed the cabin door, and climbed into the co-pilot's seat. This felt good, but I had a little trouble finding my place on the checklist.

Hal was in no hurry and gave me time to find my rhythm. In short order we were airborne with VFR Flight Following to 17,000 feet northbound. Once leveled off, Hal turned the airplane over to me. We did a few steep turns followed by an approach to landing stall. With the air work accomplished, he said, "Lets head over to Grayson County and see if you can land this thing."

After smoothly rolling it on the runway three times in a row, Hal suggested it had to be beginner's luck and that we should head on back to Addison before something goes wrong. I didn't know where all this was leading to but I was hoping the result would be a job offer.

After landing and putting the airplane back in the hangar, I began a post-flight inspection and Hal followed me around the airplane. He mentioned that he had a couple of trips coming up that he didn't have a co-pilot for and wanted to know if I was interested.

"Hell yes I'm interested!"

The owner of this Citation was a prominent, well-respected, local real estate developer and businessman who had had a flight department for at least ten years that I knew of. He owned the hangar the Citation lived in, and a pair of office buildings right down the street from Addison Airport. He owned a lot more than that as I would soon discover.

Hal gave me his flight schedule, and while most of the near future trips were simply out in the morning and back in the evening, there were a few overnight trips. We agreed on the standard co-pilot day rate plus all expenses and I would charge him my standard hourly rate when I had maintenance to perform on the Citation.

I still had plenty of time to take care of my banker friend's needs, but slowly began to distance myself from that one aircraft dealer. Although this was just a contract type of a gig, I was moving closer to flying for a living and to that Airline Transport Pilot Certificate.

For about six months, everything went along smoothly, until one day we had a mechanical malfunction. The boss was not really a Las Vegas type of person, but we had flown there for the re-opening of the Grand Ballroom at the Golden Nugget Casino, where Frank Sinatra was to be the star attraction. We were treated like royalty, escorted to our front row tables and seated, drink orders taken, while the crowd waited outside.

Unfortunately for the boss and his guests, Frank came down with a sore throat. When they announced that Willie Nelson would be performing instead, everyone at the table began questioning me as if I had something to do with the venue change. We all had a good laugh and enjoyed the show.

The following day, I left the hotel about two hours prior to departure time so I could prepare the little ol' Citation for the flight home.

The aircraft had been sitting on the hot Las Vegas ramp for about an hour with a ground power unit (GPU) hooked up, the aircraft powered up, and the air conditioner running when the boss and his guests arrived. As our passengers began getting out of the limousines, a line service technician (ramp tramp) came out to assist with loading luggage and to stand by to disconnect the GPU and marshal us off the ramp.

With the luggage securely stowed and the passengers all aboard, I pulled the cabin door closed and assumed my position in the co-pilot's seat and proceeded with the checklist. When Hal hit the Start button for the left engine, nothing happened. I immediately verified that the air conditioning system was off as he continued to push on the button as if the button was stuck or something, but the engine wouldn't start. He looked over at me as if to say, "Now what do we do? The left engine will not start."

"Hey, Chief, try the right engine." With a push of the button, the right engine began spooling up, and came right up to speed. "Now try the left engine again." Still nothing. I suggested to Hal that he shut down the right engine and motioned to the ramp tramp that we were shutting down.

Reaching over to turn the air conditioning system back on, I said, "I know what the problem is, it will take me about ten minutes, you entertain the passengers while I take care of it."

With that I climbed out of the cockpit and as I was opening the door made the announcement to our passengers, "There will be a slight delay, folks, please be patient, we will be underway shortly."

After retrieving my trusty Snap-On screw driver, a pair of dykes, and a small pair of channel lock pliers from the toolbox that was stowed in the aft baggage compartment, I crawled under the left wing and began removing an inspection panel at the wing root. With the panel partially down, I cut the safety wire that secured a cannon plug connector to the motive flow pressure

148

switch and removed the cannon plug. Using the cut piece of safety wire, I bypassed the pressure switch by inserting the cut piece of safety wire into the pins B and C on the cannon plug.

Having just jumped pins B and C, I noticed the passengers were climbing out of the aircraft and Anne leaned over to see under the wing at what I was doing "Kevin, is there anything we can do to help you?"

"Sure, does anyone have a bobby pin?"

"Oh, Margaret has one, wait just a minute."

I climbed out from under the airplane to see everybody gathered around Margaret helping to find and pull a bobby pin out of her hair. To this day I have no idea why I did this, but it seemed like a good idea at the time.

With Hal still sitting in the pilot's seat and all the passengers gathered around, I pulled out my pocket knife and began scraping the varnish off the bobby pin. I kneeled down and scratched it on the ramp a little and inspected it. With my channel lock pliers, I bent it into a more usable shape and announced, "I think this will work!"

With that I crawled back under the wing, out of view of the passengers, and put the bobby pin in my shirt pocket. A few seconds later, I emerged from under the wing and went to the little side window to the cockpit. "Hey, Chief, we are ready to give this a try, kill the air conditioner, hit the left Start button, if she starts to spool up, hit the starter disengage button to terminate the start."

I corralled the passengers to the front of the aircraft and gave Hal the finger swirl sign to hit the Start button. Much to the amazement of the boss and his guests, the engine began to spool up. I gave Hal the cut sign to hit the Start Disengage, but he must not have understood the instructions as I had to reach through the little window and hit the Disengage button myself.

"Okay, folks, just a few more minutes to put this panel back up and we will be on our way." The crowd went silent.

With the panel secure and my tools stowed in the aft compartment, I made my way to the front of the aircraft and welcomed everyone back on board. With the cabin door closed, I assumed my seat in the cockpit and re-briefed Hal to use the Starter Disengaged button to terminate the start sequence manually after the left engine came up to idle speed.

With some trepidation, he fired up the left engine and looked to me for confirmation to hit the Starter Disengage. With the left engine up and running, the right engine fired right up. I gave the ramp tramp the signal to pull the GPU plug and in short order we were on our way.

The cabin behind me was eerily quiet as we made the long taxi from Hughes Aviation Services to Runway 28 for take-off. Of ten people in the aircraft, the only person talking was me talking to ATC and running the checklist. I was beginning to worry that my emergency repairs had scared the boss and his guests. Through taxi, take-off, climb out to altitude, all was quiet. In fact, it was not until we were passing over El Paso, Texas, enroute back to Addison that anyone onboard said a word, and then the cabin erupted with laughter and lively conversation. I couldn't help but smile the rest of the way home.

When we arrived back at Addison, the boss invited his guests to meet him at the country club for dinner. Everyone was all smiles and happy as they got in their cars to leave, but no one said a single word about what happened on the ramp in Las Vegas.

I would have loved to have been a fly on the wall at the country club that night, hearing them reminisce about their pilot fixing the jet with one of Margaret's bobby pins.

Around noon the following day, my pager went off. It was Hal wanting me to meet him at the hangar. He wanted a full explanation of what had transpired the previous day.

I went into great detail, describing the motive flow pressure switch as a little fuel pressure switch that is integrated in to the engine starting circuit to make the Start sequence automatic. When the Start button is pressed in the cockpit, the starter is engaged and begins turning the engine, the ignition circuit is armed, and the electric fuel pump begins pumping fuel. When the engine rpm reaches about 10%, the pilot moves the thrust lever (throttle) from the cut-off position to idle. Through a series of switches and relays, that movement starts the ignitor plugs firing, and introduces fuel to the engine. The engine then begins to light off. When the engine reaches around 40% the motive flow pressure switch senses adequate fuel pressure and turns off the ignition, electric fuel pump, and the starter. The starter through a relay now automatically becomes a generator and the start sequence is now terminated.

What happened to us was the motive flow pressure switch stuck in the run mode and would not allow the engine start sequence to initiate. By jumping the pins B and C, I bypassed the motive flow pressure switch, which allowed the start sequence to initiate but the start sequence had to be terminated manually by pressing the 'Starter Disengage' button. There is a Service Bulletin 28-2 for this aircraft that removes the motive flow pressure switch from the aircraft completely and the relays in the electrical junction box are rewired to terminate the start sequence automatically using a speed sensor on the Starter/Generator.

He seemed happy with that reply and suggested that I order the Service Bulletin Kit and install it at the first possible opportunity.

The following morning Hal paged me again and asked that I meet him at the hangar. He informed me that he had talked with our local Cessna Citation tech rep, who had some pretty good things to say about my knowledge and experience with the Citation, and that he was in pretty good hands with me onboard.

I was pleased to hear that, but was even more grateful when Hal instructed me to hop in the truck with him and he took me to the boss's office. We met the lovely Ms. Reynolds, the boss's executive assistant, who escorted us to the big boss's office.

During this meeting, I was presented with more of the boss's background and discovered that he played an important role in bringing DFW Airport into existence and was one of the dignitaries on hand during the dedication ceremony I attended back in September 1973.

I sat there quietly as Hal briefed the boss on what the Citation tech rep had to say, and assured him that what I had done on the ramp in Las Vegas was an appropriate temporary repair. With that, discussions began regarding my full-time employment, complete with insurance and a 401K retirement package. All I had to do in return was fly the Citation and take care of her maintenance needs.

No more contract work - finally, I had become a full-time corporate jet pilot with my very own jet to love on and take care of. And, as a bonus, as long as the Citation was ready to go, I could do whatever I wanted to do.

Aside from taking care of my banker friend, I decided this would be a great time to disassemble my little Taylorcraft and perform a long overdue restoration.

Kev and Hal with Citation 550 S/N 0098 Unit 108

Chapter 17

Jet Fleet to the Rescue

For about a year, I did all the maintenance and flew every trip in that little Citation II. I was very proud of that lil gal. I took care of her like she was my very own.

One day, the boss and I were standing on the ramp next to the Citation in Hot Springs, Arkansas, after the horse races. We were waiting for the rest of the passengers to exit the FBO to board the plane when he began asking questions about all the different types of jets that were on the ramp that day.

It was one of those high-stakes race days at the track and there was at least one of every type of corporate jet made on the ramp that day. "That is a Hawker manufactured by the British, that one is a Sabreliner it was made for the military, that, sir, is a French-built Fan Jet Falcon 20, those two are Westwinds manufactured by Israeli Aircraft Industries, and those over there are Learjets, built in Wichita, Kansas, those Gulfstreams are built in Georgia."

"If you had your choice, which one would you choose?"

"Well, it depends on the mission, but if I had my choice, it would be the Fan Jet Falcon."

"Why?" he asked.

"Safety, system redundancy, cabin space, a walk-in lavatory, it is just a very well-built aircraft."

About that time, the rest of the passengers arrived at the airplane and began climbing aboard. Soon we were in line with the other jets waiting for our departure clearance.

About mid-day the following Monday, I got a call from Ms. Reynolds. "Kevin, do you know what a Fan Jet Falcon is?"

"Sure I do."

"The boss would like you to research the market, pick the best three, and then go look at them."

We searched the market for a few months and eventually settled on a Falcon 20 owned by Shell Oil Company. I had my hands full for the next several months as I babysat our new airplane through a major C Inspection, an avionics upgrade, a complete interior refurbishment, and a paint job. In addition, we had to go to Simuflite for the aircraft-specific flight training.

In addition, we still had trips to fly in the Citation and a marketing campaign to follow through with. We managed to get a deposit on the Citation with an understanding that the airplane would not be available until the Falcon was ready to enter service with us, which was at least a month or so away.

With the Citation all dolled up and logbooks loaded up, we flew to Chattanooga for a pre-purchase evaluation and a demo flight. Everyone liked the airplane, but the chief pilot was concerned that the engines only had about 500 hours to go before an overhaul was due. Their director of maintenance pointed out that at the rate they were flying, the overhauls would be at least two years away. He also pointed out that of all the Citations they had looked at up to this point, this was the cleanest one they had seen by far.

He went on to state that "somebody loves this aircraft and it shows inside the inspection panels and the aft compartment, and all the places that it really counts. This is not service center-maintained aircraft, it has been maintained by a professional corporate flight department, and it shows. There are no safety wire clippings in the belly, no hydraulic drips, no half-stripped out screws, it is exactly what we are looking for."

Overhearing that statement, I was really proud but still, we left Chattanooga without a deal that day. After arriving back in Addison, we had two more showings that week, but the next one was to be at our hangar.

While showing the Citation to the next group, we got a call from the guys in Chattanooga wanting to clarify our engine times and cycles. I told them that I was kind of busy with a potential buyer, but would be happy to pull the engine pages from the CesCom Report and fax it to them.

Shortly after I sent the fax, they called back. Hal took the call this time as I was busy with technical details regarding the aircraft maintenance status. It almost seemed as we were about to have a bidding war on our little ol' Citation II when Hal told this new crew that while they were here looking at the airplane and records, we sold it to the Chattanooga company.

Although these people here were not too happy to hear that, I was kinda proud that we sold the Citation to the first people to look at it. Essentially, we traded our Citation II even for a Fan Jet Falcon 20, and it was a bittersweet day when we flew the Citation for one last time on the delivery date to Chattanooga.

The Falcon was really a delight to fly but it took a little time and several flights to really get comfortable and proficient at finding all the switches and flying it. The trailing link landing gear made really smooth landings, but the pressurization was not as automatic as it was on the Citation. The Falcon was also equipped with an auxiliary power unit which required some management and operational understanding.

The boss and his guests loved the spacious 700-cubic-foot cabin, the eight luxurious passenger seats, and the walk-in lavatory. Unfortunately, with the increase in cabin size also came a larger cargo compartment, which meant more luggage to load and unload and longer trips.

For several months everything went fine until one Saturday morning we departed Addison for Teterboro, New Jersey, to go to some big-time horse race when the landing gear doors would not close after gear retraction.

I cycled the gear again, and I got the same indication in the cockpit, three red lights. "Whoa there, Chief, slow this thing down, our gear doors aren't closing, we don't want to rip the doors off." After a brief discussion, I switched the number 2 radio over to the Dal-Jet Unicom frequency and gave them a call. Dal-Jet was the fuel service division for Jet Fleet and occupied on the flight line side of the facility.

I asked if there were any of the maintenance guys working in the shop today and was told that yes, there were quite a few guys working back there. "Well, this is Kevin Lacey in Falcon Triple Eight Romeo Fox, and I have a gear up-lock micro switch malfunction and we will be on the ground in about fifteen minutes, please alert whoever is in charge of the shop today."

Hal was dead set against this change in plans, but we didn't have any options. We were not going to fly all the way to Teterboro with the landing gear doors open, and going back to our hangar would be half a day rounding up the help just to jack the aircraft up, and what about parts?

I switched back over to departure control, advised them of our change in destination, and requested vectors for the ILS runway 31R at Love Field. We notified our passengers of the need to divert and in short order we were pulling up on the ramp at Jet Fleet. Before I could get out of my seat and open the cabin door the maintenance tug had pulled up and hooked a tow bar on the nose gear.

As Hal came down the steps, I suggested that he escort the boss and his guests into the lobby and entertain them for a few minutes while I went to the shop with the airplane. I would report back as soon as I had some news.

With passengers deplaned, I hopped on the tug and rode back to the shop, where the big door was beginning to open and inside was a set of jacks, a power cart, a hydraulic mule, and a couple of guys already standing by.

Once inside the hangar it was all business. Without much talking, we all went to work together as we had many times in the past. Somebody was hooking up the hydraulic mule while me and two other guys installed the jack pads and manned the jacks, and somebody else connected the electrical power cart.

"Kevin, get out from under there, you're going to mess up those good clothes," gripped Stan.

"Is Kev here?" came a voice from across the hangar. "Oh shit, guys, come on, Kev's airplane is broken, let's go give him a hand."

It was a gang tackle job as we cycled the gear up one time and confirmed that my cockpit trouble shooting was right. The only thing we did not know was if the failed landing gear uplock switch was on the left or the right main landing gear.

About that time Hal came through the door into the hangar and it was plain to see that he had not expected to find the aircraft already up on jacks with the landing gear being cycled. As I turned to go over and brief him on what we were doing, Jim yelled out from the wheel well, "Hey, Kev, it's the left switch!"

Just when I got to where Hal was standing, Stan passed us by on his way through the doors. "I'll go check stock, Kev, I am pretty sure we have one, be right back."

I informed Hal that if they had a switch in stock, we would be ready to go in about thirty minutes. He really didn't believe me, but his confidence was boosted when Stan came through the door with an uplock switch in his hand. I left Hal standing there and went back to the left wheel well to retrieve the failed switch.

Just as I was returning with the old failed switch, the boss walked through the door. With the switch in hand, I explained the switch's function, where it was located on the aircraft and that a new one was being installed as we spoke. We would need to swing the gear a few times to check for proper rigging, but we should be good to go in just a few minutes.

The boss made a comment about the service we were getting. I could not have been prouder of my Jet Fleet alumni brothers. How by a stroke of luck, they all happened to be working on that Saturday, and how they rallied around our Falcon and were able to get us going again in really short order.

We were on the ground at Love Field exactly one hour, and due to favorable winds, we arrived at the airport in Teterboro only thirty minutes later than our previously planned arrival time.

It was a proud day for me, and I could never understand why Hal hated Jet Fleet so much. I guess I should feel lucky he hired me knowing that I did time at Jet Fleet.

As much as I loved my job, I still had a desire to become an airline pilot. It was a prestigious job flying for an affluent family and it had a lot of benefits. Even though they told me that I had a career for the rest of my life regardless of whether they had an airplane or not, I still had to try to become an airline pilot.

Flying corporate jets with an Airline Transport Pilot certificate and a couple of corporate Jet Type Ratings was certainly starting to look pretty good on my resume, but another requirement was that an airline applicant had to have taken and passed the flight engineer written exam.

As with all FAA written exams, the exam results expire after two years if you have not taken the practical test. After taking another weekend class, I found the flight engineer written test even easier the second time around.

Chapter 18

American Airlines Interview

Fourteen years and a lot of hard work later I had finally earned enough credentials and flight time to consider trying to get hired on with an airline.

I attended a couple of seminars and job fairs that were put on by this traveling roadshow organization who claimed to have all the inside scoop to the airline jobs. They were continuously promoting the upcoming pilot shortage. They kept saying that the airline hiring boom was just around the corner, but at those job fairs, the airline representatives would say that they were not predicting very many pilot slots for several years to come. Most airline representatives would say that they might hire ten pilots in the next two to three years. That was not very encouraging but you won't get one of those slots if you do not try.

Times were different back then. Today, if you meet the bare minimum standards, have a pulse, and can fog a mirror, you are hired.

Although I had never been a passenger on American Airlines, reflecting back to that bright sunny day in September of 1973 sitting in the cockpit of that Boeing 707, American Airlines was my first preference.

I had taken a few flights on Southwest Airlines and because of all the happy employees I came in contact with and the fun they appeared to be having, Southwest would be my second choice. Problem with Southwest was that they required a pilot applicant to have a Boeing 737 Type Rating before they would even accept your application. At the time, Southwest was only allowed to fly within Texas and the five surrounding states.

During one of these job fairs, I had collected multiple applications from every airline in attendance and spent hours filling them out and sending them in along with the twenty-five-dollar application fee. Much to my surprise, I managed to get a reply with an invitation for an interview with American Airlines. My instructions included a medical history form for me to fill out regarding the health of all my ancestors and instructions that I was not to eat anything for twenty-four hours before my interview.

As I understood it, the complete interview process at American consisted of three separate interviews all conducted on different days. Each interview lasted a full day. If they decided they liked you after the first interview, they would call you back for the second interview, and if you managed to get through that one, you would get called for a third and final interview. I had been told that it could take as long as a year for a pilot to complete the interview process and get assigned a class date if selected.

On the appointed day, I put on my favorite suit, grabbed all my paperwork and logbooks, and charged off for the interview. At that time, I held an Airline Transport Pilots Certificate with a Cessna Citation Type Rating and was flying as a co-pilot in the Falcon 20. I had a couple of thousand hours of flight time in my logbook and an Associate's Degree. In addition, I had an Airframe and Powerplant Mechanic Certificate and had recently passed the Flight Engineer written exam.

The others in my interview class included a helicopter pilot from the north east, a cute little gal with her Commercial Pilots Certificate and 500 hours in her logbook, two F-Teen fighter jocks with barely 600 hours of flying time between them, and a C-141 pilot with 1,200 hours.

This first part of the interview began with an American Airlines pep rally followed by us watching an airline promotional video. We were then all separated and sent off in different directions. I was sent to the medical department, where I was first interviewed about the family medical history form that I filled out.

Their "medical history form" was more like a family genealogy form in that it had very few questions about me, and more questions about relatives and ancestors. It was evident to me that they did not think I filled out that form honestly as I stated that the cause of death for my grandfather was "cataracts." Evidently that was a wrong answer which resulted in a deeper interrogation.

I tried to explain that when I was eighteen years old, I was away at school in Tulsa, Oklahoma, when my mom called to inform me that she was going to go to Florida to be with my ninety-five-year-old grandfather while he had cataract surgery. About a week or so later, she called to tell me that she would be there an extra week or so because grand dad had died during surgery.

That was all I knew and I tried to explain it that way, but the interviewer marked in big letters MIF by my granddad's name. At the time, I didn't have any idea what MIF meant. What about my grandma? She died of old age, she was ninety-four and simply gave out missing Granddad. That prompted the interviewer to mark another big MIF.

What about on my dad's side of the family? I had put down a question mark, because I had no idea if his parents were even alive. I did remember that back in the '60s while on a family vacation we drove all over Alabama looking for my dad's dad, but we never found him. No worries though, the interviewer had a cure for that. She put down two more big MIF's.

Lucky for me, my mom was still alive, but when they got to my dad, I had put down that he died after open heart surgery. Another MIF, even though I tried to explain that he and his brother both had rheumatic fever when they were kids. "Oh, he had a brother, is he still alive?" "No, he's dead too."

By the time that gal was finished with me, that page was all marked up with big black MIFs. I sheepishly asked what MIF stood for. By the time she finished explaining that it stood for myocardial infarction, otherwise known as heart disease or heart attack, I was ready to check myself into a hospital.

Perhaps I should have spent my spare time in medical school instead of at the airport, I might have understood the medical questionnaire and provided better answers.

Fortunately, that phase of the interview was over with and it was on to the next phase, which wasn't any better. Now we were going to get a thorough physical exam.

I felt like a lab rat being led around the facility by unhappy people in white lab coats. They drained so much blood out of me I got a little lightheaded when I stood up. At each station, I was looked at by a different person, and while I tried to make light conversation, none of them would speak to me. All they did was look at me, grunt and groan, and write on their charts. Not a single spoken word to me the entire time.

They watched me give a urine sample. They gave me a color blindness test, near and far sight vision test, and blew puffs of air into my eyes (I think that was a glaucoma test). They put me in a big soundproof box, gave me a hearing test, and then did some sort of ultra sound test on my ear drums. They poked and prodded my body in places I would rather not discuss, all without saying a word.

The whole time I was in there, I wondered if these lab coat people knew that I was only applying for a job as a pilot and had no intentions of joining the space program at NASA as an astronaut.

The final phase of my eight-hour interview was a one-on-one meeting with the lady in charge of hiring pilots. Her little office was decorated with hundreds of military squadron patches. I felt a little out of place as the only patch that I might have been able to bring to the table would have been a Civil Air Patrol patch from a few short months as a teenager that I spent in the Oak Cliff Composite Squadron.

She began her introduction by saying that "while it is a noble profession, flying a private jet full of millionaires around the country, we prefer to hire 250-hour military pilots, we pretty much know what we will be getting." She continued talking down to me as if I was not worthy to be in her presence. As I listened to her demeaning words, I wondered why she even bothered to call me for an interview.

My thoughts were that, while I do believe that our military pilots are the best in the world at delivering missiles, bombs, rockets, and other types of ordinances, what does that have to do with flying airline passengers? What an arrogant woman!

I was doing the same identical simulator check rides to the same FAA standards every year in the Falcon 20 that the American Airline pilots were doing. The primary differences were the aircraft type and weights, the switches were in different locations, and the systems were slightly different, but it was the same check ride to the same FAA standards.

But what was equally important was that I still knew how to do things like file a flight plan, work a weight and balance, plan a fuel load, book hotels, and rent cars all while negotiating a line of West Texas thunderstorms and maintaining an altitude of plus or minus 100 feet.

I had to keep reminding myself to bite my tongue as this was an interview. I simply sat and listened as she did everything short of coming right out and telling me that there wasn't a chance in hell they were going to call me back for the second interview.

I was getting to the point that I could not wait to get out of there. As instructed, it had been almost two days since I had eaten anything and after all the humiliation they dished out, I didn't think I wanted to fly for this airline anyway.

At the conclusion of the interview, I was given a big package to carry home with me. In that package was some more American Airlines cheerleading propaganda along with five self-addressed postage paid cardboard boxes with little popsicle sticks. The instructions were to go fishing in the toilet every morning for the next five days and scoop out some poop samples, put them in the cardboard boxes, seal them up, and mail them in to American Airlines.

While reading the instructions all I could think about was that this must be some sort of a test to see just how low an individual would stoop to get a flying job at American; either that or someone in their medical department had some sort of fetish that I would rather not know about.

The following morning, I was walking my little dog, Turbo, when it hit me. The mischief set in just as Turbo finished his morning business. I said, "Turbo, stay right here little buddy, daddy will be right back." I ran back to my place and gathered up one of those cardboard envelopes and a popsicle stick and returned to where little Turbo was patiently waiting.

Poor little Turbo must have been really confused as he had the funniest look on his face as he watched me scrape up his poop and put it in the cardboard box. As we continued our walk, all I could think about was getting to the post office and mailing that little cardboard box off.

Even though I got a rejection letter from American in the mail two days later, I continued to mail off one of those cardboard envelopes full of little Turbo's poop every day until my envelope supply ran out.

The more I thought about how condescending that woman was to me, the more I decided that I didn't want to work for an airline that treated its potential pilots like she treated me. Although disappointed, I was perfectly happy flying the boss and his guests around in the Falcon.

I always wondered why they never sent me a letter advising me to lay off the Purina, or perhaps I should get a little more fiber in my diet. But then it dawned on me that the way I was treated along with their new two-tiered pay scale, they probably get a lot of dog pookie in the mail.

Chapter 19

Decision Time

During my tenure with the Falcon and the family that owned it, life was comfortable. If I was not working on or flying the Falcon, I kept busy. There almost always seemed to be someone who needed a co-pilot for a day trip, or an airplane that needed some maintenance, or an airplane that needed repossessing.

If not working professionally, I would be patrolling the skies of North Texas in my T-Craft looking for places to go and interesting people to meet or flying skydivers at the local drop zone. Some of the local pilots joked about having put out a bounty on my head, as I really did have a good thing going.

During the late 1980s our flying in the Falcon had cut back dramatically as the alleged savings and loan scandal began making the news. It was not just our flight department that cut back either, it was an aviation depression everywhere. I was being called upon more and more to assist with several local corporate aircraft repossessions.

As I made my way around the local airports gathering up airplanes, I began to notice that aside from the aircraft I had captured, a large portion of the private corporate jets that I thought were safe had been sold and the larger flight departments had been consolidated to just one or two aircraft. As a result, many of my friends had lost their jobs as pilots and mechanics. It was discouraging to see all the empty hangars at the local airports.

Every day was one big resume exchange with unemployed pilots and mechanics trading resumes with each other. Funny thing though, nobody was interested in helping me repossess an airplane. They were happy to drink beer from my refrigerator and complain about being unemployed but scoffed at the thought of being paid to swipe an airplane and buying their own beer.

With the depression in the aviation industry, it seemed like the Yankee carpetbagger bankers had come to Texas and claimed that all the banks were insolvent. While they did have their poster children of crooked bankers such as Vernon Savings, Sunbelt Savings, and Western Savings, it seemed that the regulators used them as examples to consolidate all the Texas banks under the control of the big-name northeastern banks.

One phrase that I heard repeated several times was "the best way to rob a bank in Texas is to own it." They shut down almost every bank and called in all loans, including one of my favorite banks, Texas Commerce. They even shut down the bank that I was doing my personal banking with. Pretty soon, all the local banks had northeastern names and a lot of people were confused and had no idea who to pay their home mortgage to.

While I was preparing the Falcon for a trip one day, the company's CFO was the first to arrive at the hangar. As we stood around waiting for the boss and other passengers to arrive, he took note that the oil and gas company that had been renting hangar space from us had sold all their aircraft and laid off all their pilots. The Falcon and my little Taylorcraft were the only two airplanes left in the hangar.

The CFO stated that the way things were going, we would probably not have the airplane or the hangar by the end of the year. This banking fiasco had everything all jacked up. He knew the boss had said that I had a job with the company for life, but if I wanted to continue flying, I should accept the next flying opportunity that came along.

This was not exactly the best time to be looking for a corporate flying job as there really were not any, and as far as the airlines were concerned, their hiring predictions were not looking too good in the short term. Besides, I still had a bitter taste in my mouth from my experience with the Sky Nazis at American.

While flying my little Taylorcraft around to outlying airports, I had met several airline pilots, many of whom were flying for Southwest Airlines. After explaining my situation to them, they suggested that I go pay for the training required and earn a Boeing 737 Type Rating and apply for a job at Southwest. "We will put in letters of recommendation for you, no problem, you will love the job and the people, and we are going to hire seven pilots this year."

In the grand scheme of things, seven pilots was not a lot of pilots, but at the time Southwest Airlines required a Boeing 737 Type Rating just to get an interview, and that narrowed down the field of qualified applicants considerably.

So, I began calling around to inquire about Boeing 737 training schedules and costs. The best two choices were in Seattle and right there on Love Field at the Southwest Airlines training department. Seattle had a slot available in a few months but considering travel, hotels, and meals it was by far much more expensive. Southwest did not have any available training slots for over a year but they did put me on the waiting list.

At least I still had a job and had some time to plan my exit strategy. Although the Boeing 737 did not have a Flight Engineer station, I had recently renewed my flight engineer written exam in order to keep all my options open. Once again, I gathered up applications for all the major airlines and spent my time preparing them and sending them out along with their $25 application fee, a resume, and copies of my airman certificates.

Our flying in the Falcon was down to one or two trips a month, but as long as the boss was still going to the thoroughbred horse auctions and bidding big dollars on horses, I felt that my job was fairly secure for the time being.

After I returned from a trip to one of those horse auctions in Lexington, Kentucky, in the Falcon, my wife informed me that there was a message on the answering machine from a gal at Southwest Airlines and I should listen to the message.

The call was to inform me that she had a last-minute cancellation for a Boeing 737 Type Rating class and suggested that I return her call if I was still interested. I returned her call the following morning and she confirmed that she had a cancellation for a class that was scheduled to begin in a month and a half. If I wanted that slot, I needed to show up within two weeks with copies of my credentials and $12,000.

It was going to be a roll of the dice as there was no guarantee of being offered a job, and that was a lot of money to spend, not to mention the four to six weeks of time necessary to complete the training class. I consulted with my wife, who said, "Go for it!" I was pretty sure she was fantasizing about being the wife of an airline pilot, quitting her job and going to garden parties with all the other airline pilots' wives.

After almost ten years, it was difficult to say good bye to my Falcon and the folks that I was flying for. They had treated the wife and me like part of the family. They allowed me to restore my 1946 Taylorcraft and keep it in the hangar with the Falcon and as long as the Falcon was ready to go, I was free to do whatever I wanted.

I kept looking for a way to stay on the job but according to the lady in charge of payroll and benefits, in order to cash out my 401k retirement plan to pay for the 737 Type Rating class, it was necessary for me to quit my job. According to her, there was no other way.

I was hoping to find my way around that but reluctantly, I tendered my resignation and started the process of cashing out my 401k. I scoured the airport and found a T-hangar to rent for the T-Craft and began re-locating all my tools and equipment to my new playpen.

The Boeing 737 Type Rating would be the first time that I trained in an aircraft that I had absolutely no experience with. Shoot, all I knew about the 737 was that it used Skydrol for hydraulic fluid; I didn't even know what kind of engines it had. Some friends laughed at me, saying all they fly was 737s and they can hardly even get out of Texas! Or "Everybody knows that the paycheck is directly proportional to the size of the airplane, why would you want to go to Southwest?"

I was not discouraged and pressed on. The study materials handed out by the Southwest Training Department were minimal compared to all the other aircraft I had trained in. All they gave me to study was a one-inch-thick binder of material and a paper fold-out instrument panel mock-up. Compared to the two-volume three-inch binders for the Falcon and the Citation, I felt like I was cheated out of tech data on the 737.

The training program consisted of an aircraft systems ground school followed by an oral exam. Then some time would be spent in the cockpit procedures trainer and then on to the simulator. The simulator training would consist of all the maneuvers and approaches required in the Airline Transport Pilot training syllabus and that would complete eighty percent of the type rating. The final phase of the training would be to go to the terminal and get one of the 737's and take her for a spin, shooting a few approaches and landings to complete the type rating check ride requirements.

There were four of us in the class, and it seemed that everyone had some previous familiarization with the 737 except me. I bought a tape recorder and recorded the classroom sessions and took notes as fast as I could write. Each night I would listen to the recordings until I fell asleep. I wished that I had more access to system-specific diagrams such as the electrical, hydraulic, fuel, and pressurization systems, but I managed to come away with a decent understanding of the 737.

After about two weeks, we had the aircraft and systems oral exam out of the way and it was time to move on to the cockpit procedures trainer to learn the cockpit flows and then on to the simulator.

While it took me a little while to catch on to where all the switches and buttons were, my sim partner did a really good job. It was kind of like he had flown a 737 somewhere in the past or had some other experience that I was not aware of, but he was a big help to me in coming up to speed in this new-to- me airplane.

We progressed with our training and completed the simulator check rides and were scheduled shortly thereafter to do a couple of flights in the airplane for the final type rating check ride when the Director of Training came to me with a request. He wanted to know if I was willing to give up my check ride slot in the aircraft for one of my classmates.

Apparently, one of our classmates busted his simulator check ride, which threw the training plans and schedule all out of whack. They needed to do some retraining with him in the simulator and then do another simulator check ride. Problem with that was it would take a couple of extra days and he would miss his scheduled type rating check ride slot in the airplane.

Since my check ride in the airplane was scheduled for the following week, they would have time to complete his retraining and complete another simulator check ride and then use my type rating check ride slot in the airplane and finish up his training. Problem was that by giving up my slot, it would be a few more weeks before another type rating check ride slot would become available.

This guy was from out of town, living out of a suitcase in a hotel at his expense. They had not planned on any of us busting the sim check but now they needed to jam in a few more sim training sessions and as the schedule was set up, it would be a couple of weeks before their schedule would allow him to take the type rating check ride.

It was a tough decision to make but I lived close by and was not paying hotel, rental car, and additional food expenses. They told me that I would be re-scheduled for my check ride in a couple of weeks and they offered me an extra hour or two of refresher simulator time in preparation for my type rating check ride.

I thought long and hard about how I would feel had I gone to Seattle and the same thing happened to me. Hotel expenses, rental car, food, it all adds up and I was certainly sympathetic to my classmate's situation. Knowing that I would kinda be in limbo for a few weeks until my check ride, I notified the Director of Training that my class mate could have my type rating check ride slot.

Although I never saw him again, I was informed that my classmate went on with the additional training and passed his check ride followed shortly thereafter by a successful type rating check ride in the airplane.

It would be another three weeks before the training department called to get me back on the schedule. I went in one day and did an hour in the simulator and then returned later that evening for a briefing and a flight in the airplane that included shooting a couple of approaches and landings in Waco. The following evening, I returned for a briefing and the final Type Rating check ride with the FAA sitting behind me observing.

I was relieved to finally get that loose end tied up and on to the business of figuring out how I was going to earn a living.

Chapter 20

Nine One Charlie

With a fresh Boeing 737 Type Rating in my pocket and an application submitted to Southwest Airlines and no immediate plans, out of the blue, I got a call from an old friend named Tom.

Tom had been flying a Learjet 25 out of the hangar next door to the hangar that I had been flying the Falcon from. He lost his job and airplane over a year ago along with many of my friends and was now out in Carson City, Nevada, with a Lear 24 and was looking for a co-pilot for a planned cargo operation.

The aircraft would be operated under a FAA Part 135 Air Carrier Certificate based out of Florida and he was proposing to base the Learjet in Texas and fly ad-hoc cargo trips. As long as we could find the work and fly thirty-five hours a month in revenue trips, we could keep the aircraft and operate it as if it were our own airplane. In addition, due to flight and duty time regulations, I would not be allowed to perform any maintenance on the airplane. It would be going to a shop for all her maintenance needs. I was pretty happy about that aspect of this operation.

This little Learjet 24 Serial Number 160 went by the name of November Four Seven Nine One Charlie. I was not sure what all the fuss was about, but the folks associated with this new operation and the airplane seemed to be impressed that the previous owner was a famous West Coast auto dealer named Cal Worthington and his dog Spot. Being from Texas, I never heard of him.

The first order of business was for me to fly out to Carson City and do the company-required ground school followed by some flight training in the aircraft and then take the FAA-mandated FAR Part 135 Check Ride and get an FAA Form 8410. The Eighty-Four-Ten is an FAA document that is given to the pilot after the successful completion of an airman proficiency and qualification check ride.

The ground school part was easy, as I had been to Learjet school and had been a maintenance crew chief on Learjets back in the Jet Fleet days, but the flying part was another story. Unlike the docile Cessna Citation and the elegant Falcon that I was used to flying, this little crotch rocket powered by the fire-breathing General Electric CJ-610s packed a helluva punch and, weighing in at just 13,3000 pounds max gross weight, she had a climb rate of a Saturn Rocket. Along with all that performance, she also had a few nasty habits.

The first thing I was taught was that we taxi on one engine. The Lear 24 burned about the same amount of fuel sitting on the ramp with both engines running as it did at Flight Level 410 going Mach .82, or around 440 knots, so the running joke was that we were fuel critical at brake release for take-off.

During the training flights I thought that I detected a slight vibration in the right engine but was assured that this was normal for an airplane of this vintage. It was not until our initial flight to Texas that I identified a few more mechanical deficiencies in ol' Nine One Charlie. It seemed that the FC-110 autopilot and yaw damper was not near as tight as the Collins and Sperry autopilots that I was used to in the Falcon and Citation and the cabin had a few pressurization leaks which would present themselves during thrust reduction at the beginning of the descent from a high altitude.

After flying back to Texas with our new ride, we began soliciting the airplane and our services. It was a tough market to break into at first as there were several well-established operators flying cargo-configured Learjets and Falcons, but we eventually began to develop a reputation as being dependable and, for the most part, on time.

We managed to get on the call list for FedEx and UPS, which meant that we would be making regular trips to Memphis and Louisville to help with their overflow and their big upcoming Christmas rush. Both companies paid very well and would pay us to show up and return home even if we did not draw a trip and carry any of their cargo.

Kev and Tom with Learjet 24 N4791C S/N 160

Another one of the gigs we managed to get was flying back-up for an organization that had a contract with the Federal Reserve Bank flying cancelled checks from Dallas Love Field to Chicago's Midway Airport and back to Dallas. It was like a convention of around fifty Mitsubishi MU-2s and Learjets coming and going out of Midway in the middle of the night.

Chicago Midway Airport seemed to have a curse on ol' Nine One Charlie as it seemed that every mechanical incident we had originated at Midway, and it always seemed to happen on my leg to fly. Taxiing out for departure was conducted one airplane right after the other in a steady stream of Learjets and MU-2s; once you got to the runway you were usually cleared for immediate take-off.

On one particular morning, around 2:30 or 3 a.m. we were taxiing out to Runway Three One with about six or seven Learjets in front of us when the brakes went soft. The brake pedals suddenly went all the way down with no resistance whatsoever. One look at the hydraulic pressure gauge showed no hydraulic pressure. I quickly hit the electric pump and restored pressure. I told Tom that I thought we had just lost the number one hydraulic pump. We talked about our options, which at the time was simply to stay in line as there was no place to go. If anyone stopped in front of us, I would simply steer the airplane off the taxi-way into the dirt. As we neared the runway, I could feel the brakes go soft again and notified Tom. I was pretty sure we were running out of hydraulic fluid, but was not sure.

176

It got pretty busy for a few moments. Tom notified the tower of our dilemma while I fired up the number two engine in hopes of restoring hydraulic pressure with the right-hand engine driven hydraulic pump. All that did was accelerate our taxi speed, so I immediately shut the engine back down. Had we simply shut down the number one engine as well, we would be blocking the taxi-way with a long line of aircraft behind us and no way to get out of everyone's way.

We followed the Learjet in front of us onto the runway. He proceeded to take-off while we simply rolled down the runway behind him at taxi speed to the intersection of Runway Two Two, where we made a left turn off of runway Three One and down Two Two to a taxi-way that led back to the ramp.

Arriving back on the ramp, we were greeted by a marshaller who was frantically trying to direct us into a crowded parking place. I shut the engine down and coasted to a stop. We were immediately verbally assaulted by that marshaller with some of that good ol' Chicago hospitality. I am pretty sure he accused me of having sex with my mother and called me several other colorful names which I completely ignored as I suggested that his lazy union member ass go find a tug and tow us to wherever it was that he wanted us parked.

While inspecting the brakes and hydraulic reservoir, we found a trail of hydraulic fluid leading up the taxiway right up to both main landing gear. Upon closer inspection we discovered that all four brake housings had cracked and leaked all our hydraulic fluid. Upon closer inspection, it was discovered that incorrect installation of the torque plate on both landing gear caused all four brake housings to crack.

The brakes and incorrect torque plate installation happened long before we ever got the airplane at a maintenance shop in California. I felt kind of bad for not noticing the discrepancy during any one of the many pre-flight inspections I had done, as this was a serious issue. What if this failure had happened on landing, or during an aborted take-off? The results could have been a lot worse than the tongue lashing we got for having a mechanical breakdown.

Two days later, a new set of brakes had been installed and we were back in the saddle flying the same route from Dallas to Chicago and back, observing the passage of a winter storm system from Flight Level Four Five Zero.

It was one of those early winter cold fronts rapidly moving across the country from west to east parallel to our route of flight to Chicago. This cold front was producing a continuous line of thunderstorms. It was approximately a hundred miles east of our course and extended all the way from the Gulf of Mexico to the Great Lakes.

As we approached St. Louis, the line of thunderstorms had moved just east of the city, leaving the sparkling lights of the city glowing in the crisp clear air with massive thunderstorms and lightning lighting up the night sky and revealing the definition of the clouds.

At Flight Level Four Five Zero, Tom and I were well above all the weather and the turbulence enjoying the scenery and a smooth ride at Mach .82.

The Kansas City Center radio frequency had been relatively quiet until we got in the vicinity of St. Louis; then it was one airliner after the other asking for ride reports.

"Ah, Center, American 123, you have any ride reports up ahead? It is pretty rough here at Flight Level Two Eight O."

"Continental 456 requesting a different altitude, we are getting a moderate chop here at Three One O."

"ABEX 789, how is your ride at Three Five O?"

Me and my smart-ass mouth piped up and said, "Learjet Nine One Charlie is getting a smooth ride at Flight Level Four Five O."

A few seconds later a gravelly ol' voice comes over the radio and replies, "So how is that paycheck up there at Flight Level Four Five O?" The radio went silent for a few moments while I swallowed another helping of humble pie.

A few weeks later, we found ourselves back in Chicago with a pretty good snowstorm blowing through. The arrival was no big deal, but after being parked on the ramp for just a few minutes the snow began accumulating on the aircraft at a pretty good rate.

Since there were no de-icing capabilities on this side of the airport, the snowfall had most all of the Learjet crew members taking turns outside in the bitter cold sweeping the snow off their Learjets while we all waited for the freight to be sorted and distributed.

Finally, our cargo arrived and we gave Nine One Charlie one more good clean sweep with the broom to make sure all the snow we could get to was off the wings and fuselage. We climbed in, closed the door, and fired up an engine. As we taxied out, my feet were numb, my nose was dripping, and my hands were just short of being frostbitten. It sure felt good to get airborne and get the cabin heat on and head towards warmer weather.

Climbing through Flight Level Three Three Zero I felt the aircraft yaw slightly to the right. I looked over at Tom, who was sitting the in the dim glow of the cockpit lights with a cigarette hanging out of his mouth, a cup of coffee in his left hand, our flight book in his lap, and a pen in his right hand filling out our flight manifest.

"Tom, did you feel that?"

"Feel what?"

Looking at the engine instruments, "Shit, I think we just lost our right engine!"

Tom, who was always preparing me for the Learjet Type Rating check ride, replied, "Okay, Captain, what do you want me to do?"

"Call ATC, tell them we need to descend below Flight Level Two Eight Zero, grab the checklist for securing the engine, I will guard the good engine left thrust lever and start the descent. When we get below Two Eight Zero, we will get the windmilling engine start checklist and see if we can relight this puppy."

Everything went just like clockwork. We got down to Flight Level Two Eight Zero, performed a successful windmilling air-start, and began to climb to Flight Level Four One Zero. With everything back to normal, Tom went back to filling out the flight manifest while I kept the aircraft pointed in the right direction.

Suddenly, just as we were climbing through Flight Level Three Three Zero again, BANG-BANG-BANG. Only our shoulder harnesses and seatbelt kept us from jumping out of our seats. That right engine compressor stalled again, except this time it announced that it was quitting in a big way. It sounded like someone was shooting a twelve-gauge shotgun in the cabin.

After a short discussion, we decided that we would go back down and relight the engine and then run the fuel calculations to verify that we could make Dallas Love Field at Flight Level Two Eight Zero with the fuel we had onboard.

So, once again we made the request to ATC for the descent, only this time the engine would not relight with either the windmilling air-start or the starter-assisted start procedures. "Tom, I reckon you should tell Center that we need to return to Midway and open the cross-flow valve and keep my fuel balanced."

The return trip to Midway on one engine was uneventful right up until Tom turned on the landing lights and announced, "Runway in sight." I came off the dials and looked out the windshield to see snowflakes the size of softballs coming right at me. Although I could partially see the runway, the visual effects of the snowballs were just too much. "Shit, kill the lights!"

My first thought as we pulled up to the ramp was that I just thawed out and now I had to get back out in the cold again. Grabbing a flashlight, I climbed out of the cockpit and went around to the front of the right wing and looked into the engine inlet. "Tom, ya gotta come take a look at this!"

The bullet nose in front of the engine had come loose and tried to go through the engine but got jammed in the inlet guide vanes, which blocked off a significant amount of airflow through the engine, causing the compressor stall when we got up into the thinner air.

This little bullet nose in the front center of the engine is designed to direct warm engine air around the bullet nose and through the inlet guide vanes in the front of the engine to prevent ice from forming when "Engine Anti-Ice" is turned on. It is used while flying through the same icing conditions we had just been flying through.

I made an attempt to reinstall the bullet nose, but the grooves in the engine front frame that it sat in and the pin that held it in place were just too worn out. I reminded Tom of my previous observation that the right engine was a shaker, and this was a result of that vibration. Same thing would happen again as soon as we turned on engine anti-ice, the bullet nose would pop out again and jam in the inlet guide vanes.

After a lengthy discussion, we decided to top off the fuel tanks, throw the bullet in our box of spare parts, and head for Texas and let the shop deal with it. When we arrived at Love Field, we were yelled at for being late, but we called and told them and they did have a courier standing by waiting for us, so all was not lost.

We hopped back in ol' Nine One Charlie and flew over to Addison, where we left her in the hands of the maintenance shop. The next few days while Nine One Charlie was being loved on by the maintenance shop, the Christmas rush was beginning to make its presence known in the cargo world as it was "all Learjets on deck" at the main FedEx hub in Memphis and the UPS hub in Louisville.

Since we were only contracted on an "as available" basis to the outfit that had the Federal Reserve Bank run, we responded to the calls from FedEx and UPS, who paid a lot better. We would often get a call from both FedEx and UPS in the same night.

Since Memphis was closer to Addison, we would launch in ol' Nine One Charlie and fly to FedEx. Most of the time, we would get a trip, but if Memphis did not use us, we would jump in the airplane and fly to Louisville and check in with the UPS dispatch office.

FedEx would pay us to fly to Memphis and whatever trip we got and then back to Addison. If we did not get a trip, we still got paid for the round trip from Addison to Memphis and back. UPS would do the same. If we didn't get a trip in Memphis, we would fly to Louisville and check in there, and of course, they would pay us as well, so we had several times where we didn't get a trip from either FedEx or UPS but they both paid us for the round trip.

We were doing pretty well on the double dipping on nights that we did not get a trip, so to make it even better and save time on the airplane we would simply get a hotel room at some fleabag inn and spend the night. We still got paid for the round trip when we arrived in their dispatch office.

One night, we felt like we hit the mother lode. It was going to be a long night that would extend well into mid-morning, but it would be well worth it. We got a trip from Memphis to Boise, Idaho, to Seattle. That was the longest trip we had ever gotten and it would pay really well. Addison to Memphis to Boise Idaho to Seattle and back to Addison was almost 3,500 miles.

The Memphis to Boise leg went just fine, as did the flight to Seattle. Since our route was essentially over, except for the flight back to Texas, we discussed the idea of touring the Boeing Museum and getting a hotel for the rest of the day, but ol' Nine One Charlie had a few discrepancies that we wanted cleared up and was scheduled into the maintenance shop so we decided to skip all that and head back to Addison.

This leg of the trip was 1,450 miles, so we planned a fuel stop in Denver where we had cheap contract fuel. Coming out of Seattle heading for Addison Airport near Dallas, we caught the jet stream and were cooking along at 625 knots across the ground. We had gone pretty fast in ol' Nine One Charlie before, but never this fast.

As we got closer and closer to Denver, we began recalculating our fuel burn, speed, and our distance to go. It was looking more and more like we could make the trip to Addison non-stop. If we got closer to Addison and decided we couldn't make it, we always had alternatives further on down the road towards Addison such as Amarillo, Childress, and Wichita Falls. So, we continued on and flew past Denver.

Unfortunately, after passing Denver and being handed off to the next sector we were instructed to descend to and maintain Flight Level Two One Zero (FL210). Up until this point, we had been making fuel calculations every five or ten minutes, and even though we had lost most of the tailwind we still had plenty of fuel, but at FL210 our fuel burn was going to increase dramatically and we still had over 250 miles to go.

Tom got on the radio and requested Flight Level Four Five Zero (FL450) until we were 100 miles out and ATC replied, "Unable due to traffic." With that, I grabbed the Flight Manual and began looking for the best power settings and fuel burn for our new altitude while Tom got on the other radio and began checking weather at Addison and Wichita Falls. Unfortunately, it was not looking too good at Addison.

Addison weather was reporting 300 foot overcast with the wind out of the north at twenty knots and they were using the Localizer Runway Three Three approach. With that report, we knew that we would be brought down even lower and vectored all over the place, burning all our precious fuel reserves. On top of all that, the reported 300-foot ceilings were below minimums for the Localizer Runway Three Three approach.

"Okay Tom, call them back and tell them we will be diverting and let's get set up for Wichita Falls…unless you think they can switch the flow at Addison and give us the ILS to One Five."

"You sure, Kev? We will be landing with a tail wind that might be above our maximum limit." I simply nodded my head yes.

"Ah, Center, Lear Nine One Charlie, think we can get an ILS Approach to Runway One Five at Addison?" No sooner had Tom made that request than two other aircraft came on the radio and made the same request.

"Nine One Charlie, stand-by one, I will check for you."

Coming in from the northwest as we were, and landing on Runway Three Three would have required ATC to vector us through all the arrival and departure traffic for DFW and Love Field at low altitudes, which equates to high fuel burn and extended flight time. If we landed on Runway One Five they could vector us from our present position to just outside the Brons Outer Marker to intercept the Localize for Runway One Five, which would keep us out of all the DFW and Love Field traffic.

Just about the time Center came back on the radio and said "Nine One Charlie, expect ILS Runway One Five Addison," the annunciator panel "Low Fuel" light came on. Crap! We still had well over a hundred miles to go.

The Learjet is a sleek little aerodynamic airframe, and as long as you are in a slight descent and have not put the gear or flaps down, she will slide through the air a pretty long distance, but anxiety had already set in. We would be landing with minimum fuel and a twenty-knot tailwind, so the approach had to be precise and we needed to touch down at the slowest possible airspeed in order to get the airplane stopped without running off the end of the runway.

Pretty soon we were handed off to Approach Control, who instructed, "Lear Nine One Charlie, descend to twenty-two hundred, fly heading one-two-zero to intercept the Localizer, cleared for the ILS Runway One Five approach, contact Addison Tower on One Two Six point Zero at Brons." Those were welcoming words to our ears, but we were not out of the woods just yet.

The remainder of the flight was a lesson in energy management. Normally we would have the gear down and put in full flaps at Brons, and slide down the glide slope carrying around 75% power, but this time we kept the airplane clean until we were aligned on the ILS and just inside Brons and carrying around 55% power.

Just inside Brons, we went for approach flaps, and then at around 1,000 feet we went with landing gear down. You could feel the distinct drag on the airplane but there was no need to add power as we had plenty of smash to get us to the runway. We broke out of the clouds at around 300 feet and I asked for full flaps. The timing was perfect as it brought our speed right down to Vref just before touch down without ever having to add power.

As we made the left turn off the runway, the right engine belched a few times, just before I shut it down. "Tom, I will never ever do that again, next time we are stopping for fuel. If I ever suggest something like that again, you have my permission to kick my ass!"

"Don't worry, Kev, I will never suggest we do anything like that again either, the stress just isn't worth it!"

We debriefed the maintenance shop on the service required and a few discrepancies that we would like them to investigate and then left the airport for some much-needed rest.

Just about the time my head hit the pillow, my phone rang. Screw it, let the answering machine get the call. Even though the answering machine was in the other room, I could hear the message: "Kev, this is George, you gotta get back out to the airport, the truck servicing our dumpster just hit your airplane!"

Crap! Crawl out of bed, get dressed, call Tom and leave a message on his answering machine, then dial his pager and put the maintenance shop's number in so he could call the shop and off to the airport I went. Tom lived almost an hour drive from Addison while I only lived about ten minutes away.

While the shop was restacking the hangar, they parked ol' Nine One Charlie over by the dumpster to make room on the ramp so they could get other airplanes out of the hangar, and while she was parked there the dumpster truck smashed the horizontal stabilizer and elevator while backing out and stowing his forks.

We would not be flying her anytime soon. The next few weeks we spent wrangling with the insurance company, the owner of the airplane, and the maintenance shop. It would be almost six weeks before the airplane was repaired and ready for a test flight.

It was a happy day for me and Tom after returning from a successful test flight. We were back in the saddle again. While Tom went to make calls to let headquarters know that Nine One Charlie was back in service, I began making calls to all our clients to let them know we were back in business.

As we met in the middle of the hangar to brief each other, Tom advised me that he had some bad news. "We're done," he said, "they are coming out tomorrow to pick up Nine One Charlie."

"What?"

He informed me that the owner of the airplane was taking the airplane back and would be sending a crew out tomorrow to pick it up. He suggested that I go home and gather up all the flight logs and other files that I had and bring them to the airport tomorrow morning.

The following day, Tom and I arrived at the airport and loaded the aircraft logbooks and all the files we had onboard Nine One Charlie. An hour or so later the crew arrived to inventory the records we had and to fly away.

We asked if they brought our paychecks with them and they advised us that as far as they knew, we had already received our last paycheck.

"Wait a second, we haven't been paid in six weeks! You mean to tell us that we have been unemployed for six weeks now? Why the hell didn't you tell us!?"

"You guys flew the shit out of Nine One Charlie, you would be the only ones to know if the repairs were acceptable. If we told you that you were unemployed six weeks ago you would have gone and got another job and you would not have stuck around to test fly the airplane."

"Wait! What?"

With that, they gassed up Nine One Charlie and fled the scene before someone's anger issues came to a full boil.

With the loss of Nine One Charlie, there was not much left to do except to wander into the offices of other local Learjet cargo operators and pimp my FAA Form Eighty-Four-Ten and pilot services. Nobody was hiring full-time pilots and there was an abundance of self-unemployed pilots around due to the state of the economy, but if your Eighty-Four-Ten was current, they would run a company indoctrination and ground school and put you in the line-up of available pilots.

It was a tough time going from having a prestigious flying job in the Falcon to returning to the status of a freight dawg at half the pay. Based on what everyone said that I encountered at Southwest Airlines, I had felt that ol' Nine One Charlie was simply a job to hold on to until my class date at Southwest, because somewhere during the adventure with Nine One Charlie, I managed to get an interview date with Southwest.

But it wasn't to be. On a Saturday afternoon, the wife paged me to let me know that a letter from Southwest had arrived in the mail. She wanted me to come home immediately to open it, but I was engaged in a project at the airport and suggested that I would open it that evening when I got home. She was not going to have any of that. She jumped in her car and drove to the airport with the envelope in her hand.

She pulled up to the hangar and handed me the letter through the car window and with eyes of excited anticipation demanded that I open it. The letter was short and sweet and it only took a short glance to see that it was a rejection letter.

I handed the letter to her and watched her reaction as she read. Based on her expression and mannerisms I could see the disappointment, and it kind of made me feel like a failure. It was at that moment that I knew a divorce was in my future.

Chapter 21

Command Decision

Even with the loss of Nine One Charlie and the rejection letter from Southwest, I was not discouraged. One of the preferred prerequisites for the airline pilot applicant was that they should be currently engaged and actively flying, no matter what state of poverty that might put a pilot in.

Since pilots were a dime a dozen and almost willing to fly for free it made for some pretty depressing paychecks. Many retired airline and military pilots with their pensions were helping depress the pilot pay scale, as they were willing to fly for less money than the typical pay scale. I could make so much more money working on aircraft with my A&P Certificate, but flying was my passion and my toolbox was simply a means to the end.

I sent all my paperwork over to the offices of Braniff International Airways. They were attempting to re-start operations after their bankruptcy under the new name of Braniff II. Braniff had a long, colorful history in North Texas.

Some folks blamed the government and the Deregulation Act of 1978 for Braniff's fall from glory as the most profitable airline in the world, while many others blamed management's overexpansion, rapidly rising interest rates, and increased fuel costs.

I was excited to get the call for an interview with Braniff II, but for some reason I was not very confident they would be around for very long. At least it was a shot at flying a Boeing and breaking into the Part 121 airline industry. I made sure that I kept my calendar clean for the day before and the day of the interview so I would be reasonably fresh.

Arriving at the conference room of the Hyatt Hotel at DFW Airport with all my documents and logbooks, I was greeted by a gentleman wearing a captain's uniform and escorted into the conference room and asked to take the empty seat at a big round table. This was going to be an interesting interview as there were six captains sitting around the table.

One of the captains began with a short briefing about how they had restarted operations and how they planned to rebuild the airline from its current status of only operating a few airplanes. With that out of the way, the firing squad began their interrogation.

This was not a one-on-one interview; it was six against one. I was not sure if this was by design or that these guys had no manners, but one captain would ask me a question and while answering his question, one of the others would try to interrupt my answer and ask a completely unrelated question.

This went on for about fifteen minutes and I felt like I was doing a pretty good job of keeping up; that was until the guy who was looking at my logbooks asked, "I see here that you have flown a Boeing 737 a few times and you are currently flying Learjets. What is the biggest difference in flying the two airplanes?"

"Aside from the weight difference, the Learjet is much more difficult to fly precisely. To fly the Learjet well, it takes a lot more focus and concentration than it does to fly Seven Three. Airspeed control in critical phases of flight needs to be precise."

One of the captains had just taken a big gulp of coffee and nearly choked on it. Another captain began grumbling something under his breath that I could not quite hear, while the gentleman who asked the question closed my logbooks and began stacking them up, while yet another one stood up and thanked me for my time. They handed me my logbooks and showed me to the door. All I could figure was that none of them had ever flown a Learjet.

That was not how I had hoped the Braniff interview would turn out.

The corporate flight departments had yet to recover from the banking fiasco and the subsequent economic depression in aviation, but the cargo operators seemed to be unaffected for the most part. There were two Learjet cargo operators in the area, Stern Air and Cherry Air. I carried my resume, a copy of my certificates, and my current FAA

Form Eighty-Four-Ten over to both companies and did brief interviews with their Directors of Operations.

Initially, it appeared that neither Learjet operator was very interested in my services, insinuating that a former corporate pilot flying millionaires around the country in their fancy mechanically sound jet was too soft to be a freight dawg. For some reason, they discounted my time with Nine One Charlie and my past experience with the night freight outfit hauling cancelled bank checks. They even tried to use my Airframe & Powerplant Certificate against me, saying that "everybody knows that a mechanic can't fly."

Stern Air had a Learjet 24DXR, two Lear 25DXRs, a straight Lear 25, and a small door Falcon 20. Cherry Air had a Lear 24, and pair of Lear 25's, and a pair of 1121 Jet Commanders. As was the typical mission with Nine One Charlie, FedEx, UPS, and the automotive industry were the primary customers for both companies.

In keeping their payroll liabilities down, most all the pilots were contract pilots. The only full-time pilots were the Chief Pilot and the Director of Operations, which was required by the FAA and their Air Carrier Certificate.

As the cargo demand increased, each company brought in their new recruits, and their Chief Pilot or their Director of Operations would conduct a Company Indoctrination ground school. Afterwards, the pilots who had a current Eighty-Four-Ten were put on the roster as current and available, while the pilots without a current Eighty-Four-Ten had to wait around until the company decided to spend the time, money, and fuel for training flights.

Eventually Cherry Air called me and they put me in a Lear 24 Serial Number 170. It was nothing fancy and it had many of the same characteristics of ol' Nine One Charlie. After I flew a few trips for them, Stern Air called and put me in a Lear24DXR Serial Number 280. I thought the Twenty Four was a crotch rocket but this one with the Dee Howard XR modification and dash eight engines was a rocket ship and it was a blast to fly.

As was the case with Nine One Charlie, both companies had a policy that for each trip, there would be a designated captain, but the crew members would switch seats on every other leg of the trip, giving each pilot flight time in the left seat and the right seat.

After I spent several months flying for whoever called first, Cherry Air called and asked that I show up for a full day of ground school, unpaid, of course. They did not tell me what ground school it was until I arrived. They handed me some study materials and informed me that they were going to put me in the Jet Commander, which I immediately rejected. They argued that there were plenty of Learjet pilots and they would still use me in the Lear, but Jet Commander pilots were in short supply.

They also told me that after a month or so of flying the Commander as a co-pilot, they were going to send me for a Type Rating and upgrade me to Captain. I really was not interested but they sold it to me as an opportunity to do more flying and make more money, so I sat through two days of ground school and then went for a check ride and got a Second-In-Command Eighty-Four-Ten.

There always seemed to be an unspoken competition between Stern Air and Cherry Air for pilots. One company would wait until the other company spent the time and money to get the pilots current and then they would scalp the pilots away from them by sending them on a trip and using up their flight and duty time. After learning that Cherry was trying to put me in the Jet Commander, Stern Air called me up and put me through Falcon 20 ground school and a check ride.

Although I would much rather fly the Learjet or the Falcon, I made several trips in the Jet Commander with Cherry Air simply because they were the first to call. Problem was, they had me flying with a twenty-one-year-old kid who thought he was Buck Rodgers of the twenty-first century. His nose was so far up the owner's ass, that when the owner farted, his socks would inflate.

This kid was dangerous because he did not know what it was that he did not know. He made stupid decisions like flying several thousand feet above the aircraft's maximum certified service ceiling, claiming that we were saving precious fuel and we might be able to eliminate a planned fuel stop. He was saving the boss money. He would turn off the brakes' anti-skid system, which in most cases put our take-off and landing performance distances longer than the runway available. He said that he was better at regulating the braking system than the aircraft's anti-skid system was.

It was not long before I simply quit responding to my pager when Cherry Air called. Often times they would page me while I was flying a trip for Stern Air. A few weeks after I stopped responding, the owner came by my hangar one afternoon where I was noodling with the T-Craft and told me that he needed to see me in his office right away. I could tell that he was kinda pissed off at me so I told him I would be there in about thirty minutes.

When I arrived in his office, he began to dress me down and play the guilt trip on me. He said he had done all these wonderful things for me like getting me checked out in the Jet Commander and sending me on trips. He said that I was not showing my appreciation and I was not a team player. I was not responding to his calls to go fly.

I replied to his allegations by saying, "I had voiced my concerns regarding the unsafe operations of the Jet Commander and they fell on deaf ears. You do not pay me enough to fly with that kid, and he is going to get somebody hurt one of these days, and it is not going to be me."

His response was that he would set up a Type Rating check ride for me. Even though I really needed the work, I told him, "No Thanks, the Commander is a pig and I never wanted to fly it in the first place." With that I got up and walked out the door. That was the last I heard from Cherry Air.

A few weeks later ol' Buck Rogers ran one of the Jet Commanders off a runway. Not to be out done with that performance, he ran the other Jet Commander off another runway a few weeks after that. Never heard much about him after that.

Chapter 22

Crossroads

While it appeared that Stern Air somehow associated me as being in the Cherry Air camp and was not calling me very often, one of the lovely Customer Service Representatives from an FBO at Love Field that I met while flying Nine-One-Charlie informed me that there was a company at their FBO with a Diamond Jet and one of their pilots just quit. She was pretty sure they were looking for a pilot with some jet time.

After she helped me contact the Chief Pilot we arranged a meeting. He was a young guy and this was his first jet job. He was promoted to Chief Pilot just recently when the previous Chief Pilot left for greener pastures. He was pleased to see that I already had multiple jet type ratings and plenty of flight time so getting approval from the insurance company was not going to be a problem.

I was not really sure I wanted the job, as I really did not care for the Diamond Jet. The paycheck they offered was below the bottom of the pay scale, and I was not too sure about this young new Chief Pilot. We had never even been in the cockpit together so I had a few concerns with respect to our compatibility and his flying skills.

They claimed that the insurance company would require me to go to Flight Safety and earn a Type Rating in the Diamond Jet before we could even go fly together. I thought that was rather odd as that had not been the case anywhere else I had been. Because of the training cost involved, they demanded that I agree to fly for them at for at least one full year. I later found out that the insurance company would not allow the Chief Pilot to fly as Captain because he was a low time pilot, so that explained a lot.

I figured that flying a corporate gig out of Love Field during normal business hours might expose me to better corporate job opportunities in the future, so I accepted their proposal. Besides, as it was described to me, it would be a fairly light flying schedule, leaving plenty of free time for other adventures.

Perhaps my attitude towards the company and the job was soured a bit from the very beginning. The company offered round-trip airline tickets to Houston and hotel costs but would not provide a rental car (red flag) for this two-week training event. Two weeks living in a hotel with no ground transportation? I don't think so. In order to have some flexibility during this training event, I made the five-hour drive to Houston in my own car.

About a week into my training at Flight Safety, my classic black 1985 Monte Carlo SS was stolen from the parking lot of the Houston Hobby Airport Hilton Hotel sometime in the middle of the night. Learning a new airplane and doing simulator flights was a piece of cake compared to dealing with the Houston Police Department, the hotel, and my insurance company.

To pour salt into a wound, the company couldn't have cared less about my stolen classic car, all they wanted to know was if I was still on the training schedule and would I be back in time for a scheduled flight the following week. Of course, I planned to be home and ready for the scheduled trip, and I fully understood that I was on the payroll and my problems were not their problems, but geez, not one single word of compassion.

After completing the training, taking my check ride, and earning the Diamond Jet Type Rating, I caught a Southwest Airlines flight back to Dallas and rented a car so I would have local transportation until I figured out what to do about my personal ground transportation needs.

The insurance company was being impossible to deal with. Not only did I have to pay out of my own pocket for the rental car, but they were trying to deny the loss of my flight bag, which included my headset and my road trip Snap-On tool kit that was in the trunk of the car. Even more aggravating was their attitude towards my limited-edition Monte Carlo SS. They kept trying to claim it was just a standard run of the mill car without any of the performance package options. My car had long since been paid off and the insurance company was trying to pay me pennies on the dollar to settle my claim. Before I even flew my first trip for this new company, it had already cost me a considerable amount of money.

As promised, and on schedule, I arrived at Love Field at 4:30 a.m. for my first trip in the Diamond Jet driving a rental car. We departed Love Field at 6 a.m. for the one-hour flight to Wichita, Kansas. The flying part was easy. The Diamond Jet was outfitted with digital avionics and a first-generation Electronic Flight Information System (EFIS). Overall, the airplane was outfitted pretty nice, but with no ailerons and only spoilers for roll control, it flew like a pig.

The company's protocol mandated that we were to be lounge lizards at the FBO until the boss arrived for the return trip to Dallas sometime between 6:30 to 7 p.m. Our only freedom was to have the FBO's courtesy van drop us off at a restaurant somewhere close by for lunch and then pick us up when we were finished eating. Other than that, we were to wait at the FBO. To make matters worse, the pilots' lounge had a television with rabbit ear antennae that only got the three local Wichita channels.

About a week after flying my first trip in the Diamond Jet, I received a call from the Houston Police Department informing me that they found my car. First thing I did was call the Chief Pilot to verify that our schedule was still clear for the next couple of days. Next was a call to the insurance company to make arrangements to meet them at the police impound lot in Houston.

I spent a couple of days in Houston getting things sorted out and with a new set of wheels, tires, and a new stereo I was soon on my way back to Dallas in the Monster Carlo. The next order of business was to install a more advanced anti-theft device than the one I previously had.

Life was getting better now and things were going back to normal. Most trips in the Diamond Jet were one day trips. We would fly the Wichita routine a few times a month with an occasional overnight trip to Denver, Minot, Bismarck, Fargo, Gillette, Hayes, Kansas and a few other garden spots throughout the Midwest. The most difficult part of the job as the low man on the totem pole was revising all the instrument approach procedure plates.

My entire professional flying career up to this point had been performed using the paper government approach plates that came in about fifteen little booklets. When an approach plate revision came in, you pulled out that book, threw it away, and replaced it with a completely new book. It only took about five minutes to revise all the instrument approach plates for the entire country.

This flight department was using paper Jeppesen approach plates. The approach plates were stored on the airplane in ten to fifteen seven-ring binders. When revisions came in, they were individual pages, meaning that you would need to sort through thousands of pages to find the one that needed revising, pull out that page, and replace it with the revised page. It would take hours and hours updating the approach plates to airports all over the country, most of which were airports that we were never ever going to go to, but they all had to be kept current just the same. Other than that, I had plenty of time on my hands to seek other adventures.

After finishing with the approach plate revisions one day, I wandered over to the little café at the FBO next door to grab some lunch. There were always pilots and other aviators in this little café during lunch time, which made for a pretty lively crowd. While standing in line to place my order, I ran across a young married couple who said they were looking for a Learjet pilot.

They went on to explain that they were going to start a jet charter company. They had one Learjet 24 in the hangar and they had one more on the way. They were in the process of putting together their Pre-Application Statement of Intent as the first step in pursuit of their own Federal Aviation Regulation Part 135 Air Carrier Certificate. Problem was that the process could take well over a year to complete. There were several manuals to write and several qualifications necessary to meet FAA standards for an Air Carrier Certificate and they needed help.

During this casual conversation, I suggested they piggyback on someone else's Air Carrier Certificate and at least generate some revenue while working through the process with the FAA. They said that was one of their considerations but they did not know where to start or who to team up with. When I suggested that I had a few ideas, they offered me a salary to come onboard to help get it all set up. I told them that I had a job that I was obligated to, but I still had several free days every week. We agreed on a salary and a plan going forward.

I contacted the same guys in Florida that held the Certificate that Tom and I had operated Nine-One-Charlie under. They agreed to work with me on this project and we signed an agreement that was complete with a list of documents that we needed to produce along with a monthly fee that we would pay them.

There was a lot of administrative work to do. We had to ensure the aircraft met the Part 135 Air Carrier Conformity inspection requirements, and we had to write a Minimum Equipment List. The aircraft would be placed on their FAA Approved Aircraft Inspection Program and added to their Operations Specifications. Then we had to line up a few pilots, conduct a training class, and schedule some check rides.

While doing part of the Conformity Inspection I noticed that the FAA Registration Form in the airplane did not match who I was told the owner was. Come to find out, this young couple had recently sold these two Learjets to a couple of guys in the northeast part of the country on the premise that they would bring them to Texas and charter them out and make them a ton of money.

Well now that is fine and dandy, but we still needed a valid aircraft Registration Certificate to get through the Conformity Inspection process. Within a few days I was presented with two fresh pink slip Temporary Aircraft Registration Certificates. With all the conformity issues finally out of the way, the FAA Part 135 check rides with the air carrier certificate holder's Chief Pilot were conducted. In less than two months, we were officially operating on a Part 135 Air Carrier Certificate with three Captains and three First Officers. The party was short lived though, as we immediately began flying, and we were flying a lot, as in every day.

It was beginning to look like we needed more pilots and perhaps a few maintenance personnel. It seemed like we were converting the aircraft from one configuration to another after almost every flight. We were converting the airplanes' interior from cargo to air ambulance to passenger configuration. And I still had to go fly the Diamond Jet and do the instrument approach plate revisions every now and then.

We were flying each airplane around seventy to eighty hours a month. I was kind of proud of the work we had done and kept copies of everything for future reference as it was beginning to look like this little company was going to be a success story. It was not long before I noticed a substantial upgrade in the vehicles being driven by the young owners of the company. They even bragged about buying a new house.

One Friday evening, after the flying was all done, they invited everyone to the lake for a little party to celebrate. I was surprised when they ushered everyone onboard their recently purchased yacht and launched for the middle of the lake. They seemed to be doing really well for themselves as this was a pretty big boat. I should have paid more attention to the warning signs.

As time went on, I spent more time flying and managing the Learjets than I did flying the Diamond Jet. We were only doing one trip a week, and sometimes we would go two weeks without a trip in the Diamond, and the Learjets were flying almost every day.

In preparing one of the Learjets for a return trip from San Jose one Sunday afternoon, I went to the FBO and presented one of the company credit cards for payment of the fuel and services we received. The young lady behind the counter tried to run the card twice but it was declined both times. I went back to the airplane and got another credit card and it too was declined, leaving me standing there with egg on my face. The passengers were soon to arrive and I needed to get this resolved.

I made a phone call back to headquarters to try and get this all sorted out, and I was told to simply try running the cards again and if that didn't work, I should use my own personal credit card. I was pretty sure that I could hear the ice melting in their cocktails over the phone.

I was becoming really upset. I ask the gal at the FBO if she would get a representative of the aviation fuel credit card company on the phone for me. The lady on the phone informed me that the company had not made a payment in over four months and owed a substantial amount of money. Not wanting our passengers to see or hear what was going on, I simply pulled out my own credit card and paid the bill.

After arriving at Love Field, deplaning our passengers, and securing the aircraft, I gathered up the paperwork from the trip and went to the office only to find that my key didn't work on the lock. I went to the front desk of the FBO to ask why my key didn't work and was told that we had been evicted. The company had not paid rent on the office and owed tens of thousands of dollars in unpaid fuel bills. SHIT!

I grabbed the nearest telephone and called the home telephone number of the company president. He informed me that they had moved our headquarters to Addison Airport, and that I should ferry the airplane up to Addison and we would meet up on Monday to discuss all these new details.

I received a phone call early the following morning instructing me to meet up at a hangar on Addison Airport, we would be discussing my future with the company. That was kind of an ominous warning. Evidently, the company had leased a place at Addison and moved the entire office up there while I was on the two-day trip to California.

Upon arrival at the new hangar location, I was introduced to two gentlemen that I had not met or heard of before. They were reported to be the owners of the Learjets.

They informed me that they had been paying my salary for the past six months and wanted to know what they were getting in return. They had expected the airplanes to be flying several months ago and generating some kind of revenue.

As I began to explain that the airplanes were doing a lot of flying, I noticed the young company owner and his wife darting out the side door and leaving in their new car. Unfamiliar with this new office layout, I began looking in each of the rooms for my old desk. Upon finding my old desk, with these two Learjet owners in tow, I began going through all the drawers looking for all my files. They were all gone, my desk had been sanitized. I searched every desk in the place and didn't find any evidence that the airplanes were flying.

I went out to both aircraft to get the flight logs and they were all gone as well, even the Operations Manuals were missing. These two gentlemen were getting rather disturbed with me, thinking that I had been up to some sort of mischief with their airplanes. As I tried to reassure them that I had worked really hard the past six months and both airplanes were up and flying daily, I remembered that I had a flight bag in the trunk of my car.

That flight bag had a copy of the Operations Manual with both airplanes listed in it and I had copies of most of the flight logs going back to the first training flights. I also had copies of all the pilots FAA Form 8410s. I did not have a copy of the San Jose flight log but I did have a copy of the fuel receipt with the aircraft tail number on it.

In spite of the documents that I was able to produce, accusations were made that I had been robbing the company blind. I was bankrupting the company by burning thousands of gallons of jet fuel and joy riding around in their Learjets and yielding nothing that I was paid to deliver.

I argued that we were constantly changing the interior configuration and told them about all the passenger trips and cargo trips we had flown. I even offered to round up the rest of the pilots so they could be interviewed, but they were having none of that.

I told them about the Air Ambulance trip from Ft Worth to Philadelphia with an infant baby girl for heart surgery. I told them about picking up singer Frankie Lane in St. Louis and flying him to San Diego after he had a heart attack. I told them about the trip where the heart transplant crew jumped out of the airplane and into the ambulance and drove off with the wrong ice chest. I told them about the burn victim I flew from Laredo to Cedar Rapids and the trip with the DNR passenger. They did not want to hear about any of that.

During this confrontational discussion, it became clear to me that the company president and his wife had not been paying any of the company's expenses from the revenue generated from all the flights we had flown. Instead, while the rest of the crew and I had our nose to the grindstone working our asses off, they were using company funds to buy new cars, a house, and a boat.

In spite of the evidence I provided, all they wanted to know was why their airplanes were not flying revenue trips. I told them that I was not in charge of billing, that was the presidents wife's job as I understood it. It appeared that they refused to accept the fact that the couple they entrusted their aircraft to was ripping them off.

They had not been in town to witness any of these activities and were only going by what they had been told. It was my word against theirs and I had become the scapegoat. I think these two northeastern guys were beginning to have their doubts, but they fired me anyway and told me that the paycheck I received about a week and a half ago was my last paycheck.

Needless to say, I was rather pissed off. My reputation had been damaged through guilt by association with these people at the FBO at Love Field, but at least I had a current 8410 Learjet PIC letter and the job flying the Diamond Jet.

Upon returning home after that disgusting meeting, I called the Certificate holder that we were operating under and advised them that I was no longer with the company. Then I went to check my mailbox. Among other usual mail, there was a letter from my bank. In it was a company check that I had deposited a week or so ago and it was marked NSF.

I called the bank to find out what was going on and they said there were insufficient funds in the account to cover that check. Now I was really pissed off because not only did they cheat me out of a paycheck but I was still on the hook for the fuel that I paid for with my personal credit card.

I was at an interesting crossroads in my life. I just spent all this time to help get this little Learjet operation up and running and now it was gone. I was coming up on my one-year anniversary with the

Diamond Jet, and I had been planning to quit that job. And if that was not enough, my wife packed her bags and left me for more stable greener pastures.

We returned from one of those agonizing Wichita Kansas trips on my one-year anniversary date in the Diamond Jet. After sending the boss on his way and putting the jet to bed, I handed the Chief Pilot the keys to the jet and the office and wished him well. He followed me out to the truck asking what that was supposed to mean. "My one year is up, I am outta here."

He began arguing that I should stay and asked what he was supposed to do about his trip next week.

"Not my problem."

"But we are scheduled for training at Flight Safety at the end of the month!"

"Good luck."

A few days later, I wandered back over to Stern Air and gave them all my updated paperwork and they promised to put me back on the pilot roster.

A few days later, I spotted that bounced check from the Learjet company sitting on the table. Picking up the telephone, I called the bank to see if the $2,500 check would clear. When they said that it would clear, I beelined it straight to the bank and cashed it. At least it would cover most of the fuel bill on my credit card.

About two weeks later, I was at home eating dinner when there was a knock at the door. It was this little guy here to serve me papers. I supposed to show up in a courtroom at some future date in Baltimore, Maryland, as I was being sued for "conversion of funds." Unfortunately, I spent all of that $2500 and the next year fighting the case that was ultimately dismissed for lack of jurisdiction.

Chapter 23

Wrestle Mania

Stern Air was owned by a really colorful character and he was well known in these parts. It seemed like every pilot in the area had a unique "Thunder Ray" story to tell. Many of the stories were not very flattering and some contained events that were the subject of FAA investigations and potential certificate action for all involved. That was not something that anybody wished on anybody, and was not something that I wanted any part of.

The Dispatcher at Stern Air was a pretty good ol' boy who seemed to understand a lot more than he let on. One of his jobs was to make sure that there were always enough crew members available to fly the airplanes while not exceeding the FAA-mandated flight and duty times. He and I had a standing agreement that since I was simply a contract pilot, he would never call me to fly a trip with Ray.

The airplanes were butt ugly but they were all in reasonably good mechanical shape. If the airplane was not burning fuel, it was costing money. Thus, the airplanes were flying constantly, stopping only long enough to re-fuel, load cargo and perhaps do a crew change, or to spend time getting loved on in the maintenance shop.

Stern Air Fleet

The Director of Operations was a crotchety guy who seemed hold a grudge against anyone who had ever been through any kind of the formal flight training at organizations such as Simuflite or Flight Safety, and I had been through both. I always figured it was because nobody would ever spend the money to send him or if they did, he had a bad experience.

We were doing so much flying at Stern Air that dispatch started throttling some of us back because we were getting close to exceeding the maximum quarterly and annual flight time limitations set by the FAA, and with the annual Christmas push just around the corner they felt that it was prudent to reserve some of our flight time.

Almost every trip we flew, we absolutely positively had to get there right now, as was the case on one particular trip to Mexico City to pick up some car parts. We were to pick up our cargo, fly to Laredo to clear customs, then on to Detroit as the final destination.

After waiting around in Mexico City for about two hours our cargo, consisting of two little boxes, finally arrived. In short order we were on our way to Laredo. Maybe it was the unexpected delay in Mexico City or a lot of traffic at the bridge on the border, but we sat in the airplane on the ramp in Laredo for well over an hour waiting for a Customs official to show up and clear us to proceed.

Finally, I got tired of waiting and had to relieve myself. It was around 2:30 a.m. on a poorly lit ramp with nobody around so, I hopped out of the Lear and walked out by the wing tip and relieved myself on the ramp.

The customs official finally arrived to find my co-pilot and I sitting on the wing of the airplane waiting for him. He immediately began yelling to remind us that he had seen both of us before and knew that we knew better than to open the cabin door before he arrived to inspect the aircraft and our cargo.

After pointing to the two stains on the ramp and explaining that we had been waiting for over an hour, he finally settled down and went on to do his job of checking our paperwork and inspecting our cargo.

While looking over our paperwork, he asked where we had been and where the rest of our cargo was.

"It says here you have five hundred pieces; I only see two small boxes. And what is an oil level indicator?"

I reached into my pocket and pulled out a pocket knife and as I was handing it to him, I said, "You know better than that, we are not allowed to open the cargo, but you can as long as you put one of your stickers on it."

With that, he sliced open one of the boxes to reveal 250 oil dip sticks for automotive engines. The other box was identical so he didn't bother opening that one. I immediately turned and grabbed my co-pilot by the shoulder to get his attention and said, "You can never ever say a word about this to anyone, especially back home and during any of the pilot meetings."

"Gee, Kev, why not?"

"What!? Can you imagine the jokes they could make up about us? Captain Dip Stick and his Junior Birdman defy customs by peeing on the ramp! Or any other story about the flying dipsticks. The things people could come up with could be brutal."

"Oh, okay, Kev, I am with you now, don't worry I won't say a word."

The customs official laughed about that and reminded us that we needed to stay in the airplane until he arrived. He cleared us to carry on with our business. We hailed the fuel truck and in no time we were on our way to Detroit.

Flying in and out of Mexico was kinda like flying in the wild west and almost always resulted in a story of some kind. Unlike the pretty corporate jets that would fly in and out of Mexico handing out one-hundred-dollar bills to everyone they came across to make their arrival and departures go smoothly, us freight dawgs did not have that kind of cash to spread around. Dispatch would launch us with just enough money to cover the landing fees, customs and immigration fees, and to file a flight plan, and that was it.

We flew into Chihuahua late one afternoon to pick up a load of Packard-Electric automotive wiring harnesses. We made our way through the process with the airport, customs and immigration, and flight service and paid all the associated fees along the way. With all that out of the way, the only thing left to do was sit around and wait for our cargo. After a short while, I was hailed to the airport's comandante's office.

He politely greeted me and then began his shakedown. It was funny, because standing in at 5'10", I was towering way above him as he was probably only about 5'3" tall. You could tell that resting his right hand on the 45-caliber pistol strapped to his scrawny little waist made him feel invincible.

Standing behind him and off to one side was a kid with an M-16. He couldn't have been more than fourteen years old. Both were wearing green army fatigues. Needless to say, I was not very intimidated.

The comandante advised me that the airport would be closing soon and if my cargo did not arrive in time, I must pay him $300 to keep the airport open until it arrived.

Looking out the window behind him into the parking lot, I saw an old white Chevy Suburban with the tailgate down stuffed full of Packard-Electric boxes, and four or five more boxes strapped to the roof. In addition, the airline Arrival/Departure sign just on the other side of the glass showed a scheduled American Airlines flight and a few other arrivals for later in the evening.

He seemed surprised when I asked what time the airport closed. He would not tell me, but he said it would close very soon.

"Just tell me what time the airport closes, we will depart ten minutes prior to your closing."

"Ah, but Captain, what about your carga?"

"Screw the carga, I am not paying your extortion fees!"

"Oh, but Captain, you must not leave without your carga. What will you tell your customer?"

"I will tell General Motors that I was looking at their carga through the window of the comandante's office as he was trying to hold it for a three-hundred-dollar ransom!"

"Oh, Captain, is it that you have no money? That is a very nice pair of boots and that belt buckle, perhaps we can work something out."

"You can kiss my ass, I am not giving you my boots or my belt buckle. With or without my carga, I am leaving ten minutes before the airport closes, now what time will that be?"

At this point, he was speechless and did not know what else to say. He saw that his hand on his pistol did not intimidate me, nor did the kid with the M-16 and probably nobody had ever stood up to him like that before.

I returned to the lobby to my anxious co-pilot, who overheard parts of the conversation. "Kev, people disappear down here, I have heard stories. What are we going to do?"

"I don't know, but whatever it is, if I ask you to do something, do not argue, just do it."

"Okay Kev, you are the Captain, just don't get us disappeared."

A short while later, the sun was beginning to set and the runway and taxi-way lights began to come on. I was beginning to think it was time to call their bluff.

"Hey, why don't you run out to the airplane and fire up the radio and get us our IFR departure clearance."

"Okay Kev" and with that he went to the airplane. Over the speaker in the comandante's office, I could hear his radio call.

The air traffic controller asked about our cargo and he simply requested our departure clearance again.

With his second call, I exited the building and walked out to the airplane. When I got there, I climbed onboard and pulled the cabin door closed. Settling into the left seat I asked "What did they say? Did you get a clearance?"

"No, they asked about our cargo, and I simply asked for our clearance again, so far no reply."

"Tell them that we are starting our engines now and will be departing."

I reached down and turned on the beacon and nav lights and hit the start switch of the right engine. Just as that fire breathing CJ610 came to life that old beat-up white Chevy Suburban pulled up in front of the airplane. "Well, lookie there, it's our carga. Amazing how that worked."

I shut the engine down, climbed out of my seat, and opened the door. We hustled all the Packard-Electric boxes on board and strapped them down just as the comandante and his fourteen-year-old escort approached. I looked at the Suburban driver and motioned for him to get out of here. He jumped in the old Chevy and drove away.

We ignored the comandante and climbed in and closed the door. After we settled into the cockpit, it was not long before we had the right engine running again and we pulled out of our parking spot and showed that little sawed off comandante the business end of a CJ610.

"Call 'em on the radio now and see what they say."

After he made the call, the reply came back saying that the airport was closed. I knew that was a bogus claim as there was an inbound American Airlines MD-80 flight and according to my calculations they should be about ten minutes out by now.

"Tell them we are taxiing to Runway One Eight."

With that radio call, they turned off all the runway and taxiway lights. Fortunately, we were already well on our way and the airport was not that complicated so it was easy to find our way to the runway in the dark with our landing lights.

"What about our IFR clearance?"

"Just assume that we are cleared to El Paso as filed, and that is what we intend to do, fly as filed. We will call departure control once we clear the mountains. Hopefully they are not in bed with these guys here."

The airport kind of sits in a bowl at a field elevation of about 4,500 feet above sea level surrounded by mountains ranging from 5,500 to 7500 feet, which is not really that tall, but they are in pretty close proximity to the airport. Even so, those little hills are no match for the climb rate of a Learjet.

After back-taxiing down the unlit runway, we finally hit the end and turned around and lined up on the center line. Just before shoving the thrust levers forward, I briefed my co-star on this non-standard departure we were fixing to make. We needed to get as high as we could as fast as we could so as to not create any conflict with the arriving American flight, which was arriving from the north. We also needed to keep alert on the radio for any other traffic that might be out there.

"Standard call-outs, you ready?"

"Ready, Captain."

"Here we go. Setting take-off thrust."

"Power set – two good engines – no lights – one-hundred-knot cross check – V1 – rotate."

"Positive rate, gear up."

"Roger, positive rate, gear coming up."

"Yaw damp."

"Yaw damper engaged."

"Flaps up."

"Flaps coming up."

In the blink of an eye, we were airborne and climbing at 200 knots. I just kept pulling back on the elevator and trimming the airplane to try and hold 200 knots. The vertical speed indicator was pegged at a 6,000-

foot-a-minute rate of climb and the hands on the altimeter were winding up at an impressive rate.

All I had to do was wait until the aircraft was pointing north and roll the wings level and we would be on our way towards El Paso. We were climbing through 28,000 feet by the time the American flight checked in with the tower, descending through twelve thousand feet.

Damn, I loved flying these things. I might never get to be an astronaut, but this was pretty darn close to it.

Landing in El Paso, I couldn't wait to call Don in dispatch and tell him what happened in Chihuahua, but that had to wait for a while as the Customs and Border Patrol agents decided to run the dogs on us and the airplane. They even looked in the aft equipment bay, which was something they had never done before.

After being released from customs, we got the fuelers fueling the aircraft and I went to call dispatch and brief Don about what happened. I am not sure what Don did or who he called, but it was almost a year before we heard of any more shakedown attempts by the comandante at Chihuahua.

Stern Air had a lot of good people flying for them. Most, like myself, were simply waiting for the economy to turn around so we could either land a corporate flying job or move up to the airlines. Marching to the tune of that electronic leash we called a pager did not offer much quality of life. The only time you knew you would not be called was the ten hours after a trip, but after that FAA-mandated that ten-hour rest period, you were fair game. If you didn't fly, you didn't get paid.

I had just gone to bed one evening when the telephone rang. It was Don in dispatch. He began to brief me for a trip that needed to depart within an hour. The itinerary was to depart Addison and fly to Frederick, Oklahoma, pick up some car parts, and deliver them to Lawrenceburg, Tennessee, then head over to Memphis for fuel and return home. "There is just one thing, Kev, this is a Ray trip."

"Don, we have an agreement, call someone else," and with that I hung up the phone.

A few minutes later, the phone rang again. "Kev, I will give you double captain's pay if you will fly this trip for me."

"Sorry, Don, it is not worth risking my airman's certificates over." And again, I hung up the phone.

As I lay there in bed, I began thinking about the days when I get old and gray, sitting on the front porch with my flying buddies, and everyone will have a Ray story but me. If he called back maybe I should take the trip.

The phone rang for a third time. "Kev, it's Don again, please don't hang up. I will give you triple captain's pay if you will just fly this one trip for me. All the other pilots say that they have been drinking and can't fly, I really need you."

"I am on my way, Don, I'll be there in twenty minutes."

Although "Thunder Ray" had the physique of the Incredible Hulk he was reasonably soft spoken and slow moving. He had been in the merchant marines, a professional wrestler, body builder, aerobatic pilot, real estate developer and much more, all with a fourth-grade education.

By the time Ray arrived at the airport, I had the aircraft ready to go. It was a fairly short trip up to Fredrick and Ray seemed to do a pretty good job flying the airplane. His performance was not at all what I expected from all the stories I had heard.

The next leg would be to Lawrenceburg, Tennessee, and that would be my leg to fly, but after seeing that the cargo was all loaded and the cargo net was properly installed, I moved up to the cockpit only to find Ray sitting in the left seat. "Hey, what the hell do you think you're doing, Ray? It's my leg to fly!"

"I'm sorry, Kevin, I forgot." And with that Ray moved out of the left seat and over to the right seat.

It was not long before I realized that he was not very proficient at performing co-pilot duties, but that was okay as the weather was not too bad. With the cargo delivered in Lawrenceburg, we switched seats and hopped over to Memphis for fuel. Once in Memphis, Ray got on the phone with dispatch while I supervised the fueling.

With the aircraft refueled, Ray returned to the aircraft and said that we had a new assignment. He said that we needed to go to St. Louis to pick up some freight and deliver it to Flint, Michigan, and, he reminded me that it was my leg to fly.

It was a short forty-minute flight to St. Louis and we were happy to see the truck with our cargo and a fuel truck waiting for us on the ramp when we arrived. In no time at all, we were fueled up with our cargo loaded and blasting off for Flint.

St. Louis had a full load of cargo for us, so it was good to see the bobtail tuck back up to the door as we shut the engines down in Flint. That meant we would only be there a short while and we would be back in Addison in around two and a half hours.

The driver and his accomplice got out of the truck and with his Michigan union employee attitude told me that they would be in that little building over there having coffee and we should let them know when we had finished loading their truck for them.

I had seen this movie before so I replied, "Sir, you have that all wrong. We have had union grievances filed against us for helping you guys do your union jobs, so you can kiss my ass, we will be over there drinking coffee and filing flight plans, and you can let us know when you have unloaded your cargo!"

Just as he was gathering up his anger to reply, Ray, with all his bulging muscles, comes lumbering out of the cockpit and says, "Is everything okay here Kevin? I heard some words."

"Everything is fine, Ray, I was just explaining to this gentleman that he should let us know when they have finished unloading their cargo because we are running out of duty time and we need to get on our way."

The guy took one look at Ray and meekly said, "Captain, they have fresh coffee in there, why don't you get in out of the cold and have a cup, we will let you know just as soon as we are done unloading the jet."

We were only on the ground in Flint for about forty-five minutes and were soon on our way home. At around mid-morning we taxied up to the ramp at Addison. The crew that was going to fly the next trip and one of the mechanics were on the ramp with their flight bags and a fuel truck waiting for our arrival. The airplane was to be promptly fueled up and another crew was to launch on another mission.

I looked down to secure the engines and check progress of the fuel transfer as Ray climbed out of the co-pilot seat and opened the cabin door. Out of the corner of my eye I noticed that everyone was scattering in different directions and ducking for cover. What the hell?

I finished the paperwork for the trip and climbed out of the cockpit to perform a post-flight inspection of the aircraft. One by one, the pilots and mechanics came out of hiding and to the airplane. "What happened, Kev? Is Ray okay?"

"Ray is fine, why? What's up?"

"What were you doing in the left seat?"

"I was flying the airplane, what do you think I was doing? It was my leg to fly!"

"You mean Ray just offered you the left seat? He always flies every leg, he never lets anyone else fly."

"No, he climbed in the left seat when it was my leg to fly. I told him to move his ass over, this is my leg to fly. He said he was sorry and moved over to the right seat."

"You actually said that to Ray?"

"Sure did, why?"

"Can't believe you had the nerve to say that to him, he's only the owner of the company."

"That may be so down here, but up there we are crew members and there is a company policy that qualified pilots switch seats."

That trip seemed to seal my fate. For some reason, Ray decided that he liked me and every trip that he flew after that day, he requested me to fly with him. I refused as much as I could but when the flying began to slow down, I realized that a Ray trip was better than no trip at all.

Together, we made several North Atlantic crossings carrying clandestine hazardous materials for the US government to several discreet locations throughout Europe. We also made a few trips to Nicaragua. Most of these trips seemed to coincide with civil unrest somewhere in the region.

Returning from a trip one morning, I had a message on my answering machine from Eastern Airlines. I had never sent them an application but they were asking me to go to the Cooper Clinic for an interview. Cooper Clinic was a huge aerobic fitness center with a huge campus in the middle of Dallas.

Eastern was an interesting airline in that it had recently been bought by Frank Lorenzo and his Texas Air Group. They were currently in a huge labor dispute with the unions. The Machinists Union was out on strike and as a show of solidarity, the Pilots Union went on strike as well, essentially driving the airline into bankruptcy. It appeared that Eastern was trying to resume operations with non-union pilots and machinists, or as the unions would call them, scabs.

After consulting with an airline pilot friend, I called the Air Line Pilots Association Union office. I explained the unsolicited interview request that was scheduled for the following day. The guy I spoke to was cordial and asked what qualifications I had. He asked if I had applied at United Airlines, to which I replied, "Yes, twice, but I have not heard back from them."

He suggested that I go ahead with the interview at Eastern and report back to them the details of the interview. He also suggested that he would pull my application with United, and while not promising a job, he did guarantee that I would get called for an interview within the next couple of weeks.

Being from Texas, I never saw much need for a labor union, although the history books indicated there was a time and a place for unions to exist. The strife at Eastern seemed to be one of those occasions, but what I also learned from the history books is whether you are pro-union or not, never ever cross the picket line.

Arriving at the Cooper Clinic, I recognized a few local pilots while I was signing in. After taking a seat in the waiting room, I was approached by a guy who I recognized from Stern Air. I never flew with him or spent any time with him, but I did know who he was.

He sat down next to me and said that he was glad to see that I accepted his recommendation. What?! He explained that he copied the entire pilot roster from both Stern Air and Cherry Air and gave it to the Eastern recruitment team. He had been hired by Eastern a short while back and was already flying for them. He would be getting a bonus for every pilot he helped recruit. I was not too happy to hear that, but it did explain the un-solicited offer for an interview.

After a thorough physical exam and a short aeronautical test, I was taken into a little room where I was greeted by two gentlemen who handed me an airline ticket to Miami. They welcomed me to the New Eastern Airlines team and said that I came highly recommended. They told me to go home and pack a bag and head straight to DFW Airport.

They went on to explain that I was about to undergo some intensive fast-track training. I would be there for six weeks for training and since I already had a Boeing 737 Type Rating my first push from the gate would be as a Lance Captain with a Check Airman as my co-pilot for my IOE (Initial Operational Experience) flights.

It was comforting to know that at least one airline viewed me as a viable candidate and wanted to hire me, but I also knew that this was not the best pathway to the cockpit of a Boeing. And, this was an airline that was probably not going to be around for very long anyway.

I reminded them that they called me and I could not be expected to pack my bags and run away for six weeks at the drop of the hat. I needed about a week to make some personal arrangements. They really were not happy about that but they gave me their business cards and suggested I call them the following day with my estimated arrival date in Miami.

I left the interview and went home and called the Air Line Pilots Association. I did not get to talk to the gentleman that I spoke with before, but I began explaining my reason for calling all over again to this new representative. This guy was not so friendly and immediately began to dress me down for even going to the interview. It didn't matter to him that his colleague had suggested that I follow through and go to the interview and report back with details. In his opinion, I was a scab just for going to the interview in the first place.

Beginning around 11 p.m. that evening, my phone began ringing. It was ALPA representatives calling me all sorts of dirty names as soon as I picked up the phone. They called every five minutes for thirty minutes. They probably kept calling all night, but I unplugged the phone so I could get some sleep.

Chapter 24

Panama Jack

I was helping a friend who owned an aircraft maintenance shop with a C Inspection on a Falcon 10 when he came to me and asked if I wanted to deliver this little Piper Seneca III to Dunnellon, Florida.

It needed to be there by 10 a.m. the following day and they would get me to the airlines and back home. The problem was that we had to wait for confirmation that the money hit the escrow account before I could go. They should have that confirmation shortly.

Well, it was already mid afternoon, so I decided to finish up the little project I was working on and go home to clean up and grab an overnight bag. I was pretty sure that we were past the bank wire transfer cut-off time, so I didn't really think that I would be going anywhere until the following day, but I was ready to go just the same.

Finally, after several hours of waiting around, at about 9 p.m., I was given the green light to launch. I was provided with a complete set of instructions on where to go and who to deliver the aircraft to, and was told that they would get me to the airlines and provide me with a ticket home.

The airplane had a Mexican registration number of XA-PAW. Papa Alpha Whiskey was a mouthful while communicating on the radio. In most cases it was customary to take an unfamiliar airplane around the patch once or twice before launching on a long trip, especially for a cross-country night flight, but due to the circumstances and the need to make up for lost time that did not happen.

With the airplane all fueled up, a call was made to Addison Clearance Delivery for flight following and shortly afterwards I was climbing eastbound away from the bright lights of the big city. It didn't take very long to get comfortable in this airplane.

The Seneca had a stack of the latest King Silver Crown avionics complete with weather radar and an excellent autopilot. As a bonus, in flight, all the engine instruments lined up perfectly with each other. Oil temperature, oil pressure, fuel flow, cylinder head temperatures, rpm, and manifold pressure on each engine matched up. You do not see that very often in a twin engine aircraft. Just a momentary glance at the engine instruments to see all the needles aligned was all it took to verify that everything was in order. They were perfect, and the airspeed indicator sat right on 145 knots. The airplane even had an oxygen system in it that would be useful later on in the flight.

After about three and a half hours of droning along into the darkness, I was beginning to get a little tired, so I began looking for a place to stop for the night. Tallahassee was right along my route of flight and seemed like a logical stop. It had a large airport and was served by the airlines, and it had a fixed base operator that was probably open twenty-four hours. They probably even had a crew car with a hotel close by where I could get flight crew rates for the night.

From Tallahassee to Dunnellon is only about 130 miles, so I figured that I could get about five or six hours of sleep, make the final sprint in the morning, and be there on time for the 10 a.m. delivery. There was just one problem with that plan.

The FBO was closed. There was a side door that opened into what looked like a hospital waiting room, complete with stiff-back chairs and bright lights, but no telephone. As long as I was here, I may as well make the best of it. I spent the night uncomfortably sleeping upright in a chair with steel armrests under the bright lights. Apparently, the light switch was hidden away in another room.

Right around 6 a.m. the FBO employees began arriving seemingly not concerned with my efforts to get a little sleep. They let me doze in and out of consciousness for about an hour before waking me up to get my fuel order. With my fuel bill paid, they fed me a fresh doughnut and cup of coffee and sent me on my way.

The flight to Dunnellon was uneventful, considering that I was flying right into the rising sun. Once at Dunnellon, I looked around for my point of contact, whom I found in the back of a hangar packing a parachute. He was glad to see that I was a little early, so as he finished packing the parachute, he briefed me that we needed to hop in the Seneca and fly down to Tampa. That sounded like a great idea to me. They had airline service there, and I assumed that he was going to put me on an airline back to Texas from there.

As we walked to the airplane, he seemed to struggle to keep up, as he had a pretty serious hitch in his get-along. Seemed as though he had sustained a pretty serious injury somewhere in his past.

Upon arriving in Tampa, we taxied to the FBO, and upon exiting the aircraft I was instructed to go inside and wait for him. I watched as he limped across the ramp and disappeared into one of the hangars.

About twenty minutes later, he and two other people emerged from the hangar carrying several boxes heading for the Seneca. They opened the baggage door and began loading the airplane. None of my business what they were up to, my work was done here. I had done my job and delivered the airplane as instructed. Or so I thought.

Pretty soon this little old guy limped his way into the FBO and informed me that we needed to fly down to Fort Lauderdale. Well crap, this day just kept getting longer and longer and I didn't get much sleep the night before.

As we departed Tampa, the skies were filling with their typical Florida afternoon thunderstorms and the further south we went, the thicker they got and the more deviations were necessary to avoid the red and yellow on the radar.

I really began to feel like a mushroom after landing in Fort Lauderdale International. He instructed me to taxi to a facility where he went inside and picked up an overwater life raft. After picking up the survival gear, he asked me if I would like to get something to eat before I launched on the thousand-mile trip to Panama. WHAT? Wait a minute, I was only paid to get the aircraft to Dunnellon and I was told that they would put me on the airlines and send me home.

They had been keeping me in the dark and feeding me a line of crap this entire trip. Another thousand miles? How about some extra pay and letting me get some sleep? And how was I going to get home from Panama?

"Don't worry, here is a little something extra and they will take care of your airline ticket from Panama back to Miami. We have already filed your flight plan and we have your Cuban overflight permit. Stop at the Grand Cayman Island for fuel then follow the airway south. You will lose the Cayman VOR signal and will not be able to pick up the San Andreas VOR for about an hour and a half, so just do your best to stay on that last heading off the Cayman VOR and you will be fine. If anything goes wrong, just turn east and go to Kingston, Jamaica." He handed me an envelope stuffed with hundred-dollar bills.

The way this guy talked, it sounded like he had done this a time or two, and that might explain that limp that he had.

"What about all those new avionics boxes that you stuffed behind the baggage compartment panel? Are you asking me to smuggle avionics into Panama, hell, they will probably throw me under the jail house."

"Don't worry about a thing, we have someone that will meet you when you arrive and take care of everything. They will get you to the hotel and then back to the airport to catch the airline home."

Crap, looked like another ball buster of a day for me. Oh well, at least I had two Quarter Pounders with cheese and a large bag of fries and a Coke - that should hold me over for a little while.

Departing Fort Lauderdale was an adventure in and of itself. Thunderstorms were everywhere, causing ATC to issue vectors to everyone in South Florida. The radar on that little Seneca was working like a champ and I could see all the weather that I was working my way around. There were so many vectors, that after about forty-five minutes I had no idea where I was. All I knew was with all the bouncing around, my bladder was about to bust.

Looking around the cockpit for something to relieve myself into, all I could find was the cup from McDonald's that my drink came in. I was certainly glad to have a good auto-pilot to fly the airplane for me while I emptied my bladder into the cup. Having filled the McDonalds cup, I replaced the lid and wedged it between the seats so that it wouldn't spill.

Shortly after I completed that task, Miami Center called, "Papa Alpha Whiskey, climb to and maintain sixteen thousand feet and contact Habana Center on such and such frequency."

Habana Center instructed me to fly direct to a VOR (radio navigation aid) on the north side of Cuba and report reaching that fix. I spun the OBS around to center up the needle, spun the heading bug around to take me there, and decided that it was time to suck a little oxygen.

The oxygen system on the Seneca was the type that is either on or off, and no in between. In other words, when you plug the oxygen mask in, you receive a constant flow of oxygen from the bottle. It is not prudent to plug the mask in and simply let the oxygen flow constantly because you will soon be out of oxygen, and there was still about a thousand miles to go.

My plan was to conserve the oxygen by simply plugging the mask in and sucking on the bottle about every thirty minutes or so in order to make the oxygen last for the duration of the trip.

A few minutes later the VOR needle swung from TO to FROM and I called up Habana to report crossing that fix. I was instructed to track a specific radial southbound to another fix and report crossing that fix, to which I acknowledged.

As I took a few more hits off the oxygen mask, I thought how cool it would be to get a bird's-eye view of Cuba, but it was not going to happen today, as I had been in the clouds since I left Ft. Lauderdale. What a bummer. As I stowed the oxygen mask, I noticed the McDonald's cup on the floor between the seats and wondered if they had McDonald's in Cuba.

I glanced at the little side window and wondered if that McDonald's cup would fit through the window. Maybe I should send Castro a sample? After a quick comparison with the cup and the window, I decided that the cup would fit. So, without spilling a drop, I sent that cup out the window to Castro.

As I neared the south Cuban VOR fix, the clouds began to break. Not quite enough to look back at Cuba, but clear enough ahead of me to see nothing but miles and miles of open water.

The final sprint to Grand Cayman Island was pretty much uneventful and in the clear with scenic blue water beneath me. As I began my descent, I noticed some pretty tall cumulus build-ups to the south, but my attention was distracted looking at the blue water and that distinctive hook on the Grand Cayman Island.

There was almost no activity at the airport when I arrived, but I did manage to find a customs inspector who charged me twenty bucks for a quick squirt of something that smelled like hair spray from an aerosol can into the cabin. He said it was to help eradicate nonnative bugs from being imported to the island.

He then went and retrieved a fuel truck and topped off my fuel tanks. I followed him in to pay my fuel bill and check on the weather, where he proudly handed me about a quarter ream of mostly blank paper. He said it was the weather forecast for my route of flight. Problem was that their printer was mostly out of ink. A phone call to the weather service assured me that the clouds I saw during my descent were dissipating and would continue to do so into the evening and should not be a problem for me.

Piper Seneca III XA-PAW at the Cayman Island Airport

Armed with that information and a full tank of gas, I hopped back in the Seneca and departed southbound tracking the Cayman Island VOR towards San Andreas. While climbing out, the sun was just beginning to set in the west and I glanced back over my shoulder to see the city lights of the Grand Cayman Island coming on. You just don't get a view like this every day.

As I got to the top of my climb and leveled off, I noticed some color at the top of the radar screen. For the next several minutes my attention was focused on the functions of the radar. Still too far away to get a good read, I was beginning to see what looked like lightning off in the distance. It looked like some course deviations would be in order, but for now I would sit back and see if the weather forecaster was correct with the diminishing activity.

Thinking I had about thirty to forty minutes to go before any serious decisions needed to be made, I sat back and tried to relax. My gaze crossed the instrument panel and to the airspeed indicator, "What the heck? Why am I only indicating a hundred forty knots?"

Manifold pressure and rpm are exactly where they had been for the past ten hours of flying, so why were we indicating five knots slower? Oil pressure and temperature were normal, so what was going on here? Oh, wait both cylinder head temperature gauges were pegged out!

Thoughts of a double engine melt down began racing through my head as I looked back over my shoulder for any signs of the Cayman Islands. Nothing. Nothing but blackness. Crap, if those engines melted down, I would be flying a multi-engine glider.

Shit, where was that life raft? Crap, it was in the backseat. In a bit of a panic, I unbuckled my seatbelt, dove between the seats to retrieve the life raft, and placed it in the seat next to me. If I had to ditch this thing, at least I would have a chance.

After buckling my seatbelt back up I began staring at the CHT gauge. Okay, Kev, think, buddy! What am I missing here? The yellow and red weather bands were getting closer and closer on the radar and I was beginning to see more lightning flashes out the windshield. Fuel mixture? What did the exhaust gas temperature gauge say? Dang, that was all normal as well. What the hell was going on here?

Cowl flaps! Must be the cowl flaps! I grabbed one handle and it wouldn't move, so I tried the other one with the same result. My hands were tingling. I couldn't really tell in the dim cockpit light, but my finger nails looked purple.

Dammit - grab the mask, Kev! You have not had any oxygen since leaving the Cayman Islands. You have hypoxia setting in, damn.

After sucking on the oxygen mask for a little while, I reached back down to check the cowl flap handle, sliding the lever to the right and down. A-ha! I grabbed the other handle, slid it left and down. Pretty soon the airspeed crept back up to 145 knots and the cylinder head temps went back to their normal position, but now the little Seneca was getting bounced around pretty good from the weather that I had completely forgotten about.

Completely out of communication and navigation radio range, I grabbed the heading bug and rolled it around to about 100 degrees in hopes to see a gap in the weather; unfortunately, there was nothing but red being painted on the radar. I rolled the heading bug back around to about 240 degrees and found that will put me on a parallel course to that line of weather. I would just continue on this heading and try to make an end run around this line of thunderstorms, but how far west would I need to go?

Finally, after what seemed like two hours on that westerly heading, I noticed some breaks in the weather. I gradually nudged the heading bug around to the south and then on around to about 150 degrees in an attempt to get somewhat back on my original course.

Unfortunately, there were more lightning flashes out the windshield on this new heading and they were confirmed by the radar. So once again, I flew right up to the weather and then started bumping the heading bug back around towards the west, all the while wondering just how far off course I was.

Once again, I made another end run around this band of weather and turned back towards the southeast, only to find yet another line of weather, and again I drove right up to the weather and then turned back to the southwest.

As I studied the radar, I began to notice some needle movement on the VORs. The TO/FROM flag and the needles were starting to come alive. Thinking to myself, this was a good deal as I should have radio communication here pretty soon, I keyed up the microphone and made a radio call, only to hear dead silence.

Still, I kept droning along on this heading to the southwest, paralleling the line of weather and paying close attention as the VORs locked in on the signal from San Andreas. I centered up the needles on the VORs to reveal that I was west-northwest from San Andreas. The DME was simply showing dashes, meaning that I had no idea how far away I was from the VOR.

Soon there was a break in the line of weather and I turned back to the south and made a few more attempts to establish radio communication, and again nothing. But, there was another line of weather off to the southeast, so I would just maintain this heading for a while until clear of that line. It was late and I was beginning to get pretty sleepy.

Since this was my first low altitude extended overwater flight, I was trying to rationalize the lack of radio communications. It was completely understandable not to have communications while out of range, but here I was with a VOR signal, so it stood to reason that I should be able to communicate with someone on the ground. Maybe they all went to bed; after all, it was getting pretty late.

After some time had passed, I made another radio call, and I thought I heard a faint reply. I grabbed the squelch knob, dialed it all the way up, and made the call again. This time I heard a voice telling me to contact somebody else on another frequency. With the broken English and scratchy transmission, I could not understand who I was to contact, but I did get the frequency.

Just happy to finally have someone to talk to, I acknowledged the instructions and dialed in the new frequency. My radio call there was promptly replied to and was very loud and clear. "X-ray Alpha Papa Alpha Whiskey fly heading one-one-zero."

"Ah, negative, Papa Alpha Whiskey is going to maintain present heading for weather avoidance," was my reply.

"X-ray Alpha Papa Alpha Whiskey fly heading one-one-zero, you are very near Nicaraguan airspace and they will send a plane to shoot you down."

"Ah, Roger, Papa Alpha Whiskey is turning towards the east." This trip just kept getting better and better.

I cranked the heading bug around to about 150 degrees, looked back at the radar, and realized that it was either risking being shot down or making it through this line of red paint on the radar. As the airplane began to bounce around, I realized that I should probably secure the life raft in the seat next to me with the seat belt to prevent it from interfering with the flight controls. With that accomplished, I cinched my own belt a little tighter and gritted my teeth for what I knew was going to be a rough ride.

I strapped on the oxygen mask just for good measure and hung on. The noise was incredibly loud as the rain pounded on the little Seneca's fuselage and the turbulence had my eyeballs so rattled that I could barely identify the instrument panel.

Almost as if on cue, the turbulence and noise stopped and a voice came over the radio. "X-ray Alpha Papa Alpha Whiskey contact Panama Approach on such and such frequency."

"Roger, Papa Alpha Whiskey switching to Panama Approach, good day." About that time, I broke into the clear to see the lights of Panama straight ahead. The remainder of the flight and the landing were uneventful, but after that was where the next adventure began.

After landing, I requested and received progressive taxi instructions to the customs ramp, which was at the end of the terminal building. I was instructed to park inside the blue circle painted on the ramp. It appeared that there was not a soul in sight to greet me.

After shutting down the engines, I grabbed my overnight bag from the back seat, unstrapped the life raft, opened the door and moved my gear to the wing, and finished securing the aircraft. I then climbed out of the aircraft to the welcoming committee of M16-wielding kids. I was not sure where they came from; it was like they suddenly appeared out of nowhere.

They all looked to be about fifteen years old and judging by the way they handled their weapons; they were not very well trained. I wasn't sure what they were saying as they surrounded me and my gear. I was in the same clothes as I was when I left Texas, which was a nice white western-style shirt, starched jeans, ostrich skin boots, and a shiny State of Texas belt buckle.

I reached in my back pocket and pulled out my passport, but they did not want anything to do with it. They continued their animated conversation amongst themselves in Spanish and I had no clue what they were saying until I heard the letters C I A.

Upon hearing that I stood a little taller in my boots, kinda puffed out my chest a little as if to say, don't mess with me, boys, I can have you disappeared.

I picked up my bags and glared at the one who appeared to be in charge as if to say let's go, and I started walking towards the building. This must have startled them a bit as they scrambled to form up on me with three on each side, one behind me, and another one taking the lead.

We walked through a door into what looked like the typical customs baggage inspection room. There were three long stainless-steel baggage inspection tables with glass doors at the end of the room that appeared to lead to the street side of the terminal building. I noticed that there was a little white car sitting just outside the door and the driver was waving at me.

The soldiers led me to the middle table, where I dropped my gear. They simply looked at me and continued to talk to each other in Spanish. I looked back towards the door, and the little white car had disappeared.

After a few minutes, the phone in that little office rang and two of the M16-wielding kids wandered off, apparently to answer the phone. Shortly thereafter, another one headed toward the office. I glanced back towards the glass doors, and the little white car had reappeared and again, the driver was waving at me.

I picked up my bags, stared the one guy between me and the door in the eye, and walked right past him towards the door. About three steps from the door, I heard someone say something in an elevated voice, but I did not turn around to look. I hit the door, hurriedly threw my bags through the open back window of the little white car, and climbed in the front seat. The driver stomped on the gas pedal before I managed to get completely in the car, smashing my leg with the car door as it tried to swing closed.

We sped down the one-way road towards the terminal, around the loop, and back in the opposite direction at a fairly high rate of speed. I thought, great, I am finally going to get to a hotel where I can get some sleep. Just about the time that I was going to say something, he slammed on the brakes and made a hard right turn onto a bumpy dirt road and turned off the headlights.

Where in the hell was this guy taking me? "Everything is okay señor, I take good care of ju." The vegetation on the side of the road was taller than the car, and the only way for me to keep my bearings was to keep my eye on the airport's rotating beacon. After a few turns, it became apparent that we were following the airport perimeter fence.

A few turns later, we came to a screeching stop at a ten-foot-tall chain-link gate that was opened by someone who apparently had been there waiting on us. We pulled through the gate and drove just a few feet and flashlights revealed my Seneca sitting there in the darkness. He stopped the car, shut it off, and jumped out. "Come with me, señor."

Just what in the hell was going on here? My little Seneca had been moved from the customs ramp to this little airport perimeter dirt road, and they had the baggage door opened and the smuggled boxes of avionics were lying around on the ground.

"Do not worry, señor, I take care of everything for ju! Here are the aircraft's documents." He handed me the Mexican Airworthiness Certificate and the Aircraft Registration Certificate.

He loaded the boxes in the trunk of the car while the other guy closed up the baggage door and crawled inside the Seneca and fired up the engines. Without any nav lights, landing lights, or strobe lights on he poured the coals to it and took off straight ahead on the dirt road into the dark of night, blasting the crap out of us with his prop wash in the process.

Good grief, what had I got myself into? "Come on, señor, we must go!" We hopped back into the car and backed up through the gate and my driver jumped out to close the gate. We followed the dirt road back around the airport the way we came and back out onto the main drag towards town.

A few miles down the road and we pulled into a Holiday Inn. In his best attempt at English, he informed me that Eastern Airlines did not arrive this evening so my departure would be delayed by one day. He instructed me not to talk to anyone and to meet him in front of the hotel at 8 a.m., and not to worry, my room was already paid for.

As I approached the front desk, I couldn't help but notice this suspicious-looking guy standing off to the side. He was holding a two-way radio in his hand and had a Model 1911 .45-caliber pistol sticking out of his pants pocket. This guy gave me the creeps, standing behind me like that, but I got my room key from the clerk and headed for the long hallway to find my room.

This creep followed me into the hallway and took a position at the end of the hall. As I reached the halfway point in the hallway, another guy stepped out at the far end of the hall. He just stood there watching me. Like the other guy, he was holding a radio and had a .45-caliber pistol in sticking out of his pocket. I was so rattled I walked right past my room, causing me to have to turn around just to see the other guy still at the other end of the hallway.

After finding my room, I threw my bags on the floor, undressed, and crawled into bed. Even though I was very tired and it was around 3:30 a.m., it was still very difficult to fall asleep.

It seemed like my eyes had finally just closed when the phone rang. It was very difficult to understand what the animated party on the other end was saying as it was all in Spanish. The best I could determine was that they wanted to know where the Seneca was. I made several attempts to find out who I was talking to, but again could not understand what they were saying so I just hung up the phone.

It was already daylight outside and the clock in my room didn't work, so I called the front desk to find out what time it was. Holly cow, it was already 7:30. I had to get moving.

After a quick shower I left the room to make a trip down the hall to find a cup of coffee. As I closed the door behind me, the phone began ringing again. Just let it ring, Kev, and keep moving. With a cup of coffee in hand I headed out the front door of the hotel to find my driver patiently waiting for me. This was not the same guy as the previous night, but he recognized me right away and hustled me into his car and off we went.

My new chaperone's English was worse than my previous driver's English, but his driving was equally as bad. Hanging on for dear life as we sped through town, I tried to make some light casual conversation, but again, communication was difficult.

We drove off into what I believe was a northerly direction. We drove through some of the towns finest slums and out through Howard Air Force Base and into the lush tropical jungle. We drove for what seemed like hours down one-lane dirt roads and finally came to a stop at a little thatched roof hut with an open patio on the shoreline of the Pacific Ocean.

Under different circumstances, this place could be a tropical paradise. With the sounds of the jungle and wildlife on one side of the hut and the waves of the Pacific Ocean gently lapping at the shore on the other side, this could really be a relaxing place. It even had a bar.

This place was tended to by a couple of elderly well-fed Panamanian women. It was still early in the day and we were the only ones in the establishment. I did my best to relate to my chaperone that I had not had breakfast and I needed to eat.

He began an animated conversation with one of the gals, and pretty soon we were served a bowl of hot water with what looked and tasted like seaweed. It was awful. They were all smiles as my driver eagerly enjoyed his soup while I was contemplating the fact that I was going to be hungry all day.

As he was consuming his bowl of seaweed, I continued to try to communicate with him, but most efforts were in vain. Finally, one of the gals came to me and said in perfect English, "He has been instructed to keep you out of sight."

Out of sight? Out of sight from who? What was she talking about?

"This weekend is Manuel Noriega's fifth anniversary of being our president," she said. "There is going to be a big celebration and everyone must attend."

Thinking that this celebration had nothing to do with me, I reflected back to the events surrounding my arrival and wondered how I might be implicated in something I had no knowledge of. I decided to relax a little and take it easy.

Although this was a tropical paradise and I should be relaxing with an adult beverage, considering the circumstances, I thought it wise not to let my guard down. Had I been better informed, I might have been able to relax and enjoy it, but as it was, I was reasonably uncomfortable.

Knowing that I would be leaving in the morning I thought about seeing the Panama Canal and attempted to relate my desire to my driver. It was difficult communicating with him so once again the gal working the joint stepped in to assist.

"As long as I am here, I would like to see the Panama Canal."

"Sorry, señor, this is not possible, you are to be kept out of sight until Eastern Airlines."

"I really don't care, I want to see the canal."

That resulted in some animated conversation in Spanish, and it appeared that they agreed they could take me there but were going to proceed with caution and keep me out of sight. With that, off we went.

Back down the little dirt road we went, up onto a paved road that took us past the end of the runway at Howard Air Force Base and through some really bad slums. It was obvious that he was keeping me out of mainstream Panama.

Upon arrival in the Canal Zone, he reached under his seat and pulled out a pair of binoculars. We were in luck as there was a ship pulling into one of the locks. As I made my way over to watch the gates close, I noticed my driver looking through his binoculars back towards the way we came and then slowly studying everyone he saw in every direction.

It was fascinating to watch the lock doors close, the ship rise to the next level, and then the other lock door open and the ship continue on its way. For me, it was well worth the risk either real or perceived to visit the canal. It appeared that there was a canal museum but as I started to head off in that direction, my driver insisted that I not go there.

He corralled me back towards the car and off we went for a nice long roundabout drive back to my hotel. He left me with instructions not to leave the hotel and to be out front at 6 a.m. for a ride to the airport.

It was already late in the day, and the first thing I noticed when walking into the hotel was the restaurant off to the left. Finally, after having almost nothing to eat for a couple of days, it was time for some nourishment and a couple of beers.

With a satisfied belly and an extra bottle of beer in hand, I retired to my room. Once again, those creepy guys with the pistols and radios appeared in the hallway, but this time I just ignored their presence, locked myself in my room, and placed a wake-up call for 5 a.m. It took no time at all to fall asleep.

When I Emerged from the hotel promptly at 6 a.m., my driver was already waiting for me. The drive to the airport was quiet with neither of us trying to communicate.

Upon reaching the terminal, he parked the car in what appeared to be a tow-away zone and prompted me to grab my gear and get out. Once inside the terminal he asked for my passport and headed towards the ticket counter, passed between the ticket agents, over the baggage pass-through, and went through a door behind the ticket counter.

A few moments later, he emerged from behind the door and motioned me to follow him. As we approached the screening check point, he said something in Spanish to the security guard, who waved us past the check point without so much as a casual second glance. I wasn't not sure who this little guy was, but evidently he had some clout.

I followed him to the gate, where he informed me not to leave the gate area and that Eastern would be boarding in just a few minutes. With that said, he handed me my passport and a first-class ticket, shook my hand, and disappeared in the direction from which we came.

As the Eastern Airlines Lockheed L-1011 climbed for altitude, I pondered the events of the previous days. Who did I deliver the Seneca to? Did somebody steal the Seneca after I left

236

it on the customs ramp? Who were they hiding me from? Who was my chaperone and driver working for? Why did the gal at the little hut speak such good English, but was not willing to tell me anything of importance.

All I could conclude was that I had one hell of a story to tell my friends back home.

Chapter 25

A Mile of Highway

Memorial Day weekend was coming up and a friend named Bob invited us to join up with him and his wife at their house in Red River, New Mexico, for the weekend. They would be flying their Twin Comanche up a week in advance to prepare the house, stock the refrigerator, and service the four-wheelers.

We had made several trips with Bob in the past to go snow skiing, but this time it would be to ride four-wheelers through the mountains. Usually, we would fly up there with Bob in the Twin Comanche, but this time he was leaving several days before we could leave, so we would need to find our own way there.

It sounded like a lot of fun but the thought of a thirteen-hour drive one-way was discouraging. Sitting around the hangar discussing this adventure in terms of getting there, we checked with Flight Service. Although the weekend was still several days away, the long-range weather forecast indicated that it might be favorable weather to make the 550-mile trip in our little Taylorcrafts.

At the time, we had a small squadron of 65 hp T-Crafts based at Addison and would be seen on a regular basis patrolling the skies of North Texas in a three-ship formation. A friend named Rick owned a pretty little blue 1941 model T-Craft that we called "Blue," I had my 1946 model T-Craft that we called "Brown," and my younger brother owned a 1946 model T-Craft that we called "Red."

After much discussion, a few cold beers, and a review of the aeronautical charts it was all settled. Blue and I would leave on Friday morning. Our initial plan was to leave Addison Airport and fly up towards Amarillo. We would fly around and explore the Palo Duro Canyon and try to find a suitable place to land and camp out for the night, and then get up Saturday morning and fly the rest of the trip to Taos. Bob would pick us up at Taos and drive us the rest of the way to Red River. Weather and winds permitting, we planned to return on Monday.

One of our non-pilot friends named Mark, who was at the hangar during all the discussions about the trip, said that he really wanted to go with us, but getting permission from the wife might be an issue.

I was not sure what it was about this crew, but we could never leave anywhere at the planned departure time. In some cases, we were lucky if we left on the planned departure date. If we planned an 8 a.m. departure time, we would be lucky to be airborne by noon. "I need to run get some extra batteries for my hand-held radio," or "Hey, let's go get something to eat," or "I forgot my sleeping bag," or "Oh wait, I need to run to the pilot shop to get a current aeronautical chart." It was always something simple that would delay our departure, and this trip would be no different.

Finally, with a fresh weather briefing and the promise of good weather and favorable winds, it would be mid-afternoon before we were airborne and on our way. This late departure meant that we would not have much time to explore the Palo Duro Canyon before darkness set in, but it is what it is.

As we passed by Wichita Falls, we noted our time and commented on the radio that we were less than an hour out of Addison, so we were making pretty good time. With that kind of ground speed, we could make it to a little airport near Amarillo for fuel and, if time permitted, we could retreat a few miles to the Palo Duro Canyon and still camp out.

The little Brown T-Craft had two wing tanks and a center tank and would carry a total of twenty-four gallons of fuel, while the Blue T-Craft only had one wing tank and a center tank for a total of eighteen gallons. The faithful little Continental 65HP engine only burned 3.8 – 4 gallons of fuel per hour while cruising along at 95 mph.

We were pretty happy with our progress as we passed Vernon, Texas, but to the west it appeared the sun was being partially blocked by some high cirrus clouds. As we progressed further west, the sky ahead of us began to get darker and darker. The clouds began to turn an ominous dark blue-green color and then almost black.

I was beginning to get a little concerned as the radio started breaking squelch with static. I studied the aeronautical chart, looking for a safe haven, and determined that we should make a bee-line for Childress. The clouds started throwing out massive amounts of lightning bolts, but they were still a good distance away.

The winds were calm when we landed at Childress but we knew that there was a rapidly approaching storm and we needed to get the airplanes securely tied down. There were several large hangars but the airport appeared deserted. We taxied around the massive ramp looking for a place to tie down. Even though we brought our own tie-down kits with us, there was no place on the ramp to tie down the little airplanes. The thought of standing there watching our little airplanes get destroyed by this rapidly approaching storm was not too appealing.

I taxied up close to a hangar and shut the engine down and began checking the hangar's security features. Rick pulled up next to me and shut down as well. The hangar we pulled up to was really secure and I could not find a way in so I went to inspect the old Quonset hut-type hangar which was about fifty yards away. I could see inside that there was plenty of room for the T-Crafts. Running around to the side of the hangar, I found a door that was easily breached.

The gust front hit with strong winds and a rapid drop in temperature just as I was pushing the hangar doors open, spinning both airplanes around into the wind as if they were weather vanes. Mark and Rick were desperately trying to hold onto the airplanes as they were bouncing off the ground into the wind. I ran out and helped Rick push Blue across the ramp and into the hangar and then we both ran out and helped Mark push Brown into the hangar. The massive downpour of rain hit just as we were trying to close the hangar door.

After all the excitement we decided that we would be staying in Childress for the night and camping was out of the question. We found a telephone in one of the offices of the hangar and managed to secure a hotel room for the night and a ride to the hotel.

By the time we got checked into the hotel, the rain was coming down so hard, Highway 287 turned into knee-deep whitewater rapids that would have been fun in a kayak, but it had traffic slowed down to a crawl with each passing vehicle, leaving a huge wake in its path.

We called Flight Service to get an updated weather briefing for the following morning and they once again promised a great day to fly with light and variable winds along our route of flight. Of particular concern to me were the winds in the proximity of the mountains to the west but they were still calling for light and variable winds.

We reviewed the aeronautical charts and planned to leave in the morning, skip the canyon tour and head for Tucumcari, New Mexico, for a fuel stop, and then south of Sandia Peak towards Santa Fe and then north up to Taos. We called Bob to let him know our revised plans, had dinner, and went to bed.

The following morning, we were greeted with bright clear blue skies and almost no wind. Anxious to get on our way, we grabbed a quick breakfast at the greasy spoon café next door and then caught a ride to the airport.

We departed Childress, which has a field elevation of 1,925 feet, for Tucumcari, which has an elevation of 4,065 feet. We decided that we would do a gradual climb to 6,500 feet for our cruising altitude. It was tempting to divert to the Palo Duro Canyon as we neared Amarillo, but we pressed on.

After passing Amarillo I began to notice that we were beginning to travel through periods of time where I was pulling back slightly on the yoke to maintain altitude followed by a period of time where I was pushing forward to maintain altitude.

By the time we arrived in Tucumcari, the pitch corrections to maintain altitude became more and more pronounced. After fueling up the airplanes, we gave flight service another call. We were assured that we had great weather with light and variable winds along our route of flight with no reports of any mountain wave action.

I was having my suspicions based on the last leg of the flight, but we grabbed some stale candy bars from the vending machine and launched on our next leg of the flight. Although Tucumcari had a 7,000-foot runway, the field elevation was 4,065 feet and I was surprised how much runway the little T-Craft took to get airborne.

The plan was to climb to 12,500 feet for the flight to Santa Fe. That should give us plenty of terrain clearance, and I had been higher than that many times in ol' Brown so given enough time to get there, it shouldn't be a problem.

We managed to get to 12,500 feet but it was a struggle as there was some definite mountain wave action going on. We would lose 1,500 feet of altitude followed by a gain of 1,000 feet in the matter of just a few minutes. As we passed Las Vegas, New Mexico, and got closer to the mountains, we began to adjust our route of flight to the south a bit to avoid the mountains.

We discovered that by diverting left and right of course we would find areas of lift as well as sink holes, much the way gliders find lift along the mountain range or under flat bottom clouds. We were about thirty miles east of Santa Fe when maintaining altitude became very difficult.

Rick was doing better than I was as he was much lighter flying by himself with six gallons less fuel, while I had Mark with me and an extra six gallons of fuel. We managed to navigate south around an 8,000-foot mountain and although short-lived, it appeared that we were getting some lift and climbing slightly.

But soon we appeared to be in a never-ending sink hole as we were now down to about 300 feet above the trees indicating about 50 mph and steadily sinking. I knew my trusty little T-Craft with the Continental A-65 was giving me all she had, but she was counting on me to get us out of this mess.

Rick had managed to nudge himself a little further south and appeared to be doing a little better than we were when he suddenly came on the radio and said, "I got lift, Kev, I am about a quarter mile south of your position!"

I leaned forward to look to the left out the windshield and saw Rick about 500 feet above us and climbing. It was a comforting sight, but we were still in a bit of a jam and there was not much I could do but to try and get us a little further south.

We were still slowly sinking and hanging on the ragged edge of a stall. I was afraid that if I rolled into a twenty-degree bank to turn to the south, we may stall and crash uncontrollably into the trees. If we were going to crash into the trees, we were going to be in control of the crash.

We were now only indicating about 45 mph and were dangerously low. We were so low I was counting the pine needles on the trees below. I began nudging in a little left rudder to change our heading towards the south a little at a time. We would lose a little airspeed each time and I would let the speed build back up and do it again. It was becoming a desperate situation.

Racing through my mind were visuals of Mark sitting on the couch with his daughters, Miranda and Addison, beside him. The thought of them growing up without their daddy was driving me as our tires were skimming the tree tops.

We were to the point that I was trying to pick a crash line through the trees as I felt that one more kick of the rudder to the left would be the last before we could no longer stay aloft. Suddenly, to my left and about 50 feet below appeared a four-lane interstate highway.

I nudged the rudder to the left one more time and got us over the highway. Indicating around 40 mph and still carrying full power, we plopped down on the highway behind a pickup truck and in front of a maroon sedan.

Suddenly we began accelerating. It felt like someone had a rope tied to the tail of the airplane holding us back and then decided to let go of the rope. I was simply going to go along with the flow of traffic until I could find a place to safely pull off to the side of the highway but for some strange reason, that ol' hayseed driving the pickup truck in front of us decided to slam on his brakes. I knew we couldn't stop in time to avoid hitting him from behind so I snatched the T-Craft back in the air. The brakes on the T-Craft were not very good even when they were brand new.

Unfortunately, there was a bridge just a short distance ahead and I could not get over the truck and back down on the highway before the bridge so I tugged back on the yoke a little more. With just enough airspeed and just when I was sure we had it made, I noticed a single strand power wire about 15 - 20 feet above the bridge. Shit!

With almost no more speed left, I gave one more tug on the yoke and the little T-Craft responded. Just as I saw the power line pass under me, the T-Craft broke into a deep left-wing stall. Immediately, I shoved the nose over and slammed in all the right rudder and aileron I could get. Somehow the little T-Craft righted itself just as we plopped back down on the highway again.

I pulled the power back to idle and we began taxiing up the highway with what soon became a line of cars a mile long behind us. We couldn't find a suitable place to pull off the highway. Finally, near the top of the hill, there was enough room to pull off the highway.

I called Rick on the radio and let him know that were down safely on the highway and for him to go to Santa Fe and get a rental car and come back down the highway and meet us.

As we shut down the engine and got out of the airplane, we were greeted by swarms of people. They saw us land and felt like they needed to give us several Bibles and soft drinks. Most of them wanted to share their story with us regarding what they saw and take pictures with us. As we were still not even sure where we were, they informed us that we were in on Interstate 25 in Glorieta, New Mexico. Home of the National Baptist Conference Center.

The wind was probably blowing around 25 mph. As the crowd subsided, we got the tie-down kit and positioned the T-Craft so that the wings would be out of the way of the passing traffic and tied her down. With that accomplished there was not much left to do except to wait for Rick.

We got the lawn chairs out of the airplane and set them up under the left wing and were sitting there when a New Mexico Highway Patrolman arrived.

Watching him get out of his patrol vehicle, I thought he had just walked off the set of a Hollywood movie. He was tall and

245

lean, wearing a perfectly starched uniform with a big-brimmed hat that didn't seem to move in spite of the high winds. His face was tan and leathered as if he had withstood several New Mexico sand storms, and he was wearing silver mirrored sunglasses.

As he approached, he pulled a small spiral-bound note pad from his shirt pocket and looks at Mark, who was sitting in a lawn chair under the wing. "Who was driving this thing?" he asked.

Pointing at me, Mark replies in a trembling voice, "He was, Officer!"

He turned to looked at me and said, "Let me see your driver's license."

"Are you sure you don't want my pilot certificate?" I replied.

"The report I have is that you were driving an airplane on my highway, now let me see your driver's license."

"Yes sir." As I pulled out my billfold and retrieved my Texas driver's license, I looked at him, trying to gauge his demeanor, but all I could see was my reflection in his sunglasses. He jotted down all the details of my driver's license on his trusty notepad, handed my license back to me, and asked, "Anybody hurt?"

"No sir."

He began to walk around the left wing of the T-Craft looking it over as he progressed towards the fuselage. "Any damage?"

"No Sir."

He spotted the aircraft registration number on the side of the fuselage and pulled out his notepad and jotted that down, asking, "Are there any more numbers that identify this airplane?"

"Yes sir, the aircraft make, model, and serial number are right there just under the tail."

He proceeded to take down all the information and then stood up and continued his inspection around the tail, up the right side of the fuselage and around the right wing, meeting back up with me at the nose of the T-Craft.

Putting his notepad back in his shirt pocket, he looked at me and said, "I am finished here, you gentlemen have a nice day." And with that he turns towards his patrol vehicle and begins to walk away, leaving me somewhat speechless.

Just about the time he got to his vehicle he turned around and said, "By the way, what are you planning to do now?"

Without even thinking about it I replied, "My wingman made it through the pass and is on his way to Santa Fe, he will be returning with a rental car. We will be off-loading all our baggage into the rental car. Then we are going to sit here until this wind dies down, then we are going to call you guys and ask that you block off a section of this highway so that I can take off. Then I am going to fly to Santa Fe and mount up the first barstool I can find and drink until I fall off. It will probably be about an hour before sunset when we call."

"You have just one problem with that plan," he said as he reached in his shirt pocket for his notepad.

At this point I thought he was going to suggest a wrecker company or that I would be needing to disassemble the T-Craft to get it off his highway, but instead he said, "You don't have our phone number."

He scribbled down a phone number and the highway marker number and handed me the piece of paper from his notepad and said, "Call this number about thirty minutes before you are ready to go. Good luck." And with that, he got in his patrol vehicle and left.

Wow, I had no idea that he would agree to go along with my hastily fabricated plan, but he seemed to be okay with it.

After he left, a few more folks stopped by to drop off a few more Bibles and some soft drinks and the relive their account of watching us land and take off again and land again. Several took the time to pray for us and with us, and for that we were grateful.

About an hour or so had passed when Rick pulled up in a little red rental car. First thing we did was unload everything from the T-Craft into the car. We then sat around and shared our experiences with that mountain wave and the bogus weather reports of light and variable winds.

We decided that we needed to find the nearest payphone so that we knew where it was when it was time to call the Highway Patrol, and to survey my potential runway. I needed to takeoff into the wind, which meant that I would be taking off uphill.

After driving up and down the highway a few times, we found one single-strand power line crossing the highway and thought it best to park the red rental car under the powerline and use it as a marker. Looking into the low sun, I might not be able to see the power line; at least this way I would be able to see the car, and if I did not have enough smash to climb out well before I got to the car, I would just stay down low and go under the power line. The runway would be going northwest uphill, under a bridge, around a curve, and under a powerline with only a short straightaway before the highway turned sharply left and went downhill.

As the afternoon turned into evening, the wind began to die down considerably so we decided it was time to call in the state troopers. It took much longer than we anticipated for them to arrive, but when they did, they had six patrol vehicles.

These guys were hilarious. As we stood there on the side of the highway, I asked them to block the east- and westbound lanes of traffic while I taxied across the westbound lanes and the median into the eastbound lanes and then release the west bound traffic while I taxied about a mile eastbound to just past the bridge. Then I asked them to block the westbound lane while I taxied through the median into the west bound lanes to takeoff.

With the briefing over and an understanding of what we wanted to do, they began cracking jokes like "How are we going to write this up in our report?" or "Nobody at the station is going to believe us, they're gonna to say were at the doughnut shop!" and "We are never going to live this one down."

As I was climbing in to the airplane I yelled back, "Hey, fellas, don't go making any bets just yet, you haven't seen what we gotta do to start this thing!"

They stopped to watch as I strapped myself in turned the magneto switch on and yelled to Rick, "Hot and brakes!" With that Rick gave the propeller one mighty spin and the faithful little Continental came to life, chugging along at about 500 rpm. I could tell by the way the officers were carrying on that they were getting a kick out of this situation.

Just as we had briefed, they blocked both lanes of traffic while I taxied across the highway and onto the eastbound lanes. Rick followed in the red rental car until he got to the powerline and then he dodged the traffic, and jumped the median, and parked the car under the powerline.

Going downhill with a tailwind, I felt my brakes fading so I tried to stay off them as much as possible. About a quarter of a mile after passing the bridge, I slowed the airplane and pointed it to the median so the state troopers would know that this was where I wanted them to block the westbound lanes.

While waiting for them to get in position, I looked over my left shoulder to see that we were blocking some serious eastbound traffic. When the troopers gave me the signal to taxi through the median, the folks in the eastbound lanes got out of their cars to watch the take-off.

I powered up to about 1,500 rpm and did a quick check of the magnetos. Satisfied that all was good I shoved the throttle all the way in. The little Continental promptly responded to my command and began to propel me and the little T-Craft towards the bridge. This time, I would be going under the bridge.

Considering the struggle I had earlier in the day, the T-Craft accelerated nicely even though we were at an elevation of 8,300 feet. I could feel that she was ready to fly shortly after passing under the bridge but I kept her on the ground just a little longer for good measure. After gaining flying speed, I lifted her off the highway but decided to keep the airplane in ground effect until passing the red rent car and under the powerline.

After passing Rick, Mark, and the red rental car, I eased back on the yoke and she seemed to levitate into the sky without a care in the world. As I got to a little over 9,000 feet I could see just beyond that last mountain to Santa Fe. The twinkling lights of the town coming on as the sun was setting was a welcome site.

Somewhere out there is a picture of me in the little T-Craft about 3 feet off the ground with a Highway Patrol vehicle all lit up chasing me down the highway as I passed under the powerline. I have seen it but I can't locate a copy of it.

After landing in Santa Fe and securing the T-Craft on the ramp, I called Bob to let him know our status, and that we would be driving from Santa Fe and would be there by midnight.

This story could have ended a lot different than it did, and it taught me several things. Yes, I had some pretty good stick and rudder skills and I knew where the ragged edge of the T-Craft's performance was and I had to fly it on that ragged edge but, always give yourself an out and proceed with an abundance of caution.

There are many more adventures to share, but they will not all fit in one book, in fact I had to trim 5 Chapters out of this book so keep on the look out for the release of book number 2, 3, and 4.

www.ingramcontent.com/pod-product-compliance
Lightning Source LLC
Chambersburg PA
CBHW060014100426
42740CB00010B/1483